MUTUALIST MICROFINANCE

MUTUALIST MICROFINANCE

Informal Savings Funds from the Global Periphery to the Core?

Abram de Swaan &
Marcel van der Linden (eds)

aksant
Amsterdam
2006

Distributed in North America by Transaction Publishers.

ISBN 90 5260 183 6

Type setting & Cover-design: BoekVorm, Amsterdam, The Netherlands
Print: Grafisch Produktiebedrijf Gorter, Steenwijk, The Netherlands
Photo cover: Financial assistance project in Ethiopea, © Mollering/ANP

Aksant Academic Publishers, Cruquiusweg 31, 1019 AT Amsterdam, www.aksant.nl

Table of Contents

Preface

Mutual funds once flourished in nineteenth-century Europe and North America. They still abound in Asia and Africa. In recent years they have come back to European and American cities with the immigrants from overseas. The principle is simple: a number of participants each pay a contribution into the fund for as many rounds as there are contributors and at each round one player receives the total of contributions paid that time. As a result, those that get paid out early in the cycle get credit until the end, those that receive the lump sum last have lent their money all that time. Usually creditworthiness, prestige, privilege, need, lottery or discounts determine the sequence in which the players receive their disbursements.

The nineteenth century mutual funds functioned also as insurances, supporting their members in times of need with their reserves. These 'friendly societies' duly disappeared with the emergence of state social security and commercial insurance. In Asia and Africa, however the mutuals have not taken on insurance functions. Yet, they survive and even thrive among the poor, the workers, and the middle class, and they are especially popular among women. Against all expectations they are also quite wide-spread in immigrant circles in Europe, where finely-branched and easily accessible banking systems would seem to make them superfluous.

For those who get paid out early in the cycle, the mutual is a source of free credit. But why should the others accept to be paid at a late stage, having provided credit all along and run the risk that those who got paid before them would default on subsequent payments? Where living conditions make hoarding risky and banks seem remote or inaccessible, mutuals eliminate the need to accumulate large sums. As soon as it is received all the money is paid out to a single member who usually spends it right away on major expenditures. No paperwork, no permissions are required.

But there is more to the mutuals. The meetings are an occasion for the members to socialize and for the organizer to reinforce the bonds of trust and discipline. Most important of all, the reciprocal commitment helps the participants in keeping their resolve to save and ward off competing personal needs or claims from relatives. Although contemporary funds have no insurance functions, they help to strengthen the web of mutual acquaintance, confidence and solidarity among the participants. Members whose turn to collect has come may pass on the prize to members in need until their turn comes up, or they may otherwise lend, or even give them part or all of the lump sum. Thus, the mutuals may operate as an informal and ad hoc insurance scheme among peers.

In this volume, five authors describe and analyze the results of their fieldwork among mutual fund members in Hyderabad, Yogyakarta, Ayelitsa (a township near Cape Town), among Surinamese in both Paramaribo (Suriname) and Amsterdam, as well as among Senegalese Peul who migrate from Tilogne to Dakar and on to Paris. The studies are based on field observations and personal interviews.

The two senior authors and editors, Abram de Swaan and Marcel van der Linden, from the outset provided a common comparative approach, a shared historical perspective and a theoretical framework that goes back to De Swaan's earlier work on welfare arrangements in the U.S. and Europe during the Modern Era: *In care of the state* (Polity Press, Oxford, 1989). The chapter on nineteenth century mutual funds contained an analysis of the dilemmas confronting these small, autonomous associations. As they do at present, at the time also, peer pressures in these mutual funds functioned as a 'social constraint' to increase 'self constraint' on spending. Such group pressures also bolster the members' defense against the claims from relatives upon their earnings and savings, especially protecting women from the demands by their male relatives. In the Introductory chapter to the present volume De Swaan elaborates on these themes and suggests that mutual schemes provide their members with a 'proportional liquidity sequence' that allows them to meet their periodical needs for cash with the payoffs from the fund. This broader perspective, thematic, spatial and temporal, is taken up again in Marcel van der Linden's concluding chapter.

The other authors, sociologists and anthropologists, as Ph.D. students all did extensive fieldwork and wrote their dissertations with the senior authors. In this volume they sum up their results in the perspective of the common framework and the findings of their colleagues.

Erik Bähre studied mutual funds in a blighted township near Cape Town, South Africa, after the demise of the Apartheid regime. Where once mostly migrant males ran their mutual schemes, increasingly women set up mutuals of their own and in the process cemented relations among members of the same neighborhood, the same kin and village origin.

In her research on the 'kasmoni' of Surinamese both in Paramaribo and in the Amsterdam Bijlmer area Aspha Bijnaar demonstrated how these mutuals served to increase the resolve to save through reciprocal pressure. The presence of a well-developed and highly accessible banking system in the Netherlands did not diminish the readiness to 'play' in the mutual funds.

Senegalese migrants from one and the same village who now lived in Dakar or had travelled on to Paris (and even New York) were the subject of Abdoulaye Kane's study. Their 'tontines' and village associations travelled with them and kept going through rather forceful peer pressures: faxes and e-mail served to remind newly arriving youngsters to join their fellow migrants and to fulfil their duties toward their home village.

Mutual funds flourished in Yogyakarta, as Hotze Lont found in his research there, in the margin of officially sponsored self-help organizations. Explicit insurance schemes turned out to be almost completely ineffective, but the informal mutuals functioned to increase the participants' security through a complex chain of informal coping strategies of 'filling one hole with another'.

This flexibility of the mutual funds also is the main theme of Peer Smets' contribution on rotating saving associations in India, where they could be seen to adapt to their members' fluctuating circumstances, to changes in neighborhood or workplace composition and to changing political regimes or economic cycles.

In his concluding chapter, Marcel van der Linden presents a wide array of historical and anthropological evidence for the immense variety of informal, collective saving and credit arrangements. He clarifies the terminology and proposes a more fundamental typology. This allows for a comparative analysis of *threats* (internal and external) and *securities* (rules for member selection, monitoring, and sanctions), the two essential features of all mutual arrangements.

A project such as this can not do without support from outside. Financial aid came from grants by the VSB Foundation, the Royal Netherlands Academy of Arts and Sciences (KNAW), the Netherlands research foundation for the tropics (WOTRO), the directorate for development cooperation of the Netherlands Ministry of Foreign Affairs (DGIS), and the Free University of Amsterdam. Intellectual help came from many sides: Robert Ross was co-supervisor for Eric Bähre, Peter Geschiere for Abdoulaye Kane, Frans Hüsken for Hotze Lont, and the late Peter Kloos, the late Jan van der Linden, Isa Baud and Otto van den Muijzenberg supervised Peer Smets. Of course, the scholarly community of the Amsterdam School for Social Research (ASSR) over the years and in many seminars greatly contributed to the ideas in this book. Organizational and technical assistance came from José Komen and Hans Sonneveld, also of the ASSR, and Marianne Bernard, secretary at the University Professors' office. The translators, finally, helped to lift this text across the language barrier: Beverly Jackson translated the chapter by Abram de Swaan, Lee Mitzman translated the chapters by Bijnaar and Kane, Stijn van der Putte translated the final essay by Marcel van der Linden and Phyllis Mitzman did the final corrections for the other chapters.

But the greatest input, of course, came from all those people who let the researchers in on a most private aspect of their lives: their financial dealings with one another, their saving and their spending, and all the ideas, sentiments, deceptions and expectations that came with it. It is to them that this book is dedicated.

CHAPTER I

Mutual funds: then and here, now and there

Informal savings and insurance funds in the nineteenth-century West and the present non-western world

Abram de Swaan

> Hui,[1] kou,[2] kameti,[3] esso, so,[4] abo,[5] edjo, sodjodjo,[6] djodjuma,[7] mengandelek,[8] gamaiyah,[9] ajo, esusu,[10] bam, adashi,[11] chiryelano,[12] kut,[13] bouki,[14] arisan, andilan,[15] sangue, solde, comble,[16] san, box, meeting,[17] tanda, cundina, rol, rifa, bolita, mutualista, quiniela, vaca, vaquita, ronda, fuerte-pequeña, muerta-viva,[18] cuchuval,[19] pandero,[20] ikub,[21] nidi, bishi, chitty,[22] alun günü,[23] cilimba, likelimba,[24] mutualité, friendly society, mutual fund, Kasse,[25] bos, bus, onderlinge,[26] kelemba, sango,[27] songtaba,[28] natt, ndey dikke, sanni jamra,[29] ntshwa,[30] tchoua'ah,[31] stokvel, gooi gooi, umgalelo, [32] umasingcwabisane, isavings[33] lung, shwa, mikiri,[34] kye,[35] itega,[36] muvandimwe,[37] kitema, ton, paré,[38] njangi,[39] lenshare,[40] kasmonie, kasgeld, kassensi, kassi[41] pasanuku, paluwagan, xitique, pia huey,[42] xarmaneko, pianko, pitak,[43] nath, bakary, dambélé, mbotaye,[44] tegg,[45] tours, piye,[46] idir, mahaber, ekub,[47] taneh ang,[48] djarohar paisa, hini.[49]

In the course of the nineteenth century, small mutual savings and insurance funds were set up all over Western Europe and the USA, initially by craftsmen and later mainly by factory workers. Around the turn of the century, these mutuals vanished almost overnight: they were subsumed into much larger, insurance co-operatives and savings banks, supplanted by commercial insurance companies, or made redundant by the new government social insurance schemes (De Swaan 1989). Nowadays, small scale rotating savings and credit associations, or ROSCAs, are a widespread phenomenon in developing countries, and they have once again become frequent in immigrant circles in the cities of Western Europe and the United States.

The mutual fund is a phenomenon of great historical, theoretical and practical importance. Yet most of it remains almost uncharted territory. The current state of research in this area is characterized by an almost complete split between the historiography of the mutual funds in the recent past of the West and the ethnography of contemporary mutual savings funds outside the Western world. It is this division that the present volume should transcend.

In England, a number of detailed studies have been devoted to the nineteenth century 'friendly societies', and historical interest in mutual funds elsewhere has grown in recent years. Writings on the labor movement, on cooperative and mutualist movements and on migrants (especially in the United States) as well as histories of banks and insurance companies often deal quite extensively with the trials and tribulations of individual mutual associations. The first international conference devoted entirely to the subject was the *International Conference on the History of Mutual Benefit Societies* held in Paris in November 1992 (Dreyfus & Gibaud 1995; Van der Linden 1996).

Since Clifford Geertz's seminal article on modern savings funds in non-Western countries and in immigrant circles in Western cities, the research on this subject has progressed sluggishly. The clubs are described in sociological, anthropological and economic studies of agricultural workers, migrant laborers, slum-dwellers, factory girls, market dealers, rickshaw operators and road sweepers, of urban neighborhoods, informal credit services and so forth, but the first comprehensive monograph on the subject has yet to appear.

A comparative study of mutual funds in the history of the West and in present-day developing countries has never been undertaken. The two subjects were first placed on a single agenda during an informal gathering organized in December 1993 by the Amsterdam School for Social Science Research, attended by social historians on the one hand and development economists and non-Western sociologists on the other. These gatherings were the seed-bed for a number of articles on mutual funds (Van der Linden & Sluijs 1996).

The subject is enveloped in a confusion of tongues. In some countries of Western Europe, the term 'mutualism' or 'mutualité' is nowadays used to refer to private, non-profit making insurance funds governed by representatives of the members, who are at once contributors and potential beneficiaries. As a rule, these frequently vast funds fulfil an administrative function in the implementation of social insurance laws (Dumont 1993; Calisti 1982). These contemporary mutuals, like many present-day savings banks, developed from the small nineteenth century mutual savings and insurance funds managed by the members themselves. The literature on contemporary savings funds in developing countries often uses the term ROSCA to denote small, rotating mutual funds, often of a temporary nature, and again administered by the members themselves: at each turn of the cycle the sum of the deposits from the members is paid out to one of them, until all have received the 'kitty' once (Van der Linden in this volume).

This book focuses on *mutual savings funds with an informal set-up*, generally lacking a corporate personality or other legal regulations, *limited in size* (with a dozen or at most a hundred members, in contrast to the hundreds of thousands or millions of persons registered in the modern Western *mutuality)* and under the *direct management* of the members (and therefore not managed by a board of trustees, elected or not). This definition hence excludes present-day Western mutualism as a phenomenon of another order of magnitude and complexity.

Some of the small mutual savings funds use the accumulated sums to provide financial assistance to members in distress due to some deficiency or adversity, without expecting repayment; these funds fulfil an *insurance function.* Others make loans regardless of their members' individual needs, in which case it is the *savings or credit function* that predominates. Numerous varieties are conceivable – and exist – between these two extremes, such as funds that give impoverished members priority when extending credit facilities, but continue to insist on repayment. In other funds, borrowers and savers are under an obligation to provide mutual assistance to one another in emergencies. Some funds are based on the principle of solidarity and provide a 'collective' or a 'joint good', while in others all participants end up receiving a sum equal to what they have paid in (Callier 1990). Because of the immense diversity of arrangements and the complex of objectives, it makes little sense to restrict the research beforehand on the basis of the purpose or function of the funds. Distinguishing between temporary funds (which are however often reinstated again and again) and long-term arrangements is likewise a question of degree, and proves an unsuitable way of limiting the field beforehand. Furthermore, this distinction is generally related to whether the funds' activities relate more to the inherently short-term credit or the longer-term insurance function. One of the most interesting questions to be studied is precisely why in some periods and societies the funds take insurance as their prime objective, while in other times and countries saving is their first goal.

Thus the field to be studied is defined as the *small, informal, self-managing* savings fund in all its manifestations, from credit and savings association to insurance funds. As will become apparent, these three characteristics generate a specific set of shared features and problems, despite the funds' great diversity of time, place and nature.

This definition of the subject groups together phenomena that have scarcely ever been considered under a single heading before: on the one hand the nineteenth-century mutual funds run by and for workers in Europe (Hitchins 1993), and immigrants in America,[10] and on the other hand the savings funds that are found today not only in developing countries but also in the major cities of the West, where immigrants 'import' arrangements from their home countries and adapt them to their new situation (Clawson 1989).

For quite some time the comparison between countries of 'the South' and 'the North', between 'developing' and 'developed' societies, between 'the West' and 'the Third World' (and all these dichotomies sound awkward) were suspect, especially if the past of the early industrial economies was compared with the present of economies that industrialized later or less. Too often, a single road of development from the pre-industrial to the industrial phase, and beyond, had been assumed, implicitly or with so many words. In reaction to this developmentalism all historical comparison across continents became anathema. However, one need not at all assume unilinearity in development, to bring to bear the available knowledge about European or American society in the nineteenth century upon contemporary developments in Africa or Asia. The course of events in the Western past may be considered as one among many that may occur. One that was in fact observed, that may suggest questions, point to alternative possibilities, highlight contrasts. After all, comparison is not just about similarity, it is even more about difference. With this *caveat*, the comparison between centuries and across continents should proceed.

It is within the context of this extremely wide comparison, wide in terms of both historical period and social context, that the answer is sought to a series of questions of a historical, theoretical and practical nature.

As far as the *historical* aspects of the subject are concerned: in early industrial Europe, many millions of manual workers belonged to one of a host of small, largely informal, self-administered funds. Thus the mutuals contributed in large measure to the growth of a workers' culture in Western Europe, to the rise of trade unions and the development of insurance schemes and savings banks. These small, local initiatives were partly a reaction on the part of the workers to the 'civilizing offensives' aimed at them by the well-meaning bourgeoisie. This episode constitutes an essential chapter of Western European history which has recently attracted great interest, though much of it has yet to be written (International Social Security Review 1993). Nineteenth century mutual funds proved in retrospect to be a transitional phenomenon, related to a particular phase in the processes of market formation, industrialization and state formation. Although workers' families were already completely absorbed into the economy, they were also still part of a – crumbling – network of mutual care obligations among neighbors, fellow workers and relatives (often in distant home villages), which did not operate in terms of money. Mutuals partly continued, and partly replaced this network. The factory worker's existence made it increasingly difficult to resort to the land when times were bad, and made it necessary to introduce compensatory provisions. The once generous municipal support for paupers and vagrants was reduced, while there was as yet scarcely any public provision for old age, or for the breadwinner suffering sickness, accident or death, let alone for unemployment, and no compensation existed to cover the costs of medical treatment. The mutuals set out to fill some of these gaps. After a period of immense growth in the second half of the nineteenth century, the workers' funds shrank in number and size. With the commercialization of insurance and credit facilities on the one hand and the emergence of state insurance on the other, workers' funds disappeared or were incorporated into other schemes. Can similar developments, connections and time-sequences be found in present-day societies outside Europe? (Geertz 1962; Ardener 1964; Ardener & Burman 1995; Guyer 1995; Bouman 1994; Van der Linden 1996; Nzemen 1993).

The experience of the nineteenth-century working classes in Europe certainly cannot be applied wholesale to today's developing countries, but it nonetheless provides important material for comparison and for testing generalizations.

Mutual savings funds are also a highly relevant subject of study for a series of crucial questions in *social theory*. Saving is the postponement of gratification. Small entrepreneurs saved money, and still do, on an individual, or rather, family basis, and view saving as a personal virtue that is inculcated in upbringing within the family circle. Wage earners in the welfare state, however, are expected to pay contributions as a compulsory, collective form of savings, an institutionalized alternative to the insurance function fulfilled by individual savings. Whereas in the first case saving is a matter of 'self-coercion', and in the second case it is induced by 'external coercion', the participants of mutual funds are under *social constraints towards self-constraint*: they exert pressure on one another to contribute a small but fixed part of their income to the common fund at set intervals, an intermediate form of social discipline that mutuals allow us to study in what is perhaps its purest form. This coercion also works in relation to others: in societies where sharing *en famille* is taken for granted, the obligation to make deposits at set intervals provides a good excuse for withholding income from kinsmen who appeal to one's moral obligations.

Mutuals represent an intermediate form in another respect too: they function not within the family, nor in the far wider framework of a financial market or government bureaucracy, but on the basis of voluntary co-operation within a self-administered group. Rather than relying on mutual familial obligations on the one hand, or commercial insurance and public provisions on the other hand, the members rely on one another to provide insurance or facilitate savings. Viewed in macro-sociological perspective, the mutuals together make up a system of small, autonomous units, each of which is inclined to bar persons with limited means as bad risks, thus leaving out the lowest ranks: '*A system of small, autonomous, collective provisions always excludes the lower ranks – this is a sociological regularity*' (De Swaan 1989:154). By nineteenth-century mutuals and present-day savings clubs alike, creditworthiness was and is assessed on the basis of moral qualities such as 'a responsible way of living', and 'frugal habits' that will keep 'moral hazards' at bay.

When the government introduces exemptions and subsidies in an attempt to persuade funds to include the most vulnerable groups, it is in fact the well-to-do who make most use of these privileges. This was true in nineteenth-century England, where Anglican clergymen used the privileges extended to the 'friendly societies' for their own pension funds (Treble 1970; De Swaan 1989) and it is true today in India, when housewives from the educated classes contrive to obtain government loans on favorable terms – loans that are intended for the financially weak, but seldom reach them.

There is one important difference between the nineteenth-century mutuals in Europe and the United States and late twentieth-century funds in Africa, Asia and

Latin America. Among the former, it was the insurance function that predominated, whereas the modern equivalents largely operate as savings clubs. This distinction is relative, however: where the savings function takes precedence, the principal is paid out according to a schedule determined beforehand, by lottery or by auction; if insurance is the prime aim, payments are made to those who suffer a form of adversity defined beforehand: sickness or accident, or the loss of the breadwinner's income, with the money going to the surviving dependents in the event of the latter's death.

Savings funds too can take on an insurance function. This happens when a participant who has suffered adversity is given preferential treatment when it comes to paying out the principal, either out of pure solidarity or with the unfortunate participant being given the capital before his turn, with a discount being deducted and the capital still accruing him serving as security.

The administration of insurance funds is more problematic than that of pure savings funds, for three reasons:

- a rotating savings fund can be dissolved once each member in turn has received the capital accrued; the membership of mutual insurance schemes is unlimited in time, and in the case of funeral, disability and life insurance, it is in principle for life (unless the scheme has a 'buying out' option). In the case of insurance funds, therefore, money is managed and held in trust for long periods, with all the difficulties this involves, whereas in a rotating fund, the money deposited is promptly paid out to the person whose turn it is;
- insurance funds require a distinct sense of *solidarity*, which arises more easily within a homogeneous membership of people of roughly the same age and occupation and living in the same neighborhood, with their roots in the same village. Yet this same *homogeneity also leads to an accumulation of risks* and possibly to catastrophic bankruptcy (De Swaan 1989:153; Clawson 1989).
- estimating risks, calculating contributions, recording cases of damage and determining the sum to be paid out all requires actuarial and medical *expertise*, as well as a professional *distance* in relation to the fund members concerned. These two requirements *do not go together well with the mutual administration of the fund's affairs* by partners united by a sense of solidarity (De Swaan 1989:152; Mourges 1990; Lelart 1990; Pairault 1990).

In the comparative study of nineteenth-century insurance funds and contemporary savings schemes, the following may serve as a *working hypothesis*: *where misfortunes are cushioned by a system of non-monetary, mutual obligations within the extended family circle, mutual associations will confine themselves to the function of rotating savings fund. Where this insurance function is not, or no longer, fulfilled by the extended family, (nor yet by commercial or state insurance schemes), mutual associations will be assigned more insurance functions, always assuming that a fund manager is available who enjoys the trust of the participants on a long-term basis.* (Das Gupta 1996; Popkin 1979).

It will appear from the field studies that follow this chapter that insurance functions have remained the rare exception in the countries studied. At most, the participants in the rotating savings club will cede their turn to cash in on the principal and let some fellow member in acute need have it (or rather, persons in need may borrow the lump sum until their turn comes to take the kitty and they can pay off the advance with or without an added compensation in lieu of interest). Yet, migrants, like the Surinamese whom Aspha Bijnaar studied in the Amsterdam Bijlmer, or the inhabitants of the Cape Town township Ayelitsa, studied by Erik Bähre, live with much less support from their kin than was customary in their home surroundings and nevertheless have not introduced insurance provisions beyond elementary obligations to give some help to fellow members in need (under Apartheid, migrant workers in mines and factories did organize mutuals with a burial insurance). Surinamese with Dutch nationality (the vast majority of Surinamese in the Netherlands) qualify for Dutch social insurance. That may pre-empt their interest in mutual insurance. Abdoulaye Kane's 'tontines' of Haal Pulaar immigrants from Tilogne in France are hardly providential either, but they do insure the costs of transport for the remains of the deceased to their home village: burial costs were also among the first risks to be insured by the nineteenth century mutuals of the West. Hotze Lont has found a similar reluctance to collectively shoulder obligations toward members struck by adversity in the arisans of Djokjakarta. There too, burial insurances are the exception. Yet, in the course of time the members do build up 'social capital', a reputation for reliability with money and a network of fellow players who may help them over difficult times with an advance on the kitty that they expect to receive when their turn in the cycle comes.

The comparison evokes a question that ricochets back to the nineteenth century European mutuals: if contemporary savings clubs in the non-Western world do not create insurance provisions, then why did the friendly societies of a century and a half ago do so? Here, the tradition of the guild funds may have helped and also the example of the skilled craftsmen who preceded factory workers in forming friendly societies. In Asia and Africa, on the other hand, the extended families and clans continued to control and succor their kin as well they could up till the present, even if they do not always live up to the expectations and even if their support functions are slowly shrinking.

In Europe, the popularity of the small, self-governing insurance funds was short-lived and the clubs disappeared with the emergence of large commercial and governmental schemes. They were indeed a transitional phenomenon in the course of a major transition from small, kin-related or village-level arrangements to cope with deficiency and adversity towards the private and public arrangements on a national scale. The expectation was that the rotating savings clubs in the non-Western countries, too, would soon wither away, once an extensive and finely-branched banking system would cast its shadow over them. But nothing of the kind has happened and this is best explained by the collective aspects that the ROSCAs display, especially their capacity to exert social constraints upon their members that strengthen their propensity to save.

Although nothing is given away and nothing received for naught in the rotating mutual savings funds, their fundamental structure is the same as that of a cyclical system of gift exchange. A gift, as Marcel Mauss has stressed (1974), creates expectations of reciprocity, which, however, cannot be explicitly mentioned when it changes hands. The common underlying pattern is this: at a fixed moment and a fixed place the participants come together and each bring something for the person whose turn it is. But all of them will have their turn and collect from all their peers. In contemporary western society, this is the pattern of anniversary gifts in a circle of friends – an annual cycle. In rural societies, a similar pattern prevails for gift exchange at celebrations of birth, circumcision, holy communion, or marriage – in this case the cycle is generational. (In reality, the circle of participants is not always closed, it may have open ends, i.e. when people do not invite all their hosts of former celebrations or do include others who did not invite them when they held a celebration. In the former case, only time and oblivion can make up for the imbalance, in the latter, some future invitation must restore it). At some celebrations reciprocity is achieved instantly because the feast is lavish enough to make up for the gifts. Under different conditions, either the host or the visitors may end up feeling (and being considered) 'indebted'.

The cyclical and circular pattern of exchange is also found among neighbors who help one another to harvest (seasonal) or to build a barn (generational). In this case, the person whose turn has come to receive help does not reciprocate instantly and remains in debt to the others. At the end of the cycle every one will have been the recipient of neighborly assistance and everyone will have helped each neighbor: all duties and claims are 'in balance'. A dangerous moment, since there are no more outstanding claims and debts to tighten the social fabric: everything might just fall apart.

Mutual aid is an almost universal arrangement among free peasants and it resembles most closely the structure of contributions and obligations in the rotating mutual savings funds. Most likely, the savings clubs that emerged in early monetary societies reproduced a familiar pattern of mutual aid among neighbors and peers. Thus, the fact that these saving clubs are so widely spread may not be due to diffusion, but rather to local adaptation of patterns of mutual aid that emerged wherever free peasants live together. So far, almost nothing is known of the history of these mutual savings clubs outside Europe and the USA and only historical research can decide on the plausibility of this hypothesis.

Clearly, cooperation in a mutual fund, whether for insurance or saving purposes, can proffer the participants advantages which they can not realize on their own. When these mutuals have an insurance function, their collective character is obvious: an insurance capital that is owned by all members together is used to compensate the adversities which may strike any member any time. It entails a collectivization of existential risks. But even when the mutuals lack this insurance function entirely, i.e. when they function as ROSCAs. they still produce a 'joint' for their members. They allow everyone of them to accumulate through an enforced sequence of small deposits a sizable sum of money that is available and proportional to their needs at some point in time. In other words, on the one hand, for most of the time, the members display an 'illiquidity preference': they want to be pressured to deposit small amounts at set moments and be prevented from spending the balance for a given period (Shipton 1995; Papanek 1983; Dromain 1990; Liman Tinguiri 1990; Soegiarto 1993) On the other hand they reveal a liquidity preference for an adequate amount of money at a certain moment. Thus, the rotating fund provides a 'proportional liquidity sequence' to its members. This PLS can not be provided by any member alone, nor can it be undone by the defection of a single participant (although that would considerably endanger the operation of the fund). Members can be excluded from this PLS only when they fail to contribute *before* they receive the lump sum. If they fail to pay their dues *after* having collected it, they can no longer be punished. This temporal sequence is peculiar to the rotating funds and transforms the character of the enterprise in the course of the cycle. At the first turn there are n-1 creditors and a single recipient of the kitty who thereby becomes a debtor for the countervalue of (n-1) 'deposits' (having made one deposit himself) and who is to remain in debt for the remaining rounds. With each following turn another creditor receives the lump sum and is thereby transformed into one more debtor with a debt that is one deposit less than that of the preceding round and will last one round less. In the course of the cycle, a dwindling number of creditors for an amount that increases with each round finances a growing number of debtors for an amount that decreases with each round. In the final, n^{th} round the last creditor who is owed n deposits receives the kitty worth n deposits and has no debt to pay. All debtors have paid off their debts. The slates are clean and a new cycle may start.

The most sensitive phase in the cycle occurs halfway, when the outstanding debts, and therefore the outstanding credits, are at their maximum.[51] It is the moment when the total number of deposits paid by those yet to receive their principal is at its maximum, as is the sum of the deposits still to be paid by those who have already received the kitty. This is when the common enterprise is most vulnerable to defection. It is the point where 'social constraints toward self-constraint', mutual commitment and trust are most crucial. It is the moment in the cycle where the rotating fund is at its most collective.

The Proportional Liquidity Sequence that the rotating funds provide their participants with has yet another advantage over individual savings arrangements. Except for the last recipient, all members get their lump sum before they could have saved it themselves with equal deposits at the same points in time, some recipients obtaining it much earlier and the first one even right at the beginning. Of course, this extra bonus to the early beneficiaries is borne by the interest that the late recipients forego. But most people who participate in ROSCAs would not have received much interest from the bank on their meagre deposits in the first place, and they would have to pay steep tariffs for a loan if ever they got one, since bankers are likely to consider them high risk debtors. The rotating fund saves them banking fees, and under current banking rates the debtors' interest that they can spare by joining a ROSCA is much higher than the creditors' interest they must forego there. The banks must hedge against non-payment, but the mutuals can built on social constraint, reciprocal trust or 'collective social capital'. That is the underlying collective good supporting and being generated by the rotating funds.

The rotating fund ensures that members who often live in crowded homes without much protection against theft need not hoard their savings themselves, nor entrust them to someone else (safe deposits may be very hard to come by). At each turn, there is only one person with a sizable amount of cash, the recipient, who usually quickly spends it on durable consumer goods, family or ritual obligations or in the settlement of outstanding debts.

The participants in ROSCAs appear to be well aware of these jointly created advantages. They appreciate the opportunity for early credit, they like to have a sizable sum at their disposal at some point in the not too distant future, they would rather not have much cash lying around, and they enjoy the sociability of the regular gatherings with their peers (Thompson 1980). Most of all they want to be pressured into saving by their fellow members. In other words they want others to impose their own 'illiquidity preference' upon them, over and against their simultaneous inclination to spend, i.e. their preference for liquid means. Savings funds operate as a kind of 'Spenders Anonymous', in which the participants encourage each other to practice abstinence.[52]

Saving, after all, is the postponement of gratification (Barber 1957; Schneider & Lysgaard 1953) Small entrepreneurs saved money, and still do, on an individual, or rather, family basis. They view saving as a personal virtue that is inculcated in upbringing within the family circle. Wage earners in the welfare state, however, are expected to pay contributions as a compulsory, collective form of savings, an institutionalized and collectivized alternative to the insurance function fulfilled by individual savings. Whereas in the first case saving is a matter of 'self-coercion' and in the second case it is induced by 'external coercion', the participants of mutual funds have brought themselves under *social constraints toward self-constraint* (Elias 1982).The members exert pressure on one another to contribute a small but fixed part of their income to the common fund at set intervals, an intermediate form of social discipline that mutuals display in what is perhaps its purest form. This motivation crops up in all field observations and is demonstrated most convincingly in the chapter by Aspha Bijnaar.

These social constraints toward self-constraint also operate in relation to others. Tying up one's funds voluntarily by allowing a third party to impose constraints upon one's freedom to spend is also, of course, a manoeuvre intended to strengthen one's 'self-constraint' in refusing to give in to third-party demands, that is, a form of 'self-constraint to impose social constraint upon others' (Lont in this volume). In societies where sharing *en famille* is taken for granted, or where custom requires women to surrender their money to fathers, uncles or brothers, the obligation to make deposits at set intervals provides a good excuse for withholding cash against these insistent male claims.

The *practical relevance* of the research into mutual funds is related to the spread of savings clubs in present-day developing countries and among immigrants in the West. ROSCAs, along with moneylenders provide the major share of the informal credit facilities that are now receiving fresh attention from development experts (Bouman 1985; Hospes 1992; Baken & Van der Linden 1993). Efforts to arrange cheap loans through formal credit loan companies with government support for people of limited means have not always had the desired result. Because of this, there has been a reassessment of informal arrangements and experimental projects coupling mutual savings funds to formal credit institutions (Welsh 1989; Seibel 1985; Streefland 1993; Liman Tinquiri 1990).

In the rotating savings fund, the money deposited at a particular time is paid out immediately as capital to one of the members: this solves the problem of the 'safe keeping' of the fund's resources. In the case of individual saving, the money must be stored safely for a long time, with all the problems that go along with this, in a society and among population groups where banks and vaults may appear unfamiliar and remote. This raises the question of how banks or bank-like institutions can perform this safe-keeping task for what are often tiny deposits, and reinforce depositors' urge to save, without estranging this potential clientele by insisting on the usual administrative procedures, identification requirements and 'desk etiquette' (Kortenhorst & Zevenbergen 1989; Servet 1990; Financial Times July 7, 2003 and verbal comment by Arjen de Haan). Recently, numerous small-scale, rudimentary branch banks have been set up in peasant villages and slums in developing countries, often on a co-operative basis (Seibel 1985).

The mutual savings and insurance funds in Europe and the United States did not unite the weakest members of society; on the contrary, they served those who were relatively better off, excluding the financially weak as bad risks. In developing countries and among immigrants in the major cities, both the prosperous and those of limited means take part in savings clubs, whereas the rotating variant, the ROSCA, is most popular among the poor, with the poorest of all paying in and being repaid in goods such as rice. But there is always an even more vulnerable group that is excluded. Could even the utterly destitute be catered for by existing or alternative funds? Can mutual savings or insurance funds help to empower their members in the wider society? Can these funds provide an incentive to small entrepreneurs? It is often women who start a joint savings fund, using what is left of the housekeeping money. Does it help them expand the margins of their independence, to decide independently how to spend their own earnings, to trade in their own right? (Guyer 1995).

Mutual associations come 'from the people themselves' and are often intertwined with local culture. They therefore offer an alternative to a policy that stems from, and is pursued by, the state and large organizations, which inevitably come 'from outside' and intervene 'from above'. Still, combinations are entirely conceivable here, albeit not without problems: rotating funds may be regarded as the informal counterpart of those formal institutions that encourage people to save; it would be quite possible for mutual funds to decide, whether individually or as a group, to use the services of modern savings banks (Pairault 1990).

This leads us to the question of how formal institutions, which are often particularly bureaucratic in developing countries, can find some common ground with small-scale, informal and if not traditional, at least spontaneously formed arrangements. In highly developed economies, this is treated as a marketing problem for banking and insurance services. But this presupposes the full monetarization of society and the near-universal ability and willingness of the population to act as consumers, clients and account holders. In developing countries, this monetarization and businesslike approach is far from universal, and financial services for the poorest members of society must take account of prevailing attitudes and living conditions. There is much to be learnt here from the ways in which education and health care have been brought to the poorest groups. Furthermore, research into mutual funds among immigrants in Western cities seems most worthwhile. Immigrants often use formal banks and insurance companies alongside informal savings clubs and familial credit facilities; in doing so, they have developed a host of specially adapted hybrid forms that could prove extremely instructive in this connection.

Conclusion

To sum up, a comparison between the nineteenth-century European and American mutual associations and late twentieth-century funds in developing countries and immigrant circles in the West must focus in the first place on the question of why the former fulfilled insurance functions while the latter are far less likely to do so. Another area to be researched is whether the 'sociological regularity' whereby 'lower' classes are excluded and 'higher' ones privileged applies equally in non-Western countries.

As far as the funds' internal dynamics is concerned, it has to be established whether today's non-Western savings clubs find themselves facing the same dilemmas as did the nineteenth-century Western mutuals: a homogeneous membership versus the accumulation of risks this entails; self-management versus the need for administrative and possibly actuarial expertise; mutual solidarity versus the need for distance and discipline in the approach to members. It will be clear from what has already been said that the short cycles on which most ROSCAs are based help to avert long-term risks, and that the simple sequence of turns collecting deposits and handing out the principal diminish the importance of expertise and integrity. Furthermore, as ROSCAs do not have any long-term obligations to pay out money to their members, distance and discipline are required only in dealing with defaulters, and here the fact that people know each other and have a sense of solidarity actually serves to reinforce the group pressure to continue making the agreed deposits. Thus the short cycles according to which the ROSCAs operate could be regarded as a solution to the nineteenth-century dilemmas, which hence leads to the insurance function being abandoned.

The contemporary rotating savings funds provide their members with an incentive to restrict consumption and save, while providing them with a sizable sum in the near future, they offer a 'Proportional Liquidity Sequence.' In a certain sense, so did the nineteenth century insurance funds, who reinforced their members' propensity to save and held out the promise that they would receive a considerable amount one day when they would really need it. Both the nineteenth-century mutual funds and present-day savings clubs allow us to study the concept of people being under 'social constraints toward self-constraint' in its purest form, and permit the study of numerous matters in the peripheral area between communal and collective action. Mutual funds may be regarded as formative institutions in the psychogenesis and sociogenesis of the monetary and market-oriented mentality: in other words, they are transitional phenomena. But this is not to say that today's savings clubs will prove as ephemeral as the Western mutual funds, which were disbanded or taken over with the advent of commercial and public insurance. On the contrary, there is every reason to study the potential interfaces between the small, sprightly, informal savings clubs on the one hand, and the wealthy, formal credit institutions on the other, both commercial and public (or semi-public), for it is a subject of the greatest possible practical importance.

The prevalence of savings clubs and the amount of money that rotates within them are hard to determine, partly because of their informal and fleeting nature. The only way to gain a grasp of the significance and extent of the phenomenon is by extrapolating from local findings and specific field studies, and by meticulously taking stock of references – frequently casual in nature and strewn about a text – that appear in the literature of anthropology, developmental sociology and economics. Viewed in dynamic and historical perspective, a study of the prevalence of these funds thus also becomes, or becomes primarily, a study of the social diffusion of an institution: where did the funds and savings clubs originate, how did they spread, and where did they arise 'spontaneously' as a kind of 'savoir endogène' (Hountondji 1994), forming a pattern later duplicated elsewhere?

The ambivalent nature of mutual funds is also reflected by the efforts that have been made to arrive at a political evaluation of the phenomenon: were the workers' funds – and are the rotating savings clubs – instruments with which a relatively well-to-do and privileged social stratum endeavors to distance itself from 'lesser' and 'lower' ranks of society and to adopt a 'bourgeois' lifestyle? Or should these arrangements be interpreted instead as communal efforts to empower a section of society that remains relatively under-privileged, with few opportunities for advancement?

In the early European literature on the workers' funds, both these views can be found: some historians conclude that they were started by the 'respectable' workers who were finally learning how to save and to plan for the future, as befitted all good citizens, while others evoke the image of unruly proletarians who were secretly building up strike funds and learning how to conduct concerted action. The truth indeed varies from one fund to the next, and can only be determined by specific case studies. The same applies to the savings clubs of today.

The mutual funds, in all their variety, are first and foremost a local, small-scale, group phenomenon. Yet, these small clubs spread, with the same basic characteristics, over almost the entire inhabited world. They are therefore a near-ideal subject for comparative and historical study on a global scale, permitting close collaboration between the various sub-disciplines of social science.

Notes

1 China (Pairault 1990)
2 Japan (Miyanaga 1995)
3 Pakistani (in Oxford, England) (Srinivasan 1995)
4 Ewe, Gin and Ouatchie (Togo) (Soedjédé 1990)
5 Kotokoli-Kabye (Togo); ibid.
6 Akposso (Togo); ibid.
7 Kotokoli (Togo); ibid.
8 Indonesia (South Sulawesi) (Hospes 1995)
9 Egypt (Herrera, 1992)
10 Western Nigeria (Falola 1995)
11 Nigeria (Mabogunje 1995)
12 Malawi (Ardener 1995)
13 Malaysia; ibid.
14 Niger (Kiari 1990)
15 Indonesia (gen.) and Sumatra (Hospes 1995); for *andilan* cf. Dutch *aandeel.*
16 Haïti (Besson 1995); she also records the terms *susu* in Jamaica and *sousou* in St Vincent, analogous to the West African term.
17 Guyana, Dominican Republic and Barbados ibid.
18 Mexico (Vélez Ibanez 1983)
19 Guatemala; ibid.
20 Peru; ibid.
21 Ethiopia (Bouman 1994)
22 India (Bouman 1989)
23 Turkish Cypriots (Khatib-Chahidi 1995)
24 Zaïre (Yaoundé, 1993)
25 France, England and Germany (De Swaan 1989)
26 The Netherlands, the nineteenth century and earlier (Timmer 1913)
27 Central African Republic (Nzemen 1990)
28 Mauritania (Zombre Coulibaly 1992)
29 Wolof (Senegal) (Diagne1978-1982)
30 Bamileke in Cameroon (Bouman & Hospes)
31 Bamileke in Cameroon (Nzemen 1993)
32 South Africa (Burman & Lembete)
33 South Africa (cf. Dandala & Moraka 1990; Bähre 1996)
34 Umueke Agbaja, Southeast Nigeria; ibid.
35 Korea (Light & Zhong Deng)
36 Kikuyu in Kenya (Nelson)
37 Ruanda (Desroche 1990)
38 Congo, Togo, Chad (Pinardel Tchaptchet 1988)
39 Cameroon (Niger-Thomas)

40 Thailand (Steinwand)
41 Suriname, also in the Amsterdam Bijlmermeer ward (Van Wetering 1999; Bijnaar: oral communication)
42 Encountered without any indication of its origins (Henry, Tchente & Guillerme-Dieumegard 1991) The last three terms probably originate from the Philippines, Mozambique and Thailand respectively.
43 Kurdish (Goran Baba Ali oral communication).
44 Wolof (Lelart 1995)
45 Wolof (Kane, in this volume)
46 Haal Pular (Kane, in this volume)
47 Ethiopia (Gerdes 1975)
48 Javanese in Surinam (Bijnaar: oral communication)
49 Hindustani in Surinam (idem)
50 Here, *America* stands for Latin America, where – especially in Chile – workers' mutuals were of great importance (cf. Grez Toso 1993) 3, 29-52); on present-day Mexico and Mexicans in the United States (cf. Velez-Ibañez)
51 The total amount owed, y, at turn x in a cycle of n turns, $y = x.(n-x)=-xn-x^2$, is highest when $dy/dx=0= n-2x$; $x= \frac{1}{2}n$, or half way the cycle.
52 Moneylenders often play a similar role in developing societies. They not only demand (and sometimes even extort) payment from defaulters, but also exert pressure on them to work; they are always close at hand to advise, monitor activities and provide encouragement.

References

Ardener, S.
1964 'The Comparative Study of Rotating Credit Associations.' *Journal of the Royal Anthropological Institute*, 94(2):201-29.
1995 'Women Making Money Go Round; ROSCAs Revisited.' In: S. Ardener & S. Burman (eds), *Money-Go-Rounds. The Importance of Rotating Savings and Credit Associations for Women*, 1-19. Oxford: Berg.
Baken, R.-J. & J. Van der Linden
1993 'Getting the Incentives Right': Banking on the Formal Private Sector. A critique of Current World Bank Thinking on Low-Income Housing Delivery in Third World Cities', *Third World Population Review*, 15(1):1-16.
Barber, B.
1957 *Social Stratification. A Comparative Analysis of Structure and Process.* New York: Harcourt.
Besson, J.
1995 'Women's Use of ROSCAs in the Caribbean: Reassessing the Literature.' In: S. Ardener & S. Burman (eds), *Money-Go-Rounds. The Importance of Rotating Savings and Credit Associations for Women*, 263-288. Oxford: Berg.
Bähre, E.
1996 *We Organize Each Other: Financial Self-help Groups and Civics in the Townships of Cape Town*, South Africa, unpublished MA Thesis Utrecht University, Utrecht.
Bouman, F.J.A.
1985 'Indigenous Savings and Credit Societies in the Third World: A Message.', *Quarterly Journal of International Agriculture*, 24(4):181-218.

1989 *Small, Short and Unsecured.Informal Rural Finance in India.* New Delhi [etc.]: Oxford University Press.

1994 'Informal Rural Finance: An Aladdin's Lamp of Information.' In: F.J.A. Bouman & O. Hospes (eds), *Financial Landscapes Reconstructed: the Fine Art of Mapping Development,* 105-22. Boulder [etc.]: Westview Press.

Burman, S. & N. Lembete

1995 'Building New Realities; African Women and ROSCAs in Urban South Africa.' In: S. Ardener & S. Burman (eds), *Money-Go-Rounds. The Importance of Rotating Savings and Credit Associations for Women,* 23-47. Oxford: Berg.

Callier, P.

1990 'Informal finance: The Rotating Saving and Credit Association – an Interpretation', *Kyklos,* 43: 273-276.

Calisti,L.

1982 *La mutualité en mouvement.* Paris, Editions Sociales.

Clawson, M.A.

1989 *Constructing Brotherhood. Class, Gender and Fraternalism.* Princeton: Princeton University Press.

Dandala, H.M. & K. Moraka

1990 *A Book on Burial Societies: Masingcwabisane – Are Bolokaneng.* Braamfontein: Skotaville.

Das Gupta, R.

1996 'Social Security and Mutual Assistance in Late Colonial India: A Preliminary Account.' In: M. Van der Linden, *Social Security Mutualism*: 555-575. Berne: Peter Lang.

Desroche, H.

1990 'Nous avons dit *tontines.* Des tontines Nord aux tontines Sud, Allers et retours.' In: M. Lelart (ed.), *La tontine. Pratique informelle d'épargne et de crédit dans les pays en voie de développement,* 1-24. Montrouge: John Libbey Eurotext.

De Swaan, A.

1989 *Zorg en de staat, Welzijn, onderwijs en gezondheidszorg in Europa en de Verenigde Staten in de nieuwe tijd.* Amsterdam: Bert Bakker.

Fatou Diagne,

1978-82 *Les tontines à Dakar.* Dakar: Ministère de l'éducation nationale.

Dreyfus, M. & B. Gibaud (eds.)

1995 *Mutualités de tous les pays.* Paris: Fédération Nationale de la Mutualité Française.

Dromain, M.

1990 'L'épargne ignorée et negligée. Les resultats d'une enquête sur les tontines in Sénégal.' In: M. Lelart (ed.), *La tontine. Pratique informelle d'épargne et de crédit dans les pays en voie de développement,* 161-162. Montrouge: John Libbey Eurotext.

Dumont, J.P.

1993 'Mutualism in the World: Ignorance, Inequalities and Market Pressures.' *International Social Security Review,* 46:99-108

Elias, N.

1982 *Het Civilisatieproces; Sociogenetische en psychogenetische onderzoekingen.* Utrecht/Antwerpen: Het Spectrum.

Falola, T.

1995 'Money and Informal Credit Institutions in Colonial Western Nigeria'. In: J.I. Guyer (ed.), *Money Matters. Instability, Values and Social Payments in the Modern History of West African Communities,* 162-187. Portsmouth, NH and London: Heinemann.

Geertz, C.
1962 'The Rotating Credit Association: A "Middle Rung" in Development.' *Economic Development and Cultural Change*, 10(3):241-63.
Gerdes,V.
1975 'Precursors of Modern Social Security in Indigenous African Institutions.' *Journal of Modern African Studies*, 13:209-28.
Grez Toso, S.
1993 'The Mutual Benefit Movement in Chile from its Origins to the Present Time (1853-1992).' *International Social Security Review*, 46, 3:29-52.
Guyer, J. (ed.)
1995 *Money Matters. Instability, Values and Social Payments in the Modern History of West African Communities.* Portsmouth, N.H and London: Heinemann.
Henry, A., et al.
1991 *Tontines et banques au Cameroun. Les principes de la Société des amis.* Paris: Karthala.
Herrera, L.
1992 'Scenes of Schooling: Inside a Girls' School in Cairo.' *Cairo Papers in Social Science*, 15(1):60-61.
Hitchins, K.
1993 'Mutual Benefit Societies in Hungary, 1830s-1941.' *International Social Security Review*, 46, 3:79-98.
Hospes, O.
1992 'People that Count: The Forgotten Faces of Rotating Savings and Credit Associations in Indonesia.' *Savings and Development*, 16:371-400.
1995 'Women's differential Use of ROSCAs in Indonesia.' In: S. Ardener & S. Burman (eds), *Money-Go-Rounds. The Importance of Rotating Savings and Credit Associations for Women*, 127-148. Oxford: Berg.
Houtondji, P. (ed.)
1994 *Les savoirs endogènes. Pistes pour une recherche.* Paris: Karthala.
International Social Security Review 46 (3) (special edition 1993).
Khatib-Chahidi, J.
1995 'Gold Coins and Coffee ROSCAs; Coping with Inflation the Turkish Way in Northern Cyprus.' In: S. Ardener & S. Burman (eds), *Money-Go-Rounds. The Importance of Rotating Savings and Credit Associations for Women.* Oxford: Berg.
Kiari, L.T.
1990 'Epargne et crédit informels en milieu rural au Niger: l'activité des tontines et des gardes-monnaie villageois.' In: M. Lelart (ed.), *La tontine. Pratique informelle d'épargne et de crédit dans les pays en voie de développement*, 177-202. Montrouge: John Libbey Eurotext.
Kortenhorst, K. & K. Zevenbergen
1989 *The Common Man's Money Matters. The Case of Autonomous Savings and Credit Associations (India).* Amsterdam: CASA Werkdocument No. 18.
Lelart, M.
1990 'Une tontine mutuelle dans l'Administration béninoise.' In: M. Lelart (ed.), *La tontine. Pratique informelle d'épargne et de crédit dans les pays en voie de développement*, 53-80. Montrouge: John Libbey Eurotext.
1995 'Les pratiques informelles d'épargne et de crédit: une approche économique.' In: J.M. Servet (ed.), *Épargne et Liens sociaux. Études comparées d'informalités financières.* [cahiers Finance Éthique Confiance], 85-104. Paris : Association d'Eco Financière.

Liman Tinguiri, K.
1990 'Épargne et crédit informels en milieu rural au Niger: l'Activité des tontines et des gardes-monnaie villageois.' In: M. Lelart (ed.), *La tontine. Pratique informelle d'épargne et de crédit dans les pays en voie de développement*, 177-202. Montrouge: John Libbey Eurotext.
Light, L. & Z. Deng
1995 'ROSCA Participation among Koreans in Los Angeles.' In: S. Ardener & S. Burman (eds), *Money-Go-Rounds. The Importance of Rotating Savings and Credit Associations for Women*, 217-240. Oxford: Berg.
Mabogunje, A.L.
1995 'The Capitalization of Money and the Credit in the Development Process: The Case of Community Banking in Nigeria.' In: Jane I. Guyer (ed.), *Money Matters. Instability, Values and Social Payments in the Modern History of West African Communities*, 277-296. Portsmouth, NH and London: Heinemann.
Mauss, M.
1974 *The Gift. Forms and Functions of Exchange in Archaic Societies.* London: Routledge and Kegan.
Miyanaga, K.
1995 'Economic Kou (ROSCAs) in Japan: a Review.' In: S. Ardener & S. Burman (eds), *Money-Go-Rounds. The Importance of Rotating Savings and Credit Associations for Women*, 149-162. Oxford: Berg.
Mourgues, N.
1990 'Réflexions sur les mécanismes financiers des systèmes tontiniers.' In: M. Lelart (ed.), *La tontine. Pratique informelle d'épargne et de crédit dans les pays en voie de développement*, 245-266. Montrouge: John Libbey Eurotext.
Nelson, N.
1995 'The Kiambu Group in Nairobi.' In: S. Ardener & S. Burman (eds), *Money-Go-Rounds. The Importance of Rotating Savings and Credit Associations for Women*. 49-70. Oxford: Berg.
Niger-Thomas, M.
1995 'Women's Access to Credit in Cameroon.' In: S. Ardener & S. Burman (eds), *Money-Go-Rounds. The Importance of Rotating Savings and Credit Associations for Women*. 95-110. Oxford: Berg.
Nzemen, M.
1993 *Tontines et développement ou le défi financier de l'Afrique* 16, 101, Yaoundé: Presses Universitaires de Cameroun.
Pairault, Th.
1990a 'Formes traditionelles de tontines chinoises.' In: M. Lelart (ed.), *La tontine. Pratique informelle d'épargne et de crédit dans les pays en voie de développement*, 81-94. Montrouge: John Libbey Eurotext.
1990b 'Sociétés de tontines et banques des petites et moyennes entreprises à Taiwan.' In: M. Lelart (ed.), *La tontine. Pratique informelle d'épargne et de crédit dans les pays en voie de développement*, 281-308. Montrouge: John Libbey Eurotext.
Papanek, H.
1983 *Implications of Development for Women in Indonesia: Selected Research and Policy Issues.* Boston: Center for Asian Development Issues.
Popkin, S.L.
1979 *The Rational Peasant: The Political Economy of Rural Society in Vietnam.* 47. Berkeley [etc.]: University of California Press.

Schneider, L. & S. Lysgaard
1953 'The Deferred Gratification Pattern: A Preliminary Study.' *American Sociological Review*, 18:142-149.
Servet, J.-M.
1990 'Les tontines, formes d'activités informelles et d'initiatives collectives privées en Afrique.' In: M. Lelart (ed.), *La tontine. Pratique informelle d'épargne et de crédit dans les pays en voie de développement*, 267-280. Montrouge: John Libbey Eurotext.
Shipton, P.
1995 'How Gambians Save: Culture and Economic Strategy at an Ethnic Crossroads.' In: Jane I. Guyer (ed.), *Money Matters. Instability, Values and Social Payments in the Modern History of West African Communities*, 245-276. Portsmouth, NH and London: Heinemann.
Soedjédé, D.A.
1990 'L'épargne et le crédit non structurés au Togo.' In: M. Lelart (ed.), *La tontine. Pratique informelle d'épargne et de crédit dans les pays en voie de développement*, 200-210. Montrouge: John Libbey Eurotext.
Soegiarto, H.N.
1993 'The Embeddedness of Money, Moneylenders and Moneylending in a Javanese Town. A Case Study of Bantul-Yogyakarta Special Province.' (doctoral dissertation, Universität Bielefeld).
Srinivasan, S.
1995 'ROSCAs among South Indians in Oxford.' In: S. Ardener & S. Burman (eds), *Money-Go-Rounds. The Importance of Rotating Savings and Credit Associations for Women*, 199-208. Oxford: Berg.
Seibel, H.D.
1985 'Saving for Development. A Linkage Model for Informal and Formal Financial Markets.' *Quarterly Journal of International Agriculture*, 24:390-398;
Steinwand, D.
1994 'Money Lending and Modern Times: Informal Credit in Thailand.' In: F.J.A. Bouman & O. Hospes (eds), *Financial Landscapes Reconstructed: the Fine Art of Mapping Development*. 298-299. Boulder: Westview Press.
Streefland, P.H.
1993 Credit and Conscientization: Effects of Different Development Approaches in Bangladesh. *Public Administration and Development*, 13:153-169.
Tchaptchet, F.P.
1988 *Communautarisme et solidarité Africaine: l'expérience associative Camerounaise.* Paris: thèse de 3e cycle, Paris VIII, UFR sociologie.
Thompson, E. P.
1980 *The Making of the English Working Class.* Harmondsworth: Penguin.
Timmer, E.M.A.
1913 *Knechtsgilden en knechtsbossen in Nederland: arbeidersverzekeringen in vroeger tijden*, (Diss. Universiteit van Amsterdam). Haarlem: Kleynenberg.
Treble, J.H.
1970 'The Attitudes of Friendly Societies towards the Movement in Great Britain for State Pensions, 1878-1908.' *International Review of Social History*, 15:266-299.
Van der Linden, M. & J. Sluijs
1996 *Onderlinge Hulpfondsen. Historische en etnografische essays.* Amsterdam: IISG.
Van der Linden, M. (ed.)
1996a *Social Security Mutualism. The Comparative History of Mutual Benefit Societies.* Bern [etc.]: Peter Lang.

1996b 'De historische logica van onderlinge arbeidersverzekeringen.' In: *Onderlinge Hulpfondsen*, 23-44. Amsterdam: IISG.

Van Wetering, I.

1999 'ROSCAs, Ethnicity and Strategy: Suriname Creole Women's Saings Clubs in Amsterdam.' In: R. Barot et al (eds), *Ethnicity, Gender and Social Change*. 60-77. Houndsmill: MacMillan.

Vélez Ibanez, C.

1983 *Bonds of Trust: The Cultural System of Rotating Credit Associations among Urban Mexicans and Chicanos*. New Brunswick, NJ, 1:25-26.

Welsh, B. et al (eds)

1989 *Banking the Unbankable. Bringing Credit to the Poor.* London: Panos Publ.

Zombre Coulibaly, G.M.M.

1992 *Les tontines féminines à Ouagadougou (Burkina Faso): Une alternative d'entraide face à la crise environmentale.* Dakar: Université Cheikh Anta Diop.

CHAPTER 2

Changing interdependencies and the state

How financial mutuals have changed in South Africa

Erik Bähre

Introduction

Financial mutuals are very widespread and popular among Africans in South Africa. It was not uncommon for Africans in Cape Town – the place where I undertook most of my fieldwork – to put aside more than half of their income in these saving- and credit associations or insurance schemes. In South Africa, financial mutuals have not disappeared and in my view are not likely to disappear like they have largely in Europe and the United States, or as expected by modernization theory. But financial mutuals did change, particularly in the late 1980s and 1990s. During apartheid, financial mutuals were predominantly insurance schemes consisting of male migrants from the same area in the Eastern Cape. With the breakdown of apartheid, the variety of financial mutuals increased as more savings and credit arrangements emerged. Also the type of participants changed. Participants were increasingly women and, contrary to men, they were not migrants from the same area in the Eastern Cape, but neighbors. How did this change occur? What led to the changes of the type of identifications on which financial mutuals were founded, and the kinds of financial mutuals? Why did these changes take place simultaneously? Based on ethnographic fieldwork and the limited amount of historical sources on this subject, I will attempt to reveal the nature of these changes, as well as reveal its causes.

Let us first turn to existing approaches that deal with financial mutuals and change and see how these approaches can help us to understand South African financial mutuals. Geertz (1962) was probably the first to develop a general theory about financial mutuals. Geertz expected that these migrant organizations were eventually going to disappear. He argued that migrants needed financial mutuals to overcome the differences between their traditional rural society with a modern urban society: 'the rotating credit society is such a middle rung in the process of development from a largely agrarian peasant society to one in which trade pays an increasingly crucial role' (Geertz 1962:262). He expected that modern financial institutions, such as banks, were eventually going to replace financial mutuals. His argument was that financial mutuals took over some of the functions of kinship in an urban area. Financial mutuals were expected to have an adaptive function because they helped people to overcome the discrepancies of the traditional and modern worlds and finally lead to the rationalization and modernization of people. According to Geertz (1962:259):

> A form of symbiosis between the 'traditional' social structure of the immigrants and the more 'rational' one into which they have been suddenly projected has made possible the immigrants' adaptation to the new economic and political tasks with which they are faced, while at the same time minimizing the strain of transition and social transformation.

Financial mutuals were expected to overcome the tensions between traditional and modern society and once the migrants had adapted themselves to modern society these organizations were expected to disappear and modern financial institutions, such as banks, would replace financial mutuals.

History has proven that these assumptions were wrong. Financial mutuals still thrive in most parts of the world, even when banks are present and also among people who have lived in the city all their lives. The popularity of financial mutuals in South Africa cannot be fully attributed to the absence of a banking system. Many participants of financial mutuals are employed in the formal economy and receive their salary at the bank. Some financial mutuals deposit their savings in a group account at the bank. Although banks treat poor people with suspicion and their services often do not meet the demands of the poor, the banking system is widely used in South Africa, also by participants of financial mutuals.

Geertz, and many others, attempted to embed financial mutuals in a theory of change. However, as part of modernization theory that was en vogue at that time, it was wrongly presupposed that people developed along a linear path towards rationalization and individualization.[1] Geertz (1962:261) also argued that '[t]he theoretical as well as the practical interest of the association [financial mutual] lies in its ability to organize traditional relationships in such a way that they are slowly but steadily transformed into non-traditional ones'. But financial mutuals among the Xhosa in Cape Town were not based on traditional forms of solidarity. Participants of financial mutuals were not part of a particular clan, kin-group, church, or age group. On the contrary: the members of financial mutuals barely knew one another and were often new neighbors. If financial mutuals are not based on traditional forms of solidarity, on what are they based? If it is not a clear-cut case of traditional relations transforming into modern ones, then how do relations change?

Financial mutuals were expected to disappear in the third world once modernization had done its work. This evolutionary approach to financial mutuals, or societies in general, was probably inspired by the disappearance of financial mutuals in Europe and the United States. In 19th century Europe and the United States financial mutuals disappeared largely, only to revive recently among migrant communities, such as those studied by Bijnaar and Kane (this volume). Studies by, among others, Van Genabeek (1996), Van der Linden (1996a; 1996b), and De Swaan (1996a; 1996b), have revealed the rise, as well as fall, of financial mutuals in the western world. De Swaan (1996) utilizes Elias' (1982) concept of figuration to explain that changing interdependencies and moral orientations towards the poor were fundamental to the collectivization of care arrangements in Europe. Mutual aid societies were an important transitory phase but eventually declined by the end of the 19th century due to organizational weaknesses that were inherent to the interdependencies of members. Moreover, state enforced collective arrangements provided an alternative and a sense of belonging that transcended older identifications (see also Van der Linden 1996b).

De Swaan (1996b:12) applied Elias' concept of social constraint toward self-constraint in describing this aspect of financial mutuals.[2] Late 18th and 19th century migrant workers resorted to financial mutuals as traditional forms of solidarity became insufficient. Workers mutuals provided insurance against unemployment, death and illness. Moreover, the social constraint toward self-constraint in these organizations agreed with notions of civilization among its participants. This concept encompasses the ability of the participants to save in the absence of fellow participants, as well as the social constraint offered by fellow members who force one another to put money aside for the financial mutual. Participants of financial mutuals constrain themselves from spending their money in anticipation of the social constraint by fellow members who rely on the money.

How do the evolutionary perspectives contribute to an explanation of the changing mutuals in South Africa? Financial mutuals in South Africa have changed, not disappeared, which is markedly different from Geertz's assumptions about the future of financial mutuals and the demise of financial mutuals in Europe and the United States in the 19th century. Nevertheless, South African mutuals need to be analysed by unravelling the interconnectedness of state transformation and interdependencies. By revealing the impact that the apartheid and post-apartheid state had on migrants' interdependencies, it will become clear why financial mutuals went to these specific changes. Financial mutuals cannot be studied as if they existed in a socio-political vacuum. One gains insight in the changes that these arrangements undergo by putting state transformation and shifting interdependencies at the core of the analysis. One must consider the impact that capitalism, the apartheid state, as well as the post-apartheid state have had on the Xhosa economy and the constitution of social relationships. First, I will briefly highlight the incorporation of the Xhosa people into the colonial and apartheid political economy. Second, the impact on relations among kin, neighbors, and migrants from the same area will become clear. I will examine how new relations emerged among migrant men in Cape Town, how these relations offered the social constraint to accumulate money, and how these relations were effected by the abolishment of apartheid. Furthermore, the gendered dynamics of apartheid and post-apartheid migration will be revealed and set against the establishment of financial mutuals by women.

In order to establish financial mutuals one needs money. Therefore, to study financial mutuals one needs to examine what the consequences of the fairly recent introduction of money were for the Xhosa society. Money was introduced as part of the package deal of colonialism and capitalist expansion. The political economic change that took place in South Africa from the 18th century onwards was one from a kin-ordered mode of production to one in which the capitalist mode of production became important. A kin-ordered mode of production meant that kinship relations were central to social labor: 'Put simply, through kinship social labor is "locked up", or "embedded", in particular relations between people. This labor can be mobilized only through access to people, such access being defined symbolically' (Wolf 1982:91). Due to capitalist expansion, the capitalist mode of production started to play a major role. Capitalists were in control of the means of production. Laborers had to sell their labor power, often at a low price for capitalists to accumulate (Wolf 1982:77-78). These modes of production did not necessarily present different types of society, or evolutionary stages, but are 'constructs with which to envisage certain strategic relationships that shape the terms under which human lives are conducted' (Wolf 1982:100).

Earning money

As early as 1777, Xhosa worked as domestic and agricultural servants, and sometimes as slaves, in the Cape Colony. In return, they were paid in 'beads, brass-ware and brass plates, and sometimes in articles of clothing' (Gardner 1835:174 cited in Cock 1980:174). Slavery was abolished in 1834, but the many economic and political pressures either forced Xhosa men and women to start or continue working as wage laborers or offered them new economic opportunities. The colonial conquest by the British army in the mid 19th-century forced many Xhosa off their lands and led to the foreign control of Xhosa chiefs. The occupation of their lands and subjugation of chiefs made it increasingly difficult for them to survive on land and livestock. The spread of lung sickness among cattle in 1855 contributed to a further collapse of the Xhosa economy and society, 'killing two-thirds of the stock in some areas and virtually wiping out the herds of even cattle-rich chiefs' (Ross 1999:51). For most, it became impossible to maintain a subsistence economy: cash income through wage labor became vital for survival.

The rise of a millenarian prophecy in the mid 1800s revealed, as well as further intensified, the already desperate situation of the Xhosa. According to a young girl named Nongqawuse, the 'end of the world' as they knew it could be stopped. She prophesized that their lives would change for the better if they destroyed the harvest and remaining cattle. Only total destruction would cause the Whites to leave, grain pits to fill up, and herds of cattle to return. Her prophecy led to the mass destruction of cattle and grain in 1857 and left a tremendous human tragedy in its wake (Ross 1999:51-52; see also Peires 1989). According to historical sources, between 20,000 and 40,000 Xhosa died of starvation: some even reported incidences of cannibalism (Cock 1980: 202; Ross 1999: 52).

Natural disasters, especially the droughts of 1876 to 1878 and 1912 (Cock 1980:203; Beinart 1982:75-78), and rinderpest epidemics resulted in a continued destruction of the Xhosa subsistence economy. For example, in Pondoland the 1912 draught and East Coast fever spread by ticks brought about deaths of cattle on a large-scale. In roughly five years (from 1911 to 1915) heads of cattle plunged from almost 280,000 in number to just over 54,000. A main source of income was thus lost and the use of cattle for the establishment of conjugal and affinal relations must have been under serious threat. To prevent further spread of East Coast fever, the movement of cattle was severely restricted and cattle dipping was introduced. In 1915, a cattle dipping tax of five shilling was introduced, but regular cattle dipping was only enforced by around 1920. These measures (restricted movement and the dipping of cattle) resulted in an increase in cattle, which in turn caused its own problems. The increase of cattle, combined with the restrictions on transport for cattle to other markets, led to a decline in the price of cattle by the end of the decade. The decreasing income levels must have been felt even more harshly due to the taxation per homestead which was already introduced in 1895. Due to the vulnerability of agriculture, failure of cash crops, starvation of cattle, and taxation, young men decided to leave their homes and work in the mines, cities, or White-owned farms (Beinart 1982:36, 75-78, 94, 173). The scale of labor migration was massive:

> According to the 1936 Census Report, about 54 per cent of the adult male population of the reserves was absent ... over half the Keiskammahoek [which is a district in the Ciskei] population consisted of those too old, too young, or too ill to earn wages (Bundy 1979:225).

Whatever was left of land and cattle was further threatened by apartheid's 'betterment schemes' that started in the 1930s (Wilson & Ramphele 1994:220). Basically, the 'betterment schemes' was forced villigization: 'the movement of people into villages, the excising of old lands and the demarcation of new fields, the establishment of crazing camps, and nothing more' (McAllister 1996:13). Particularly in the former Ciskei, I came across villages that at first glance appeared to be remote, picturesque, subsistence-based communities, but which were actually rural slums created through betterment. During a funeral in such a small and remote village, I asked a resident how old the village was, to which he replied: 'Oh, this village is very old. It was built in the early 1960s.'

Changing consumption patterns made it also less viable to live off land and cattle alone. Colonial authorities attempted to incorporate Africans into the colonial economy by introducing new consumer products (Burke 1996). They regarded Africans as a potential market for goods like soap and clothing. They also attempted to 'civilize' Africans by installing desires that were thought to be absent during the pre-colonial past. The new consumer products could only be purchased with cash obtained through wage labor, which was to the advantage of colonial authorities in search of cheap labor (Burke 1996:83-90).[3]

In the early 1980s in the Libode district of the Transkei, for example, more than half of the population had no cattle at all, while only 10 per cent owned more than ten beasts (Wilson & Ramphele 1994:72).[4] An African female wage laborer expressed the increased reliance on cash in the following way: 'we [Africans] can cope. You can put a black person in the forest and just leave water with him or her. We can manage because there is a lot we can do. But now we are chained without money' (Cock 1980:109).

Conquest incorporated Xhosa into the colonial economy and simultaneously marginalized them within that economy: wages were low and working conditions were horrible. Furthermore, as early as 1828 legislative measures restricted the free movement of Xhosa in order to regulate the flow of African laborers (Cock 1980:204). Migrants in Cape Town initially lived scattered across the city's poorest areas, but by the end of the 19th century they were forced to live away from Whites in townships on the outskirts of Cape Town (Cole 1987:5; Ross 1999:97-98).

Influx Control, as these policies on the restriction of African movement and labor were called, forced Africans to live in a few reserves which, in 1926, comprized no more than 13 per cent of South Africa (Ross 1999:88). The Urban Areas Act of 1923 restricted Africans from residing in urban areas by deporting 'those who were habitually unemployed, those who had no honest livelihood, and those who were idle, dissolute, or disorderly' (Davenport 1969 in Wilson 1972:160). Between 1954 and 1985, Cape Town was governed by yet another policy restricting African movement, namely the Coloured Labour Preference Policy. It had to make sure that the city would be virtually unoccupied by Africans: 'The intention of the Department of Native Affairs was to phase Africans out of the Western Cape ... and incorporate Coloureds by giving them labor preference' (Goldin 1987:87).

The implementation of the racist labor policies depended too some extent on the demand for laborers. From 1968 to 1974, an increased demand for labor led to a loosening of the enforcement of these policies. During the economic recession, repression was enforced more severely (Cole 1987:9). Labor policy was, however, not always carried out according to an economic rationale. For example, in the 1960s the government had decided that the number of Africans in the Western Cape had to be reduced by 5 per cent per year. White farmers were upset and feared a shortage of skilled farm laborers. Their protests were put aside and the number of Africans was reduced (Wilson 1972:19-20).

Against the enforcement of legally embedded discrimination, migrant labor became pivotal for survival: 'In 1929, 46.6 per cent of the taxes paid in by residents in Pondoland were collected outside the home district of the payer, showing that at least that percentage of males over 18 years were away from home' (Hunter 1979:108). In the Ciskei and the Transkei, households greatly depended on remittance from migrant laborers. For example, in 1982, in households with less than an annual income of R1,500, two thirds of the income came from such remittances (Wilson & Ramphele 1994:62-63). War, taxation, slavery, the introduction of new consumer products, political domination, 'betterment schemes', in combination with natural disasters, such as droughts and cattle diseases, have made it inevitable, and desirable, to have money in contemporary South Africa.

The data on the composition of the urban population are notoriously unreliable and frequently contradict each other. One of the causes is that many Africans defied apartheid legislation and lived in the city illegally. Therefore, they had good reason to hide from a population census.[5] Government authorities also modified the numerical representation of Africans in Cape Town for administrative purposes: it followed that those who did not officially exist did not need public services and, therefore, the urban African population was intentionally underestimated (cf. Lee 1999:60). Bearing these precautions in mind, the available data indicate that the African population in Cape Town grew, despite apartheid legislative efforts to prevent its doing so. According to Monica Wilson and Archie Mafeje (1963: 2), in 1911 only roughly 1,500 Africans (1.5 per cent of the urban population) lived in Cape Town, which increased to just over 30,000 (8 per cent) by 1946 and, according to Francis Wilson (1972:70) 55,000 Africans lived in Cape Town by 1971.[6] The number of pass law contraventions provides another indication of levels of urbanization and the attempts by the state to control African migrants. The number of pass law contraventions in South Africa rose from just under 50,000 in 1921 to more than 600,000 in 1970 (Wilson 1972:232).[7] And '[I]n greater Cape Town ... between 1962 and 1967 the number of people convicted rose by over 80 [per cent] from 8,434 to 15,367' (Wilson 1972:164). Because of the desperate economic situation, many Africans continuously tried to find employment outside of the homeland at the risk of being caught, detained, fined, and sent back to the Bantustans.

For African women, it was even more difficult to live in the city than for African men. The Bantu Urban Areas Act of 1964 ruled that women had to receive permission to join their husband in the city. Furthermore, if a 'section 10 woman' – a woman permitted to live in the city under section 10 of this act – would marry a 'homeland man', the apartheid state forced her to leave the city and join her husband in 'his homeland'. In the house of assembly in 1969, Froneman, who later became the Deputy Minister, defended the discrimination of women by arguing that one 'must not be burdened with superfluous appendages such as wives, children and dependants who could not provide service' (Cock 1980:245). In 1911, in Greater Cape Town there were almost four African men for every African woman, which decreased to two African men for every woman in 1951 (Wilson & Mafeje 1963:5).[8] The status of women in the city was much more insecure than that of men. Because most women were living in the city illegally, could not work legally, and often had no place to stay, they depended heavily on their husbands (see, amongst others, Oliver-Evans 1993:70-81; Ramphele 1989).

In 1986, the Abolition of Influx Control Act put an end to numerous apartheid laws that restricted the movement and labor of Africans. The inability to enforce the pass-laws and, finally, the abolition of these laws in 1986 made it easier for African men and women to live in the city and search for a job (see Robertson 1990). This led to a distinctive transformation in the urban demographic landscape.

The African urban population rapidly increased after the abolishment of apartheid, thus contributing to the already existing housing problems.[9] Population growth and a housing shortage meant that the poverty in which most Africans lived slowly became visible to the Whites living in Cape Town. For most Whites during apartheid, townships were places one only saw at a far distance while driving on the highway. For example, Langa, the oldest township in Cape Town that still exists today, could only be seen in the distance if one drove on the N2 Highway. A few hundred metres of grassland used to separate the highway from the township. Another attempt by the apartheid government to conceal the poverty was to place the better houses on the side lining the highway, while the worst housing conditions remained in the interior areas and invisible to Whites passing by in their cars. In an attempt to camouflage the presence of Africans even further, the power station in Langa was, and still is, called Athlone Power Station, after the adjacent Coloured area, Athlone. In the last years, the townships have become more visible. In 1995, one could witness how Africans used the grass fields between the townships and the highway to build their makeshift dwellings, made of corrugated iron, wood, cardboard, plastic, or other affordable building materials.

Influx Control discriminated against women in particular, which forced many women to stay in the Bantustan and rely on the remittances sent by their husbands. Remittances, however, were frequently irregular, too little, or nothing at all (cf. James 1999a:77; Moodie 1988:251). After Influx Control was abolished, many women left the Bantustans. While urban female-headed households had been relatively few in numbers due to apartheid policies, they started to increase due to the arrivals of many migrant women.[10] A conjugal familial unit – a husband and wife living together, perhaps with children – was less prevalent, and the absence of husbands meant that many children were illegitimate according to civil or customary law (Burman & Lembete 1995:28, 46; Longmore 1959).

The above does not provide a complete picture of the impact of the changing political economy and the introduction of money. My aim, however, is only to delineate the general process of colonial conquest and capitalist economy (especially the introduction of money, wage labor, taxation, new consumer items, war, apartheid legislation), and natural disasters (drought, lungsickness among cattle, East Coast fever). The political and economic changes had a tremendous impact on livelihoods of Xhosa, sources of income, household relations, and conceptions of the world. They also led to financial mutuals that were at the crossroads of three very important types of relationships (kin, migrants from the same area, and neighbors) and money.

Changing kinship relations

Pressure on land, the demise of cattle, and an increasing reliance on migrant labor put all kinds of pressures on people who depended on each other. It challenged the way people depended on each other, such as the increasing powers of young men, women, and even children, because they earned some money.[11] It could help people escape certain inequalities, but also led to new forms of oppression. Similar to Wolf's (1999) description of the gift giving institution of the potlatch among the North American Kwakiutl, new income generating activities and drastic political changes gave previously marginal people the opportunity to acquire status and challenge dependencies.

The shortage of land brought on by foreign conquest caused homesteads (*imizi*) to become smaller (Beinart 1982:98). In the 1930s there were people who still remembered that homesteads used to consist of up to twenty married men with their wives and children, while in the 1930s a homestead was more like a nuclear family (Hunter 1933:273). Also, the introduction of the plough made large homesteads with many female laborers less important for economic survival. A Xhosa chief expressed the relationship between labor and technological innovation when he saw a plough at work as '[t]his thing that the white people have brought into the country is as good as ten wives' (Hunter 1979:202).

The different manner in which hut tax and dipping tax were levied also stimulated homesteads to become smaller. Hut tax was levied on the number of huts –with each wife occupying a hut – within a homestead and the head of the homestead was responsible for paying this tax. It put him in a precarious situation: although he had to pay the tax, also for the wives of his sons, it was difficult for him to claim his sons' wages. The tax made it financially more attractive for the headman to let his sons establish their own homesteads and let them pay their own taxes. From 1913-1915, the administration enforced an additional 'dipping tax' on cattle treated against East Coast fever. The dipping tax depended on the number of adult men living in the homestead: homesteads with less male members had to pay less tax. The tax made it financially more attractive for the headman to let his sons establish their own homesteads and let them pay their own taxes (Beinart 1982:98).

In addition to tax, homesteads also became smaller because men had left in search of jobs. People's reliance on kin relations had thus decreased, a trend aggravated by forced resettlement. Instead of being able to rely on kin, Xhosa households were increasingly confronted with, and dependent on, neighbors that were not related to them (Hunter 1979:60; McAllister 1985:130). Among other initiatives, neighbors established co-operative work arrangements, such as the ploughing company where neighbors assisted each other during the agricultural cycle (McAllister 2000). The dependency on neighbors was also reflected in ritual practices:

> The increase in [ritual] beer drinking, probably gradually from about the 1920s onwards, coincided with, reflected and provided normative or ideological support for the changing nature of rural production, in which neighborhood and a sense of community replaced kinship as the major organising principle. Neighborliness did not arise as a new social principle, but it became more important as the kinship system weakened (McAllister 1997:306).

There are contradictions within the literature on the consequences of these changes for marriage and relations established by marriage. Before cash income played a major role, marriage took place through the transference of bridewealth (*ukulobola*). According to Hunter (1933:263) most marriages were not arranged, and if they were arranged it was with consent of the lovers. But Hunter, as well as others, also described the practice of *ukutwala*, which was the kidnapping of the bride with the parents' consent, which does not imply the bride's consent (Hunter 1979:189; Laubscher 1959:266; Moodie 1988:239).[12] An older woman in Cape Town told me that she was lured into marriage with a bicycle that she received for her birthday. At the time, she was very pleased by this tremendous gift and went for a bicycle ride with her brothers. It was a big shock for her when she ended up in a nearby village where she was forced to marry a complete stranger.

Parental control over conjugal relations was also reflected in the control over marriage cattle. Hunter described how each daughter was allotted to a son. This practice was called *ukushaka*, which means 'to link' or 'to put together'. The *lobola* that was received when a daughter married was allotted to this specific son. This meant that the marriage of a man greatly depended on the marriage of his sister and the allotment by his parents (Hunter 1979:122-123). Kuper, however, argued that in the period from 1880–1930 the Xhosa were an exception in the region because they did not practise allotment (Kuper 1982: 36). These different findings might not necessarily reflect different practices and might rather be due to a different degree in parental control over cattle and marriage. Customs such as *ukushaka* were probably practised in different ways and adapted to particular circumstances. The fragmented pieces of information that are available make it tempting, yet also dangerous, to develop a structural analysis and generalize the scattered findings to society at large. But even if *ukushaka* was not commonly practised, *lobola* did enhance parental control over young men and women. Moreover, cattle were a constitutive element of the establishment of parental rights over children: *lobola* incorporated the wife's children into the father's patrilineage.

The advantage of bridewealth payments was that they could support a married woman in a dispute with her in-laws:

> 'Well, if you are not *lobola*, what do you do when your husband misuses you, since you have no home (*ikhaya*) to run to?' Any home that has benefited from a woman's *ikhazi* is bound to give her support and protection, and women frequently take advantage of this right by running back to their own people (Hunter 1933:263).

Many women had good reasons to run away from their affines. Her new home was strange and many felt that the practice of *ukuhlonipa*, or avoidance, was degrading to them, even if they agreed with it from a moral point of view.[13] A wife had to show respect by avoiding words, names, and letters that related to her husband's clan. She was given a new name which, if the woman was unlucky, was not flattering. She had to behave respectfully towards her husband's relatives by walking slowly, talking softly, often by sitting on a mat on the floor instead of on a chair, and through strict dress codes.

Because of virilocal residency, a married woman was, and still is, an outsider within the homestead of her husband. As a relative stranger, a woman was felt to be dangerous (Hammond-Tooke 1962:113; Hunter 1933:267). Subsequently, her affinal relations were particularly vulnerable to witchcraft: many of the witchcraft allegations concerned the relation between a woman and her husband's brother's son and, according to Wilson, especially between a woman and her mother-in-law (Hammond-Tooke 1970:30-31; Wilson 1952:173 in Hammond-Tooke 1970:30).

Wage labor provided new forms of economic power and marginalized the use of cattle for the establishing of kin relations. As young people earned cash, parental authority over them was undermined and elderly men had less to say about their marriage. Young people did not depend on their fathers or a chief for marriage cattle and instead bought their own. Subsequently, elders complained that they were no longer respected. Although wage labor led to the financial independence of young men, their prolonged absence during labor migration also made men more hesitant to set up their own homesteads (*umzi*) and, as an alternative, left their wives with their parents (Beinart 1982:96-103; Hunter 1933:270; 1979:59-60, 177). The *lobola* payments in cattle were replaced by *lobola* payments in money that was still spoken of as cattle. Marriage negotiations still made use of vocabulary steeped in cattle terms and the monetary value of particular beasts was negotiated (cf. Comaroff & Comaroff 1990:209).

Parents had some control over the marriage of their children, but because marriages rarely took place anymore in practice, parental control over their children's choice of partners was weakening.[14] For example, in the 1930s in East London, over half the children were illegitimate, both according to civil and customary laws (Hunter 1933:273). Hunter attributed these findings to the high costs of children in a money economy, while children in a subsistence economy contributed through labor. The illegitimacy of children could also be due to the weakening paternal control over children due to declining flows of cattle that established or confirmed conjugal relations between spouses and consanguineal relations with children.

The oppressive regime that women had to suffer from their affines might have become worse. As I mentioned above, *lobola* was helpful for women in disputes with affines. The absence of *lobola*, as well as an increased distance between the homestead of the wife's parents and that of her affines, made it difficult to involve them in a dispute. In addition, many husbands were away as migrant laborers and left their wives under the control of the husbands' parents or siblings. Furthermore, civil marriage might have marginalized the parental role in disputes between spouses, possibly not always to the advantage of the wife.

At the same time, financial autonomy gave women new freedom to choose a partner and decide if they wanted to marry. In general, women told me they were very reluctant to marry because it would subject them to affines, while a boyfriend could be left much easier. This, in turn, had consequences for relationships with children. As Bank found among the Xhosa in East London: '[F]atherhood is conceptualised in very materialistic terms – the image of a 'good father' is a man who can support his family financially' (Bank 1997:175).[15] Unemployment, the decline of marriage and *lobola*, fears of independent women, and the man's inability to control his wife's sexual behavior during his absence made it difficult for him to assert fatherhood, amongst others embodied through initiation. Women frequently had the sole responsibility over children. Thus, the distribution of income between a husband and wife, or girlfriend and boyfriend, became increasingly contested.

A migrant man often left his wife in the care of his brother (see also Wilson & Mafeje 1963:84). This could create tensions because the migrant could fear that his brother would sleep with his wife during his absence. Tensions between brothers also increased if a younger brother had to hand over his income to his father, which would later be inherited by the oldest brother (Wilson & Mafeje 1963:84). But, as far as I could see during my research, many parents were so poor that nothing substantial could be inherited. Nevertheless, the fear of one sibling 'stealing' the inheritance, even if it was not there, was vivid.

The tensions with – and often absence of – brothers and fathers meant that migrant men had to rely more on others:

> The effect of these conflicts [between full brothers] appears to be that a man feels more free with his home-boys than with his brothers or parallel cousins; there are fewer strings attached to co-operation with them. Between sisters, and brothers and sisters, there are no similar rivalries, and relationships between them are easy in the changing, as in the tribal, society (Wilson & Mafeje 1963:84).

Niehaus' (1994:118) research among residents of the Qwaqwa district revealed that 'in Southern Africa it is rather siblings who stay together while conjugal pairs are dispersed'. Spouses were often away as migrant laborers and many relations had broken up, which meant that support among siblings became more important, although sibling ties were not free of conflict either.

Migrant men of one home

The changing kinship dependencies and, in some respect, the downright breakdown of kinship relations contributed to the emergence of new social networks. Apartheid legislation brutally classified Africans in two categories.[16] One category was allowed to stay permanently in the city, while other Africans were only allowed to stay as migrants as long as they were employed and under strict control of the Labour Bureau (Lee 1999:16-18). These laws had a tremendous impact on the living conditions of the – mostly male – African migrants. Under apartheid fellow male migrants frequently lived together and organized financial mutuals with *abakhaya*. *Abakhaya* means 'those of one home' and migrants who identify each other as originating from the same area refer to each other as *abakhaya*. The collapse of apartheid changed the relevance of *abakhaya* identification for organizing financial mutuals. Men had more freedom to move and live where they pleased, and women were increasingly migrating to Cape Town. In this process, the significance of *abakhaya* relations for financial mutuals changed. *Abakhaya* were not necessarily neighbors anymore, which caused a demise of *abakhaya*-based financial mutuals. Although *abakhaya* were not that important anymore for financial mutuals, by examining *abakhaya*, the experience of migrants in Cape town comes into relief.

So what was the migratory experience like? Migrants were only allowed to live in overcrowded male hostels and had to leave their families back home. Wilson & Ramphele (1994:128) gave the following description of living conditions in the 1980s:

> There are many men in South Africa whose address is not some street number identifying a house, nor even a room number to locate where he might stay in a boarding house, but a bed number to identify where he may be found in a maze of concrete bunks which accommodate perhaps 90 men in a single room.

Although the regrouping of migrants in urban areas was not unique to South Africa, the apartheid administration strengthened the regrouping of Africans. Africans who came from one area were forced to live in one room in a specifically designated barrack. Each room had its own official registration number and people from one particular area, such as the Umtata district in the former Transkei, were forced to share one room. The residents would often paint the area code of the licence plate, such as CCY for Umtata, on the door to indicate their place of origin (Wilson & Mafeje 1963:50). In line with the logic of indirect rule, each room had to elect a convenor (*isibonda*) that was recognized by the local township authorities. The convenor was responsible for managing disputes within the room and could be called upon for disciplinary evictions (Ramphele 1989:396-397).[17] Many Xhosa migrants also lived illegally in the city in overcrowded squatter camps where they were subjected to police harassment (see for example Cole 1987). Nevertheless, the clustering of 'those of one home' (*abakhaya*) in one room must have had an important effect on their organizations.

Pressures from family and friends back home also strengthened *abkahaya* identifications. For those who stayed behind in Emaxhoseni, or 'the land of the Xhosa', there was always the fear that the migrant worker would fail to return with the desperately needed cash: 'The special nightmare of Xhosa peasant families …is *ukutshipha*, absconding – the vanishing of a man in town, leaving his kin at home without money remittances and without news of him' (Mayer & Mayer 1974:179). For a migrant worker's wife, it was virtually impossible to make a successful claim on her husband's wage. Therefore, whenever a migrant left, his neighbors and village elders stressed the importance of remittances at public beer drinking rituals. The speakers reminded the migrant that he depended on them and was leaving in order to build the homestead in a material, religious, social, and moral sense (McAllister 1980: 208). A migrant was told to constrain himself financially and abstain from relations with 'town women' who would '"eat" his [the migrant's] money and induce him to forget about his wife and home' (McAllister 1980:211).[18]

The social pressure executed at public beer drinking rituals contributed to the identification of fellow migrants with their areas.

Men from one particular area of 'the land of the Xhosa' (Emaxhoseni) often shared one overcrowded room in one of the barracks. They ate together, cooked together, and made monthly contributions in order to buy groceries together (Mayer & Mayer 1974:101-104; Wilson & Mafeje 1963:49). Mayer and Mayer (1974) show how an *abakhaya* in East London established a close-knit community. New migrants were initially taken care of by their fellow *abakhaya*, with whom they could reside in the hostels. They purchased food together and unemployed *abakhaya* could join in the communal meals in return for the performance of domestic tasks.[19] In case of illness and disease, the *abakhaya* would also help each other: 'Each group of Red amakhaya [sic]... forms a community of its own' (Mayer & Mayer 1974:99). Living and eating together in groups of home-people established some level of social control. The social control of *abakhaya* kept migrants in line with the expectations of migrant labor: to save money for the homestead without spending it on women and alcohol in the city.

The extent of social control among *abakhaya*, however, should not be exaggerated. It has been estimated that around 1970 migrants in Cape Town spent about a quarter of their income on hard liquor (Wilson 1972:180). Nevertheless, *abakhaya* relations were an important type of identification. Whenever migrant men lived in closely knit networks these networks and identifications constrained them from illicit behavior, at least to some degree (Mayer & Mayer 1974; Wilson & Mafeje 1963:47; see also Delius 1993:130). A migrant man said about the dangers of not living among *abakhaya* in Cape Town: 'Living in a flat [not among *abakhaya*] induces people to spend too much money... I am not a bee, I cannot eat honey while still making it' (Wilson & Mafeje 1963:39). Moreover, migrants told me that inappropriate behavior could easily reach the ears of kin in Emaxhoseni due to gossiping *abakhaya*.

The inadequate reinforcement of apartheid laws on migration, the abolishment of many laws on migration in 1986, and the first democratic elections of 1994 caused migration and residence patterns to undergo transformations. When my fieldwork took place, Xhosa migrants could move freely and were not forced anymore by law to live in Cape Town's overcrowded, badly maintained hostels. Migrants built their shacks in illegal settlements, or rented a shack, or space, in the backyard of someone's brick house in a formal and serviced township. For about R200 a month, the migrant could rent a small shack and use electricity, water, and sanitation facilities of the main house. Subsequently, the co-residence and organization of *abakhaya* had largely seized to exist. Apart from one barrack in the township Guguletu, I did not encounter *abakhaya* living, eating, or cooking together the way Wilson and Mafeje (1963) and the Mayers (1974) had encountered in the past. The confinements of the hostels under apartheid caused *abakhaya* and neighborhood relations to overlap, but the democratization process meant that neighbors were not necessarily *abakhaya*, and that *abakhaya* increasingly lived scattered throughout different parts of Cape Town. This, in turn, caused a decreased interest in migrants to organize among *abakhaya*. The national Reconstruction and Development Programme (RDP) of the post-apartheid government also dispersed *abakhaya*. The RDP provided the poor with a housing subsidy that was allocated according to seniority: those who lived the longest in an informal settlement had the first right to a housing subsidy. This made it difficult for migrants to influence where they lived and made it less likely to have *abakhaya* as neighbors.

I only came across one ROSCA that was organized by *abakhaya*. The male members each put in R500 per month. Of the burial societies with a fund, half were organized by *abakhaya* because recent migrants no longer established these burial societies in their new settlements. In fact, in the new settlements they did not organize any *abakhaya* burial societies. The burial societies that were organized by *abakhaya* were much older, up to thirty or more years, and had their meetings in the older and established townships. One of them had even changed its rules and was now open to everybody whether they were *abakhaya* or not. The *abakhaya* burial societies were open to newly arrived *abakhaya* migrants who were willing to travel to the meetings in different parts of the city.[20]

With the end of apartheid, *abakhaya* relations had become less important for the organization of financial mutuals. *Abakhaya* relations no longer overlapped with neighborhood relations and therefore the vital social constraint mechanisms among *abakhaya* diminished.[21]

Before continuing with neighborhood relations – as markedly different from kinship and *abakhaya* relations – it is important to point out the relevance of *abakhaya* relations after apartheid. Although they no longer established financial mutuals together, migrants still identified with *abakhaya*. Insight into the identification of fellow *abakhaya* contributes to an understanding of the migratory process. Life in hostile Cape Town, after all, was primary out of a concern with people back home in Emaxhoseni. The money was saved for and spent on people back home, which was the place for initiation, burial, ancestors, and the place where many children grew up.

Abakhaya identifications were grounded in several, not necessarily exclusive, categories. One was the district or region where one came from, which was often the magisterial district (see also Wilson and Mafeje 1963:47). *Abakhaya* burial societies were often based on magisterial districts. *Abakhaya* could also be those that went to the same town to buy groceries. A migrant from Ciskei, who was a member of an *abakhaya* burial society, said: 'First, *abakhaya* are the people from the same village. Second, they are people from the same district where you stay. These are the people who shop in the same town. Also, the whole Ciskei are *abakhaya*'. A teenage girl, who had been listening to our conversation while lying on the bed, added: 'now the whole Eastern Cape are *abakhaya*. The Ciskei and Transkei don't even exist anymore.' Another woman argued that Ciskeians amongst each other were *abakhaya* because there were so few Ciskeians in Cape Town and so many Transkeians: 'Yes, we do neglect Transkeians, but they are from behind the [Kei] river and they are therefore not *abakhaya*.'[22] If migrants were further away from home, more people were regarded as *abakhaya* (see also Wilson & Mafeje 1963:47-49): 'if I would be overseas [in Europe] and meet someone from Jo'burg, he would also be *umkhaya*.'

Through greeting, people found out if they were *abakhaya*. If people met each other and greeted they asked: 'Where do you come from?' If one knew a person and saw him or her regularly this only meant 'what have you been doing?' If, however, one just met someone, the question related to the place of belonging. In such a case, the answer would refer to an area 'back home', mostly in the former homelands Transkei and Ciskei. Another way to ask about a person's home was: 'Where is your umbilical cord buried?' The umbilical cord was plastered in the wall of a rondawel in the homestead, or at least supposed to be plastered there, even if someone was born in Cape Town. Thus, the umbilical cord connected the migrant with the homestead.

During many casual conversations people explored if they knew someone from his or her area of origin. Discussions often developed around these mutual acquaintances. For example, Mimi and my research assistant Edith introduced themselves at Mimi's *umgalelo* meeting. Both asked where they lived in Cape Town, to which clan they belonged, what their family situation was, and where they came from. After some time, Edith delightedly told me that she had shared a home area with Mimi. For some years, Edith had lived with her brother in a particular town in the Qobo Qobo district where she also attended secondary school. Edith had just found out that Mimi's brother lived in exactly the same town. Both were very pleased that they found a place in Emaxhoseni (the place where both their brothers lived) through which they could relate to each other. Conversations in which people elaborated on where they used to live and go to school and who they know occurred all the time.

During the many months of research, I met only one African who stated that he was from Cape Town because he was born in the township Langa. He felt that he did not belong to a place in Emaxhoseni and found people's identification with Emaxhoseni exaggerated. Most Africans who were born in Cape Town did not consider themselves to be Capetonians and would have felt it an insult to be considered Capetonians. Instead, they identified with a particular region in Emaxhoseni, although some had visited this area only once or twice in their life, or not at all. If one wanted to point out that someone misbehaved, a rhetorical 'where do you come from?' made the point. The insulting answer implied by this question implied was 'you come from nowhere'. You have no home and behave without a show of respect to others.

The many moves that people had made in the course of their lives from place to place made *abakhaya* identifications personal and flexible. Instead of having one town or region of origin, there were often many places to which people felt they belonged. This started in early childhood. Under Influx Control, many children were forced to leave the city and sent home (Mayer & Mayer 1974:271), but it was also the case that children often grew up in Emaxhoseni after the abolition of apartheid laws (for example see Jones 1993:57). Children often moved between different households, depending on if a household had sufficient money to care for the child, if parents felt that the money they sent was spent on the child, and if they felt that the child was not ill treated (Spiegel 1987:120-127). Many parents could not take care of their child because they had to work. Crèches, if available at all, were too expensive, far away, poorly facilitated, or had no qualified staff. Parents also wanted to protect their children against the dangers of Cape Town. They worried that their child would join a gang or become a victim of violence. The Mayers' (1974:271) findings on attitudes to rearing children in town still apply almost forty years later: '"Town is no fit place for a child". Rearing children there was supposed to mean loss of parental control, with disastrous consequences for the child's morality, especially in the fields of sex, work, and crime.'

Maqashu and his wife, for example, sent one child old enough to attend school to relatives in the Eastern Cape. They also had a toddler, but he was easier to take care of and could temporarily be left with neighbors. Maqashu worked as a security officer and brought home about R800 a month. The family struggled to get by. Maqashu's wife told us (Edith and me) that they had been unemployed for about six years. They survived because they could get food on credit from a local shop. They repaid the debt to the shop owner with R250 per month. Another R100 was spent on public transport in order for Maqashu to commute to work. The relatives in the Eastern Cape also needed money to buy food and clothing, and pay for school fees for their child. Every month the parents had to send R250 through postal order, which left them with only R200. Although the financial problems of this family were severe – they were also regarded by neighbors as poor – they could not have the child with them and stop sending money. Maqashu's wife had to look for a job and she felt that Cape Town was a terrible place for children to grow up. This is only one example of how important relations with people in Emaxhoseni were. Children often grew up with different relatives in different towns where they attended different schools.

Upon their return to Cape Town, these moves and memories determined who was *umkhaya.* The moves between Cape Town and Emaxhoseni were also visible in the composition of the age pyramid of Africans in Cape Town, based on the 1996 census. Less then 5 per cent of the African population was between ten and fifteen years old, while the age category of fifteen to nineteen years represented about seven percent of the urban African population. This increase is accounted for by the trend that at this age young people left Emaxhoseni in order to find employment in Cape Town.[23]

Government institutions under apartheid regulated labor through labor bureaus, which limited the migrant's opportunity to introduce an *umkhaya* to his employer (Wilson & Mafeje 1963:51). According to a small sample that concerned employment from the mid-1980s to the early 1990s, about two-thirds of the migrants said they had found employment through the labor bureaus. Only 19 per cent found a job by word of mouth. Once apartheid and its labor bureaus were abolished, more people found a job by word of mouth (Oliver-Evans 1993:39). The abolishment of apartheid could have led to an increasing mobilization of *abakhaya* in the migrant's quest for employment. If I asked whether *abakhaya* helped each other find employment in Cape Town, this was mostly confirmed (see Wilson & Mafeje 1963:51). But when I asked them for an example – maybe they had found a job for an *umkhaya*, got a job through *umkhaya* relations, or knew of someone who got a job through *umkhaya* relations – they could not give it. High unemployment made it very difficult to find a job for anyone and if people knew about a job, they preferred to introduce a relative, a neighbor, or a member of the church. The contrast between ideology (finding a job for *abakhaya*) and practice (the inability to provide *abakhaya* with jobs) was also because *abakhaya* lived widespread in Cape Town and were rarely neighbors.

But *abakhaya* did try to help each other a little bit, for example by passing through messages and money on visits back home. Sometimes they were left in charge of a child on the same taxi home, a task sometimes also left to the driver. *Abakhaya* were more likely to attend a festivity or funeral of an *umkhaya*. Although the social support migrants gave to *abakhaya* was limited, people did try to help each other and cherished the relationships with people who knew their home, school, or relatives.

Common relations (such as family members, ancestry, shared acquaintances) and places (such as magisterial districts, shopping centers, and rivers) were important to migrants who had to survive Cape Town's threatening triad. The hostility of Cape Town contributed to the identification among *abakhaya*. The city was a dangerous place where migrants could not feel at home. During apartheid, many illegal migrants tried to find a job in South Africa's industrial areas and took the risk of police detention, torture, and deportation to the Bantustans. Their illegal settlements could be bulldozed any time and, especially under the state of emergency, the powers of the state and the police were incredible. The police did not address crime in the African settlements, which made them even more vulnerable. After apartheid, police were often absent as well or, if they were available, people were afraid that they co-operated with criminal groups. In the Western Cape Province, the average murder rate in 1997 was eighty murders per 100,000 (SAIRR in Cape Times 1998). In the African townships, such as Guguletu and Langa, the murder rate is even higher, up to 120 to 150 murders per 100,000 in the early 1990s (Bähre 1996a:85; Ramphele 1991:267). In the Western Cape in 1999, eighty-one murders and 160 rapes per 100,000 people were reported (SAPS 2000). Many rapes, however, were not reported due to lack of confidence in the judiciary system and fear of public stigmatization. A survey of 4,000 women in Johannesburg revealed that one in three had been raped the past year (BBC 1999).[24]

The occurrence of rape and murder in Cape Town is presently likely the highest in the world. Although the role of the police has changed in post-apartheid South Africa, the risk of poor, semi-literate migrants becoming victims of one or more of these crimes were tremendous, and actually unavoidable. For this reason alone Cape Town was not regarded as a home. Who wants to give up hope and realize this is the place one will live permanently? The hostility of the city made migrants reluctant to feel at home and contributed to the identification with *abakhaya* and stressed the relationships with home in Emaxhoseni.

That Xhosa took the hostility of the city seriously was evident in the preparations taken when they left the Eastern Cape. Those who were about to leave invoked the ancestors for assurance of their co-operation and assistance. They also had a special medicine, called 'medicine for war' (*ubulawu*), which provided protection. McAllister (1980:215) notes that 'ubulawu ensures good luck, the favor of one's employer and protection from accidents, assaults and other misfortunes that might befall one at work'. The shiny and slippery sap of a particular aloe was used. This aloe was called *intelezi*, which meant 'good fortune in escaping danger', while *ubutelezi* meant slipperiness. As this name indicates, it helped a migrant to escape danger and slip out of difficult situations. Previously, *intelezi* was used to treat the army prior to battle but the new battle had become labor migration to Cape Town (McAllister 1980:214-215).

The interdependencies between migrants and their families at home were strengthened by the hostility of the city, the dangers of the migratory process, and the importance of ancestry located in the area of origin. It was a terrible ordeal to live in the city or to be initiated and buried in such a hostile place. Upon arrival in Cape Town migrants rarely organized the beer drinking ritual that would introduce their new place to both the neighbors and the ancestors, who in return would provide protection. By neglecting this ritual, they risked the withdrawal of ancestral protection. Only once had I noticed that a migrant brewed beer and invited his neighbors for this ritual. It was not a great success, however, because many neighbors felt that they were not invited properly. They gossiped that they were not invited properly on purpose. They spread a rumor that the neighbor did not want them to attend it in order to limit the costs of the ritual.

At times, migrants told me about the large luxurious homes that they were building in Emaxhoseni. They conveyed images of large square brick houses with corrugated iron roofs and beautiful furniture – as opposed to the traditional round huts made of grass and clay with a thatched roof. These were presented as the real homes and, therefore, it was useless to invest in a shack in Cape Town. Nofurniture, for example, used the R1,360 from her *umgalelo* (ASCRA) for her home in the Umtata district in the former Transkei. She lived in Cape Town for ten years but preferred to invest her money in a four room house and nice furniture in Emaxhoseni. The place was empty and her children, who stayed with relatives in the same compound, took care of the place but did not live there. She still wanted to go back home: 'I will be buried there.' She had not introduced her shack in Cape Town to the ancestors through a beer drinking ritual. She wanted to finish her home in Emaxhoseni before she would buy furniture for her place in Cape Town. Obviously, the beer drinking ritual was never going to take place, and Umtata would always be her home, even if it was only as an ancestor.

To sum up, in the 1990s the identification of *abakhaya* was still important but did not govern migrants' lives like it did in the 1960s. It is possible that, during apartheid, migrants overemphasized what they were able to do for *abakhaya* in order to conceal their inability to help people. But there were nevertheless significant changes. With the breakdown of apartheid, *abakhaya* were not neighbors anymore, which made it less likely to use *abakhaya* relations as support networks. *Abakhaya* did try to help each other out, but opportunities were limited. Furthermore, under apartheid the intersection of *abakhaya* with neighborhood relations provided social constraint that was vital for financial mutuals. When apartheid ended, this form of regulation ceased to exist and relations in the city became more diverse. This, in turn, caused a decrease in the relevance of *abakhaya* relations for financial mutuals.

Although *abakhaya* were not often neighbors anymore and had loosened the ties of mutual co-operation, *abakhaya* identifications were still pivotal to the migratory experience. The analysis of *abakhaya* identifications reveals how important home was for the migrants in Cape Town. The identification with home had religious significance, especially concerning relationships with the ancestors. It also had an economic dimension, because the identification with home revealed the economic and social interdependencies between migrants and their kin in Emaxhoseni. The hostility of Cape Town, moreover, made it even less attractive to set up a permanent life there. Labor migration, also after apartheid, was a treacherous and insecure experience in itself. Xhosa migrants were willing to endure it because they hoped to make some money, but not because they liked Cape Town.

Female neighbors

Under apartheid, women often depended on their husbands or boyfriends in order to live in the city; the illegal women depended on men for income and shelter. They had to be submissive to their men because, in case of disagreement and social tensions, the men had the authority to stay, while women could not make any claims. Unmarried women competed with wives or with other unmarried women over men with a job and lodging (Ramphele 1989).[25] Thus, men were initially central to the migratory process of women (James 1999b:48-58). Women migrated in order to join their men – for social and economic reasons – or in order to earn money for their dependants. As James (1999b:49-50) wrote on women who moved from the Northern Province to the Johannesburg and Pretoria area:

> All these women, whether married or not, relied on individual, usually male, family members, related either by blood or by marriage, to bring them to town and to connect them into broader networks after arrival. It was because female migration from the Northern Province was not undertaken by groups of people ... that they were tied, at least at the start of their migrant careers, to husbands or male kin and to the home-based networks to which they belonged.

After some time, James (1999b:62-63; 1999a) describes, the Sotho women did not want to depend only on the home-boy networks of the men, and instead established their own groups based on home relationships. By establishing *kiba* groups, migrant women set-up their own identification with 'those of one home' (James 1999b: 62-63;1999).

Female Xhosa migrants joined their husband's burial societies in Cape Town, but did not establish distinct female *abakhaya* burial societies. Unlike the Sotho women that organized around identification of home-people, Xhosa women in Cape Town did not organize around home-people. Although *Abakhaya* were definitely important for Xhosa women, they did not lead to the establishment of women's organizations. The difference between Sotho and Xhosa women could be due to the social constraint that was needed to form financial mutuals. For the Sotho women's *kiba* groups, social constraint was probably less important because there was no money that needed to be controlled. Xhosa women did not organize financial mutuals with *abakhaya* because they did not offer social constraint, while the neighbors did.

When the apartheid laws were not enforced anymore, women increasingly migrated to Cape Town.[26] These women, unlike the illegal migrants during apartheid, were able to set up their independent homes in the city. Their neighbors were only incidentally *abakhaya* and social constraint toward self-constraint had to be sought within the neighborhood and not among *abakhaya*.

Although neighborhood relations were very important for the organization of financial mutuals, they have received little scholarly attention in South Africa. In South Africa, critical social scientists were particularly interested in political struggles, as well as the uses and abuses of 'community' for policy purposes: '"Community" is a political term – perhaps the political term ... "Community" is the ideal for the future, the structure of utopia, the expectation of heaven, the legitimate goal for a truly democratic politics' (Thornton & Ramphele 1988:29). The preoccupation with political struggles focused on 'community', but 'neighborhood' was implicitly apolitical and, therefore, not worthy of much attention.

The 'neighborhood' as an analytical category is undervalued, despite the fact that it is very important to the Xhosa. The neighborhood is also a site of political struggle. During apartheid, for example, neighbors established street committees, organized rent boycotts, consumer boycotts, stay-aways, and tried to take over functions from local government (Seekings 1992:217-222). Street committees tried to establish some rule of law in their neighborhoods by arbitrating in petty fights between neighbors. Notwithstanding this role of neighborhoods, these initiatives were easily drawn into the debates on 'community'.

'Neighborhood' and 'community', however, were not the same. Neighbors were people with whom one interacted on a daily basis, while the community encompassed a much larger group of people whom one generally did not know, excepting local leaders and other prominent figures. Generally, those who lived in the same street were identified as neighbors. But some streets were very long or had a sharp curve so that residents of one street were not necessarily neighbors. Still other streets were very short, like a dead-end street, and therefore the residents of that street regarded themselves more easily as neighbors of residents in the adjacent street.

The neighbors' children played with each other and formed a vital link between neighbors. They were sent for messages, bought eggs, bread, cigarettes, or alcohol at the *spaza* shop (local store) down the street. Children were an important source of information for their parents who asked them about the latest gossip in the street. Occasionally, there were birthday parties where all the children of the neighborhood were invited. Their mothers would come along to dish out cake, biscuits, and lemonade and would give presents to the beautifully dressed birthday child. Neighbors also asked one another for favors. It was common to ask a neighbor for some money, such as R10 for a taxi or paraffin for cooking. This was considered a loan, but both neighbors often knew that it would not be returned. One could perhaps return the favor whenever the neighbor needed some help. Neighbors also kept an eye on each other's children or homes. Some even gave the key to the door to a neighbor who could let visitors or a child into the house. Moreover, neighbors tried to help one another find jobs, much more than *abakhaya* did.

Neighbors were well informed about the lives of those living next door. Corrugated iron and cardboard were far from soundproof and the small houses were very close to one another. Sometimes neighbors literally could overhear what their next-door neighbors were saying while they were inside their houses. Moreover, the confined space meant that many quarrels took place outside for everybody to observe. Neighbors visited each other, gossiped, and had tea or chicory coffee. It was rare to stay for a meal. If one would visit neighbors around dinner time, one forced the neighbor to offer some food. It would have been very impolite of the host not to offer anything, but also very painful if he or she had hardly anything to give. There were jokes about the strategies people devised to avoid sharing food. One suggestion was that it was best to start eating one's meat immediately, or instead hide it under the potatoes, just in case a visitor would arrive. Another option, I was told jokingly, was to offer a visitor one's spoon: 'here's my spoon. Come and share a meal with me'. The hope was that a visitor would decline the offer to use the same spoon. Some visitors had the reputation for abusing hospitality. They would 'accidentally' arrive when neighbors were eating. When the visitor was offered food, he or she would say: 'no, I'm not so hungry, just some meat is fine'. Mostly, however, neighbors tried to avoid causing embarrassment by adapting eating times or visits. I never encountered anybody eating, except at my research assistant's place, and during funerals and festivities. This was quite telling if one takes into consideration that people lived in a one- or two-roomed house and had little opportunities to hide while eating.

Neighborhood identifications showed a flexibility that resembled *abakhaya* identifications. When I asked Edith to indicate on a map who her neighbors were she marked a large section covering about 110 plots, with a rough estimate of about 400 residents. She felt, however, that the selection was to some extent arbitrary because other people, who lived further away but with whom she had contact, were also her neighbors. Another woman told me that someone who lived almost on the other side of the settlement, about five to ten minutes walk away, was also her neighbor: they used to be close neighbors in the past and, after they moved apart, they continued to consider each other as neighbors. The identification of neighbors was thus based on a combination of social and physical proximity.

Because neighborhood identifications were fairly flexible, they formed a practical basis for organising groups together: there were never too many or too few neighbors to form a financial mutual. Neighbors established all kinds of financial mutuals together, except for the fairly large burial societies with a fund, they were a convenient group of people to work with, and moreover, joint activities, such as collecting money for a funeral or forming a financial mutual, helped to define the neighborhood. Thus, financial mutuals were not only based on neighborhood relations, but they also identified people as neighbors. Especially among migrants who had only recently moved into a particular area, financial mutuals could help them to get acquainted.

Burials in particular led to a definition of neighborhood. The collection of money discerned who were considered neighbors. The collection engaged people in reciprocal relations that were regarded to be constitutive of neighborly relations. In other words, being neighbors was realized by doing neighborly activities. Noxolo, who was involved in such a collection among new neighbors, told me that the person whose door she could see from her own place were her neighbors. If she saw the entrance to their place, she could see who was walking in and out and what everybody was doing, which made them her neighbors. There were about a dozen shacks that one could see across the street from her whom she identified as neighbors. The residents on her side of the street were also Noxolo's neighbors, although she could not see their doors. Right behind Noxolo's shack was an open field. Noxolo could look across the field and the adjacent street into the residents' houses, so they were therefore also her neighbors. Noxolo, furthermore, was not the only one to collect money for the funeral; women in streets further away collected money, and they were considered neighbors of the deceased as well.

Especially in new areas among new residents, financial mutuals helped to establish neighborly relations. Although feelings of solidarity and mutual support were important, one should not neglect the social tensions that could exist among neighbors. After all, an important function of financial mutuals was to provide social constraint to its members. This social constraint was supposed to feel as a restriction, that was not always convenient or pleasant. A conversation that I had with participants of a financial mutual clearly illustrates the importance of social constraint. I had joined a financial mutual with my research assistant and some of her neighbors. After the five of us had each contributed R200, I told them the story of Ulysses and the Sirens that Elster (1979) has used to explain the mechanism of bounded rationality in which 'binding oneself is a privileged way of resolving the problem of weakness of will' (Elster 1979:37). I described how Ulysses and his crew had to manoeuvre their ship past the sirens whose tempting songs would lure them to the cliffs and cause their death. Only by sealing the ears could the crew ignore the sirens and survive. But Ulysses desperately wanted to listen to the seductive voices of the sirens without risking his life and the lives of his crew.

Upon his request, the crew tied him to the mast of the ship so he could listen to the sirens without danger. The crew had deafened themselves by sealing their ears and could safely pass the dangerous cliffs. Thus, upon his own request, Ulysses could be constrained by the deafened crew and enjoy the sirens' songs. He was aware of the pitfalls of temptation and therefore asked his crewmates to constrain him.

I asked the organizer of our *umgalelo*, Grandma Doris, if our *umgalelo* worked like that. 'Oh, yes', she replied enthusiastically; 'I know that story from the bible. It is exactly like that! We push each other to save money.' This was one of the great advantages of financial mutuals above other financial arrangements. One could join a group voluntarily and the social constraint of fellow members would make sure that one would not spend all the money but use it for the contribution to the financial mutual (cf. Ardener 1995:7; Bijnaar 1998:343-344; 2002:104-110; this volume; De Swaan 1996b:12; Rowlands 1995:113-114).

Conclusion

Three kinds of social relations were central to financial mutuals: kinship, *abakhaya*, and neighbors. These relations were not static, but changed considerably over time. In this respect, the dramatic impact of colonialism and capitalism on the Xhosa economy can hardly be overestimated. It led to drastic economic changes, such as the introduction of wage labor, money, taxation, and the availability of new consumer items, as well as political changes, such as those brought on by war, apartheid legislation, and natural disasters that undermined the subsistence economy, including drought, lung sickness among cattle, and East Coast fever. A society with a kin-ordered mode of production changed into a society in which the capitalist mode of production became dominant.

Due to these political economic changes social relations altered drastically. The elders' position was challenged due to the decrease in customary marriages; young men and unmarried women had greater autonomy due to the money they earned themselves; dependencies between husbands and wives were fraught with new tensions due to no longer adhering to *lobola* and the prolonged absences of migrant men; children increasingly became a financial burden; competition between full-brother's changed, and new demands were made on newly available money. Furthermore, compounds became smaller and people were often forced to resettle in the Bantustans. Such changes meant that reliance on neighbors increased and that neighbors, both in urban and rural areas, were less likely to be kin.

In order to support themselves and their families, many Xhosa tried to find work in urban and industrial centers outside of the Bantustans. Cape Town was governed by the Coloured Labour Preference Policy, which resulted in a minority African population and a further marginalization of Africans in the city. The migratory process led to the establishment of a new type of relations among the Xhosa migrants, namely those based on the identification of *abakhaya*, i.e. 'those of one home'. In order to understand why migrants were in cities such as Cape

Town, one has to be sensitive to what 'home' meant to migrants. The male migrants – under apartheid it was even more difficult for women to migrate – identified with each other due to a shared notion of origin, which coincided with responsibilities towards home, such as building the homestead and a commitment towards the ancestors. The threatening experiences of migration made home even more important, and also in post-apartheid South Africa, the threatening triad of violence, economic insecurity, and volatile relations did not make migrants feel at home in the city. Instead, it urged migrants to emphasize and possibly romanticize the home they left in the Eastern Cape.

Apartheid policy forced the male migrants that originate from one area – often accompanied by 'illegal women' – to live together in one room; *abakhaya* would live together, eat together, cook together, and exercise social constraint over one another. These *abakhaya*/neighbors offered the social cohesion and constraints that were needed to form financial mutuals. Financial mutuals, at least to some extent, ensured that migrants did not abscond during their stay in the city but returned home with gifts and presents for their kin. They also made sure that, after death, the migrant's body was returned home for a proper burial.

The breakdown of the apartheid laws loosened *abakhaya* relations. Although *abakhaya* identifications were still important, they did not lead to financial mutuals anymore. Instead, neighborhood relations became increasingly important as a type of social relation that was independent of kin and *abakhaya*. Consanguinity no longer meant physical proximity. This was because migration of women to Cape Town coincided with the further separation of *abakhaya* relations and neighborhood relations. The end of apartheid brought with it a change in urban demographics from mainly single men living in barracks, to households, often headed by females, in newly established neighborhoods. The neighborhood was central to the organization of the migrants' social life, including the care of children and forms of mutual care. The social constraints that neighbors offered gave women more possibilities to organize their money in financial mutuals.

The structural changes in the three types of relations (kinship, *abakhaya*, and neighbor) were accompanied by new structural tensions between people who depended on each other. Financial mutuals figured prominently in these tensions because it influenced the allocation of money within the wider kinship network and helped to establish new personal bonds between neighbors. This is one of the major attractions of the study of financial mutuals. Financial mutuals were central to the establishment, as well as people's understanding, of *abakhaya* and neighborhood relations in the city. Moreover, the study of financial mutuals revealed how, by allocating money, migrants tried to establish, maintain, or challenge kin relations.

The concept of social constraint toward self-constraint brings to the fore the social processes which people seek and submit to voluntarily. Elster (1979) highlights the weakness of will that calls for the binding of people. He calls for a theory of 'imperfect rationality' that includes the weakness of will, and people's awareness of this weakness. The person knows the limits of his rational behavior and solves the lack of willpower through pre-commitment. De Swaan (1996a: 1996b) pointed out the importance of social constraint toward self-constraint in financial mutuals. Members of financial mutuals are able to constrain themselves from spending money in anticipation of sanctions by fellow members, who they would have to face at the meetings or in the neighborhood.

There are, however, severe problems if one uses Elster's theory on bounded rationality, as well as the concept social constraint toward self-constraint in the South African context. 'Lack of willpower' and 'self-constraint' assume control over money and that it is spend due to personal weakness. But the data on Xhosa migrants revealed that control over money was very difficult, particularly for women. It was, for example, common that members of the household would steal money. Clearly, such loss of money was not due to a weakness of will. Another problem was that neighbors, colleagues, partners, and family members constantly called on each other for help.[27] It was very difficult or plainly impossible to refuse assistance, especially if one had money to help someone. The only more or less legitimate way to refuse help was to have no money. Saying *'andinanto'*, which means 'I do not have anything' was the only acceptable response.[28]

By creating new and immediate social constraints in a financial mutual, migrants tried to dodge the social constraints of kin, neighbors, or colleagues. It was especially difficult for women to circumvent claims of kin, particularly those by a husband or in-laws. Therefore, financial mutuals not only offered social constraint toward self-constraint, but also social constraint against social constraint. Xhosa migrants used financial mutuals to reposition themselves within changing configurations of social constraint. The advantage of new forms of social constraint and new interdependencies was that flows of money could be manipulated to some extent. Consequently, the popularity of financial mutuals among women should be attributed to gendered social constraints, and not because women had a weaker will than men, or had less self-constraint.

The case of financial mutuals among Xhosa migrants in Cape Town has revealed that it is very insightful to pay close attention to changing interdependencies and state transformation for the analysis of financial institutions. Only if one takes these at the core of the analysis, one can understand why financial mutuals changed the way they did, and why they have not disappeared. Contrary to expectations, such as those formulated by Geertz (1962), financial mutuals did not replace or build on older forms of solidarity. Rather, people were able to organize their money in with people who lived in close proximity. But the type of people that lived in close proximity drastically changed over time as part of the colonization process and apartheid policy. Furthermore, this case reveals that one should be very careful to regard financial mutuals as a 'middle rung' in development, or as part of a civilization process. People participated in financial mutuals because it was a way to create social constraint against social constraint. Financial mutuals were part of the battle over scarce money that was constantly in danger of slipping out of control into unwanted directions.

Notes

1 See also Kerri (1976) and the discussions following his article. Another publication that was central to the debate was by Ardener (1995 [1965]) who paid attention to the origin and spread of financial mutuals. Meillassoux (1968), however, revealed some of the less adaptive aspects of financial mutuals among migrants in Bamako, Mali. More recently and increasingly, interest in financial mutuals has been revived and new questions are being posed. Many studies of financial mutuals give insight into dimensions of poverty and insecurity. It is expected that knowledge about these informal groups will make it possible to support these groups or build new ones in order to combat poverty. See, for example, Bouman (1978), contributions in Adams and Fitchet (1992), contributions in Bouman and Hospes (1994), Hospes (1997), Smets (2000; 2002), Lont (2000b; 2002), Kane (2001a; 2001b). The poor are no longer pictured as irresponsible and untrustworthy people who do not know how to handle money or debts. Instead, many studies reveal the creativity and sophistication of the poor. Attention is also paid to women's participation in financial mutuals and to what extent financial mutuals empower women. See, amongst others, the contributions in Ardener and Burman (1995), Kappers (1986), Lont (2000a), Ross (1990), Van Wetering (1987).

2 See Elias (1982:239-259). See Bijnaar (1998; this volume) for an analysis of social constraint toward self-constraint in ROSCAs among Surinamese Creoles.

3 Burke somewhat overemphasizes how new tastes were transferred and forced upon people by the colonial authorities. However, similar to the maroons in Suriname (Thoden van Velzen & Van Wetering 1991:24) new consumer products were also eagerly embraced.

4 Based on Hendricks' 'preliminary notes on land and livestock in Libode'. N = 12,854. Research in 1974 in the Transkei revealed that 'almost half the households surveyed owned no cattle at all' (Leeuwenberg 1977:2 in Bundy 1979:229). The survey took place among 757 households.

5 An example of these problems can be found in Wilson and Ramphele's book (1994:92). They compared unemployment among Africans in Durban and Cape Town. In Durban's townships, depending on the definition of unemployment, between 16 and 29 per cent of the Africans were unemployed. In Cape Town, this was a remarkably low 6 to 9 per cent. At the time of the survey in 1982-3 the pass-laws were still enforced in Cape Town, while they were not enforced in Durban, which, according to Wilson and Ramphele, explains the lower level of unemployment in Cape Town. They argue that the restrictive pass-laws discouraged Africans to move to Cape Town. It could also be, however, that the pass-laws inhibited African migrants from telling the truth about their illegal employment status and therefore create the false impression that unemployment in Cape Town is low.

6 Not all migrants came from the Bantustans. 'Between 1936 and 1951 … five times as many of the [African] urban newcomers came from white farms as from the reserves' (Bundy 1979:234).

7 Historical sources differ about the amount of pass-law contraventions. According to Savage (1984:11 in Jones 1993:235n9) seventeen million pass-law arrests and prosecutions were made between 1916 and 1982 while Wilson (1972:232) mentions at least nine-and-a-half-million convictions and prosecutions between 1921 and 1970.

8 Lee (1999:67) shows how, in Langa, the female population decreased between 1965 and 1970 due to the council's policy to make Langa a township for male bachelor migrants. As a consequence of this policy, the male to female population ratio rose as high as 6.3:1 in 1970. Ramphele (1989:399) found that in the mid 1980s the male to female ratio

among hostel dwellers was 2:1. In the Transkei, the ratio had fallen from 73 men per 100 women in 1946 to 66 men per 100 women in 1974. The decline in the number of men and women in the age group 25-29 years was even stronger: from 36.1 to 28.9 men per 100 women (Clark & Ngovese 1975 in Bundy 1979:229-230).

9 Ramphele has calculated that the average bed occupancy – people sharing one bed – in the single sex hostels in three African townships of Cape Town (Nyanga, Guguletu, and Langa) in the mid 1980s was 2.8. In the hostels of Nyanga on average, every four residents had to share one bed among each other (Ramphele 1989:396).

10 'Forty per cent of the children had lived apart from their fathers for 48 per cent of their lives', reports Reynolds (1989:35) on children living in the squatter camp Crossroads in Cape Town in the 1980s. In Crossroads it was relatively easy to live with fathers compared with the male bachelor hostels, which made it likely that children spent even less time overall with their fathers.

11 See, among others, Comaroff and Comaroff (1990) on South Africa, Geschiere (1983) on Cameroon, and Hutchinson (1996) on Sudan.

12 See also Hammond-Tooke (1962:100-102) on consentient and forced marriage.

13 For a detailed description of *ukuhlonipa* among the Xhosa in 1979, see Kuckertz (1997). A shortcoming of his structural analysis is that he fails to note the contestations around this practice. For many of the women I spoke with the practice of *ukuhlonipa* was an important reason not to get married. See also Mager (1999:178-179) for a critical examination of *ukuhlonipa* among the Xhosa in the period 1945-1959.

14 It might be that, similar to the Nuer, cattle bought with money that was earned through labor migration was less vulnerable to claims from the extended family than cattle that had a 'social origin' (marriage and inheritance) (Hutchinson 1996:26, 89-90). See also Geschiere's (1983:629) observation that, notwithstanding drastic economic changes among the Maka in Cameroon, the elders, at least formally, were pivotal in the negotiation of bridewealth.

15 See also Sharp and Spiegel (1985) who compare the erosion of kinship and neighborhood relations in two villages.

16 Section 10 of The Natives (Urban Areas) Consolidation Act No. 25 of 1945 was particularly important.

17 In their influential book *Townsmen or Tribesmen*, Philip and Iona Mayer (1974) fail to take apartheid legislation and rule into consideration in their analysis of the difference between 'townsmen' and 'tribesmen', 'read' and 'school' people. They fail to mention the legal position of the convenor (*isibonda*) and ignore the legal distinction between residents and migrants under Section 10, although it must have been an important dimension of processes of identification and social organization. In a discussion of their work, Bank writes that 'The *abaqaba* ['red', 'traditional'] migrants completely rejected these urban social institutions and set out to 'encapsulate' themselves in close-knit, social networks based on their links with *amakhaya* (home-mates) in town' (Bank 1999:397). But this 'rejection' of urban social institutions took place within the context of apartheid legislation that forced Africans out of the cities, or designated them to live in specific rooms in the barracks based on their place of origin. In his fierce critique of the work of the Mayers, Magubane (1973:1713) wrote: 'The "urban/tribal" antithesis must not be studied apart from its social content, but rather in its economic, technological and political setting'.

18 Here, 'to eat' has a double meaning. It refers to the consumption of money as well as to sexual relations between male migrants and town women (see also Bähre 2002a; 2002b).

19 Trustworthy elders in the hostel block were asked to safeguard money for their fellow *abakhaya* to prevent them from spending it. The money was kept in a goatskin purse

called *ufelemntwini*, which means 'die for a person'. The elder would have to be killed before the purse could be taken from him (McAllister & Deliwe 1994:51 in Bank 1999:401). It could be, however, that the safeguarding of money by one elder was not a very common practice (personal communication McAllister).

20 These burial societies most closely resemble financial mutuals in 19th century Europe because of their emphasis on insurance and their financial structure.

21 This also explains why there were still some burial societies with a fund among non-neighbors: if a member failed to contribute, the burial society could simply reject his or her claim. In contrast, with Cape Town, women migrants in Johannesburg still organized dancing groups (*kiba*) with fellow home-people (James 1999a; 1999b). The reason for this discrepancy between Cape Town and Johannesburg could be due to the involvement of money in financial mutuals, which made social constraint necessary. The absence of social constraint would have fewer consequences for the participants of the dancing groups.

22 See also McNamara (1980:317-319) on the separate interaction of Transkei and Ciskei migrants.

23 Based on a 10 per cent sample of the Cape Metropolitan Area component of the Population Census conducted by SA Stats in October 1996 (CMC 2001). The authors mistakenly contributed the small 0-4 age group as 'characteristic of a population with a decreasing fertility rate' or undercounting. In 1991, in the Ciskei the African population between ten and fifteen years old was 13.8 per cent and the African population between fifteen and twenty years old 12.9 per cent (SAS 1997, table 1.19). Such comparisons, however, are problematic and should only be seen as a rough measure that a declining fertility rate was not the cause of the CMC findings. Research by Reynolds (1989:35) on the illegal squatter camp of Crossroads in the 1980s revealed that: 'In all, the children spent more than half of each of their lives in Cape Town… [T]hey had spent on-tenth away from their mothers and one-third away from their fathers.' See also numerous contributions in Burman and Reynolds (1986).

24 The NGO CIET Africa carried out the survey. The Western Cape, the province in which this research took place, has the highest number of rapes reported in South Africa. In 1997 there were 170.5 rapes and attempted rapes reported per 100,000 people, which is an increase since 1994 by 24 per cent (SAIRR 1998:28-29, 44; Cape Times 1998; SAPS 1998).

25 See Mager (1999) for a detailed examination of women's position in the Ciskei from the mid 1940s to the end of the 1950s. For the sexual dimension of the migratory process in the Rand, see Bonner (1990; 1995) and in the South African mines see Moodie (1988; 1994).

26 Although women moved to Cape Town in order to look for a job, in 1996 half of the African women in Cape Town were unemployed. A third of the African men were unemployed, while 5 per cent of White males were unemployed (CMC 2001).

27 For the constraints that kin could put on those who had some money, see Ardener (1995:7) and De Swaan (1996a:12).

28 The strategy to make it more difficult to spend money and easier to save has also been called the illiquidity preference (Bouman 1994a:117; Shipton 1995:257-259). Lont (2000b:167-168; this volume) has examined the benefits and limits of illiquidity in urban Indonesia.

References

Adams, D.W. & D.A. Fitchett (eds)
1992 *Informal Finance in Low-Income Countries.* Boulder: Westview Press.

Ardener, S.
1995 'Women Making Money go Round: ROSCAs revisited.' In: S. Ardener & S. Burman (eds) *Money-Go-Rounds. The Importance of Rotating Savings and Credit Associations for Women,* 1-19. Oxford/Washington D.C.: Berg.

Ardener, S. & S. Burman (eds)
1995 *Money-Go-Rounds; The Importance of Rotating Savings and Credit Associations for Women.* Oxford/Washington D.C.: Berg.

Bähre, E.
1996 'We Organise Each Other: Financial Self-help Groups and Civics in the Townships of Cape Town, South Africa.' unpublished MA thesis, Utrecht University.
2002a *Money and Violence: Financial Mutuals among the Xhosa in Cape Town, South Africa.* PhD thesis, University of Amsterdam.
2002b 'Witchcraft and the Exchange of Sex, Blood, and Money among Africans in Cape Town, South Africa.' *Journal of Religion in Africa,* 32:300-334.

Bank, L.
1997 'The Social Life of Paraffin; Gender, Domesticity and the Politics of Value in a South African Township.' *African Studies,* 56(2):157-179.
1999 'Men with Cookers: Transformations in Migrant Culture, Domesticity and Identity in Duncan Village, East London.' *Journal of Southern African Studies,* 25(3):393-416.

BBC
1999 *World: Africa. Sexual Violence on the Rise in South Africa.* BBC News.

Beinart, W.
1982 *The Political Economy of Pondoland 1860-1930.* Cambridge: Cambridge University Press.

Bijnaar, A.
1998 'Wat je zaait, zal je oogsten! Dwang en zelfdwang in Creools-Surinaamse onderlinges.' *Amsterdams Sociologisch Tijdschrift,* 25(3):329-370.

Bonner, P.
1990 'The Politics of Black Squatter Movements on the Rand, 1944-1952.' *Radical History Review,* 46(7):89-115.
1995 'African Urbanization on the Rand Between the 1930s and 1960s: its Social Character and Political Consequences.' *Journal of Southern African Studies,* 21(1):115-129.

Bouman, F.J.A.
1978 'Indigenous Savings and Credit Societies in the Third World: a Message.' *Development Digest,* XVI(3):181-218.
1994 'Informal Rural Finance: an Aladdin's Lamp of Information.' In: F.J.A. Bouman & O. Hospes (eds), *Financial Landscapes Reconstructed: The Fine Art of Mapping Development,* 105-122. Boulder: Westview Press.

Bouman, F.J.A., & O. Hospes (eds)
1994 *Financial Landscapes Reconstructed: The Fine Art of Mapping Development.* Boulder: Westview Press.

Bundy, C.
1979 *The Rise and Fall of the South African Peasantry.* London: Heinemann.

Burke, T.

1996 *Lifeboy Men, Lux Women; Commodification. Consumption, and Cleanliness in Modern Zimbabwe.* London: Leicester University Press.

Burman, S. & N. Lembete

1995 'Building New Realities; African Women and ROSCAs in Urban South Africa.' In: S. Ardener & S. Burman (eds), *Money-Go-Rounds. The Importance of Rotating Savings and Credit Associations for Women*, 23-47. Oxford: Berg.

Burman, S. & P. Reynolds (eds)

1986 *Growing Up in a Divided Society: the Contexts of Childhood in South Africa.* Johannesburg: Ravan Press.

Cape Times

1998 *Western Cape is Crime Hot Spot: SA Winning War on Violent Crime.* In: Cape Times. Mail and Guardian

CMC (Cape Metropolitan Council)

2001 *A Socio-Economic Profile of the Cape Metropolitan Area: Cape Metropolitan Council.*

Cock, J.

1980 *Maids and Madams. A Study in the Politics of Exploitation.* Johannesburg: Ravan Press.

Cole, J.

1987 *Crossroads: the Politics of Reform and Repression 1976/1986.* Johannesburg: Ravan Press.

Comaroff, J. & J.L. Comaroff

1990 'Goodly Beasts, Beastly Goods: Cattle and Commodities in a South African Context.' *American Ethnologist*, 17(2):195-216.

Delius, P.

1993 'Migrant Organization, the Communist Party, the ANC and the Sekhukhuneland Revolt, 1940-1958.' In: P.D.P. Bonner & D. Posel (eds), *Apartheid's Genesis: 1935-1962*, 126-159. Braamfontein/Johannesburg: Ravan Press, Witwatersrand University Press.

De Swaan, A.

1996a *Zorg en de Staat: Welzijn, onderwijs en gezondheidszorg in Europa en de Verenigde Staten in de nieuwe tijd.* Amsterdam: Bert Bakker.

1996b 'Onderlinges toen en nu, hier en daar. Informele spaar- en verzekeringskassen in het negentiende-eeuwse Westen en in de tegenwoordige buiten-westerse wereld.' In: *Onderlinge Hulpfondsen. Historische en etnografische essays.* M. van der Linden & J. Sluijs (eds), 9-22. Amsterdam: Stichting Beheer IISG.

Elias, N.

1982 *Het civilisatieproces: Sociologische en psychogenetische onderzoekingen.* Utrecht: Het Spectrum.

Elster, J.

1979 *Ulysses and the Sirens. Studies in Rationality and Irrationality.* Cambridge/Paris: Cambridge University Press.

Geertz, C.

1962 'The Rotating Credit Association: A "Middle Rung" in Development.' *Economic Development and Cultural Change*, 10:241-263.

Geschiere, P.

1983 'Bruidsprijzen bij de Maka in Kameroen: Marxistiese theorieën en de praktijk van antropologies veldwerk.' *Ter Elfder Ure*, 26(3):604-638.

Goldin, I.

1987 *Making Race: The Politics and Economics of Coloured Identity in South Africa.* Cape Town: Maskew Miller Longman.

Hammond-Tooke, W.D.
1962 *Bhaca Society: a People of the Transkeian Uplands, South Africa.* Cape Town/London/New York: Oxford University Press.
1970 'Urbanization and the Interpretation of Misfortune: A Quantitative Analysis.' *Africa XL,* (1):25-39.
Hospes, O.
1997 'New Studies on Informal Finance: Exploring The-state-of-the-art and the Art of the State.' *Savings and Development,* XXI(1):5-18.
Hunter, M.
1933 'The Effects of Contact with Europeans on the Status of Pondo Women.' *Africa,* VI:259-276.
1979 *Reaction to Conquest. Effects of Contact with Europeans on the Pondo of South Africa.* Cape Town: David Philip.
Hutchinson, S.E.
1996 *Nuer Dilemmas. Coping with Money, War, and the State.* Berkeley/Los Angeles: University of California Press.
James, D.
1999a '*Bagagsu* (Those of my Home): Women Migrants, Ethnicity, and Performance in South Africa.' *American Ethnologist,* 26(1):69-89.
1999b *Songs of the Women Migrants. Performance and Identity in South Africa.* London: Edinburgh University Press.
Jones, S.
1993 *Assaulting Childhood: Children's Experiences of Migrancy and Hostel Life in South Africa.* Johannesburg: Witwatersrand University Press.
Kane, A.
2001a *Les caméléons de la finance populaire au Sénégal et dans la diaspora: Dynamique des tontines et des caisses villageoises entre Thilogne, Dakar et La France.* PhD thesis, University of Amsterdam.
2001b 'Diaspora, villageoise et dévelopment local en Afrique: le cas de Thilogne association development.' *Hommes et Immigrations,* 1229 (Janvier-février):96-107.
Kappers, S.
1986 *Sitanani: Let's Help Each Other. Women and Informal Savings-, Credit-, and Funeral Organizations in Swaziland* – an Exploratory Study.
Kerri, J.N.
1976 'Studying Voluntary Associations as Adaptive Mechanisms; a Review of Anthropological Perspectives.' *Current Anthropology,* 171:23-47.
Kuckertz, H.
1997 '*Ukuhlonipa* as Idiom of Moral Reasoning in Mpondo. African Studies.' In: P.McAllister (ed.), Special Issue: *Culture and the Common Place;* Anthropological Essays in Honour of David Hammond-Tooke, 311-348.
Kuper, A.
1982 *Wives for Cattle; Bridewealth and Marriage in Southern Africa.* London/Boston/Melbourne/Henley: Routledge and Kegan Paul.
Lee, R.
1999 *African Women, Urban Areas and the Development of the Apartheid State: the Case of Cape Town, 1945-1970.* M. Phil. University of Oxford.
Leeuwenberg, J.
1977 *Transkei: a Study in Economic Regression.* London: The Africa Bureau.

Longmore, L.
1959 *The Dispossessed: A Study of the Sex-life of Bantu Women in Urban Areas in and Around Johannesburg.* London: Jonathan Cape.
Lont, H.
2000a 'More Money, More Autonomy?: Women and Credit in a Javanese Urban Community.' *Indonesia,* 70:83-100.
2000b 'Finding the Right Balance: Financial Self-help Organizations as Sources of Security and Insecurity in Urban Indonesia.' *International Review of Social History,* Supplement, 45:159-177.
2002 *Juggling Money in Yogyakarta; Financial Self-help Organizations and the Quest for Security.* PhD, University of Amsterdam.
Mager, A.K.
1999 *Gender and the Making of a South African Bantustan: A Social History of the Ciskei, 1945-1959.* Oxford and Cape Town: James Currey and David Philip.
Magubane, B.
1973 'The 'Xhosa' in Town, Revisited Urban Social Anthropology; A Failure of Method and Theory.' *American Anthropologist,* 75(5):1701-1715.
Mayer, P. & I. Mayer
1974 *Townsmen or Tribesmen: Conservatism and the Process of Urbanization in a South African City.* Cape Town/London/New York/Toronto: Oxford University Press.
McAllister, P.
1980 'Work, Homestead and the Shades: The Ritual Interpretation of Labor Migration among the Gcaleka'. In: P. Mayer (ed.), *Black Villagers in an Industrial Society; Anthropological Perspectives on Labor Migration in South Africa,* 205-253. Cape Town: Oxford University Press.
1985 'Beasts to Beer Pots – Migrant Labor and Ritual Change in Willowvale District, Transkei.' *African Studies,* 44(2):122-135.
1996 'Traditional Settlement, Cultural Identity and Rural Development in the Transkei.' In: P. Blunt & D.M. Warren (eds), *Indigenous Organizations and Development,* 7-20. London: Intermediate Technology Publications.
1997 *Ritual and Social Practice in the Transkei.* Special Issue: *Culture and the Common Place;* Anthropological Essays in Honour of David Hammond-Tooke, 279-309.
2000 'Maize Yields in the Transkei: How Productive is Subsistence Cultivation?' Occasional Paper Series: *Land Reform and Agrarian Change in Southern Africa.*
McNamara, J. K.
1980 'Brothers and Work Mates: Home Friends Networks in the Social Life of Black Migrant Workers in a Gold Mine Hostel.' In: P. Meyer (ed.): *Black Villagers in an Industrial Society; Anthropological Perspectives on Labor Migration in South Africa,* 305-340. Cape Town: Oxford University Press.
Meillassoux, C.
1968 *Urbanization of an African Community; Voluntary Associations in Bamako.* Seattle/London: University of Washington Press.
Moodie, T.D. (with V.Ndatshe & British Sibuyi)
1988 'Migrancy and Male Sexuality on the South African Gold Mines.' *Journal of Southern African Studies,* 14(2):228-256.
Moodie, T.D. & V. Ndatshe
1994 *Going for Gold; Men, Mines, and Migration.* Volume 51. Berkeley and Los Angeles: University of California Press.

Niehaus, I.

1994 'Disharmonious Spouses and Harmonious Siblings; Conceptualising Household Formation Among Urban Residents in Qwaqwa.' *African Studies*, 53(1):115-135.

Oliver-Evans, C.

1993 *Employement and Urbanization: The Impact of the Abolition of Influx Control in the Western Cape.* Cape Town: Southern Africa Labour and Development Research Unit.

Peires, J.B.

1989 *The Dead Will Arise: Mangqawuse and the Great Xhosa Cattle-killing Movement 1856-7.* Johannesburg: Ravan Press.

Ramphele, M.

1989 'The Dynamics of Gender Politics in the Hostels of Cape Town: Another Legacy of the South African Migrant Labor System.' *Journal of Southern African Studies*, 15(3):393-414.

1991 *The Politics of Space: Life in the Migrant Labour Hostels of the Western Cape.* Doctoral thesis, University of Cape Town.

Reynolds, P.

1989 *Childhood in Crossroads: Cognition and Society in South Africa.* Cape Town and Johannesburg: David Philip.

Robertson, M.K.

1990 'Black L & Tenure: Disabilities and Some Rights.' In: A.J. Rycroft et al. (eds), *Race and the Law in South Africa*, 119-135. Cape Town: Juta & Co.

Ross, F.

1990 *Strategies Against Patriarchy: Women and Rotating Credit Associations.* B.Sc.Hons., University of Cape Town.

Ross, R.

1999 *A Concise History of South Africa.* Cambridge: Cambridge University Press.

Rowlands, M.

1995 'Looking at Financial Landscapes: A Contextual Analysis.' In: S. Ardener & S. Burman (eds.) *Money-go-rounds; The Importance of Rotating Savings and Credit Associations for Women*, 111-124. Oxford/Washington D.C.: Berg.

SAIRR

1998 1997/1998 Survey. Johannesburg: South African Institute of Race Relations.

SAPS

2000 Specific Crimes per 100 000 of the Population for the Provinces During the Period January to December 1999: SAPS.

SAS

1997 South African Statistics 1995. Pretoria: Central Statistical Service.

Seekings, J.

1992 'Civic Organizations in South African Townships.' *South African Review*, 6:216-238.

Sharp, J.S. & A.D. Spiegel

1985 Vulnerability to Impoverishment in South African Rural Areas; The Erosion of Kinship and Neighborhood as Social Resources. *Africa*, 55(2):133-152.

Smets, P.

2000 'ROSCAs as a Source of Housing Finance for the Urban Poor: an Analysis of Self-help Practices from Hyderabad, India.' *Community Development Journal*, 35(1):16-30.

2002 *Housing Finance and the Urban Poor: Building and Financing Low-income Housing in Hyderabad, India.* PhD thesis, Vrije Universiteit Amsterdam.

Spiegel, A.
1987 'Dispersing Dependants: a Response to the Exigencies of Labor Migration in Rural Transkei.' In: J. Eades (ed.), *Migrants, Workers, and the Social Order*, 113-129. ASA Monographs. London/New York: Tavistock Publications.
Thoden van Velzen, H.U.E. & W. Van Wetering
1991 *The Great Father and the Danger; Religious Cults, Material Forces, and Collective Fantasies in the World of the Surinamese Maroons.* Leiden: KITLV Press.
Thornton, R. & M. Ramphele
1988 'The Quest for Community'. In: E. Boonzajer & J. Sharp (eds.), *South African Keywords: The Uses and Abuses of Political Concepts*, 29-39. Cape Town/Johannesburg: David Philip.
Van Genabeek, J.
1996 'Dwang en vrijwilligheid; Onderlinge verzekeringen in Nederland, sedert de middeleeuwen tot circa 1860.' In: M. Van der Linden & J. Sluijs (eds.) *Onderlinge hulpfondsen; historische en etnografische essays*, 45-69. Amsterdam: IISG.
Van der Linden, M.
1996a 'Introduction' In: M. Van der Linden (ed.), *Social Security Mutualism: The Comparative History of Mutual Benefit Societies.* 11-38. Bern: Peter Lang.
1996b 'De historische logica van onderlinge arbeidersverzekeringen.' In: M. Van der Linden & J. Sluijs (eds), *Onderlinge hulpfondsen; historische en etnografische essays*, 23-44. Amsterdam: IISG.
Van Wetering, I.
1987 'Informal Supportive Networks: Quasi-kin Groups, Religion and Social Order Among Surinam Creoles in the Netherlands'. *The Netherlands Journal of Sociology*, 23(2):92-101.
Wilson, F.
1972 *Migrant Labour.* Johannesburg: South African Council of Churches and SPRO-CAS.
Wilson, F. & M. Ramphele
1994 *Uprooting Poverty: The South African Challenge.* Cape Town/Johannesburg: David Philip.
Wilson, M.& A. Mafeje
1963 *Langa; A Study of Social Groups in an African Township.* Cape Town/London/New York: Oxford University Press.
Wolf, E.
1982 *Europe and the People Without History.* Berkeley/Los Angeles/London: University of California Press.

CHAPTER 3

As ye sow, so ye shall reap!

Kasmoni in Suriname

Aspha Bijnaar

Context of the Surinamese kasmoni

Suriname, a former Dutch colony, is situated north of Brazil. Paramaribo is the capital. The country has over 450,000 inhabitants, comprising various ethnic groups. Descendants from indigenous people, African slaves and Asian contract workers, or rather Creoles, Hindustanis and Javanese are the largest population groups. In addition, Surinamese society includes Indians, maroons, Chinese, Buru (descendants of Dutch farmers), Jews and Lebanese. This study is focused on the Creole population group.

In literature about the Caribbean, analyses of countries such as Suriname reflect the perspective of their tradition of slavery, which underlies their current social structure (see e.g. Jansen 1986:20-23; Wekker 1994:59-74). On the one hand, this past has given rise to richly hybrid cultures in their own right in the Caribbean countries. On the other hand, these cultures have a tragic inner disunity. Historically, Suriname has been exploited by foreign firms that snapped up the profits without investing in the country. To this day the country primarily supplies commodities such as bauxite. Local industries are rarely developed, and Suriname continues to rely on imports. These imports of food and luxury goods consume a large share of the national budget. The population has grown accustomed to a Western consumer lifestyle. Local merchants, who earn a good income from this lifestyle, perpetuate this unproductive situation with the help of clientelist politicians.

Because of this political and economic structure, Suriname has a longstanding dependence on financial aid, which arrives mainly from the former colonial power of the Netherlands. Other problems include ongoing budget deficits, huge foreign debts and rampant inflation as a consequence of the economic recession that started in the 1980s. This economic slump has brought about an extensive informal economy in Suriname, in which several informal arrangements such as ROSCAs, ASCRAs, money lending and nearbanking figure prominently.

Kasmoni, a type of ROSCA that may have been widely used by Creoles as early as the days of slavery (see Bijnaar 2002:39-52), actually thrived during the economic slump toward the end of the twentieth century. The system has grown increasingly popular among Surinamese Creoles. Although Creoles are the chief users of kasmoni, other ethnic groups participate as well. With the Creole exodus toward the former colonial power of the Netherlands around the Surinamese independence in 1975, the kasmoni went along as a cultural asset and helped the Creoles get their bearings in their new surroundings.

Nearly one third of the Surinamese Creoles presently contributes to the kasmoni.[1] The system is as follows: 12 confidants deposit a predetermined amount each month for up to 12 months. This sum, which is known as *anu* (meaning 'hand'), is distributed to one of the participants each month, until each one has had a turn. The first recipient is the borrower: he receives a loan to be repaid over the following months. The final recipient is the saver and receives the savings accumulated in previous months. Because each participant is supposed to receive the kitty at some point, each feels compelled to pay his dues on time every month. Each cycle lasts one year on average, after which another kasmoni is started up. The sequence of distribution is determined by a raffle or by mutual agreement. The person who manages the kasmoni may receive financial compensation for services rendered.

Deposits average 50 euros a month. Depending on their personal need, depositors may contribute double, half or even quarter deposits. Assuming an average deposit of 50 euros, over 2 million euros in cash is circulating every month.

Most participants are working or middle class. Women outnumber men in kasmoni. Although they are in the minority, men account for 30 percent of the participants. Kasmoni are formed among family members, friends, co-workers and acquaintances. Most kasmoni in Suriname are organized at the workplace, such as in homes for the elderly, cafeterias of large companies and at supermarkets, schools, post offices and banks.

Kasmoni are informal financial arrangements that are not regulated in Suriname. As such, they lack protection against defaults on payment and embezzlement. Why do so many Creoles join kasmoni?

Rationales for ROSCAs

The worldwide popularity of ROSCAs has been attributed to various factors, none of which fully explain the practice. While the British anthropologist Ardener highlights the importance of ROSCAs within cultural traditions of mutual aid, the American sociologist Callier has noted their economic function in obtaining fast credit on reasonable terms, and De Swaan focuses on group discipline in savings. These views derive from four subordinate rationales, in which cultural, economic and sociological perspectives complement one another.[2]

The first culturally-based rationale reflects the views of Ardener, who associates ROSCAs with mutual solidarity. Ardener situates the ROSCA system within traditions of reciprocal support among families, neighbors and co-workers, who respond more adequately to local needs than the formal banking institutions with their cumbersome procedures. ROSCAs serve as a form of insurance in highly cohesive communities. Other authors note that community ties are not only a condition for joint economic activities, but that joint savings plans enhance community awareness as well (Bouman 1994:275). Participants enjoy gathering to make their deposits, consult each other about the course of the cycle and engage in joint activities.

The second rationale reflects Callier's position and emphasizes the purely economic aspect of the ROSCAs. Like Ardener, Callier observes that the informal nature of ROSCAs makes them better equipped to meet the needs of their members than formal financial services are. In his view, certain groups join ROSCAs because of the rigid requirements and bureaucratic obstacles of official financial institutions (Callier 1990:276. Also Bouman 1985; Falola 1995; Hospes 1996). Callier adds that the system serves other economic purposes besides support in case of need: many members aim to save or borrow money to purchase more expensive items for personal use.

The main motive for preferring ROSCAs to banks, according to Callier, derives from the logic of collective action and concerns the 'reduced waiting time' for members to receive payments (Callier 1990:275). The 'reduced waiting time' of ROSCAs is indeed a significant economic advantage. Members whose turn for a payout comes early obtain the total sum sooner than they would through a savings account at a bank or cash hoarded in a piggy bank or under their mattress. If the payout moment is early in the ROSCA cycle, the depositor receives the sum before he or she has saved the total amount and repays what is left during the remaining periods. Depositors with an early payout turn thus acquire credit quickly and easily without needing to satisfy the bureaucratic terms of a bank loan. Members often plan the time of receipt to coincide with expenses they anticipate, for example for celebrations, ritual activities and purchases of durable consumer goods.

The timing of receipt is a personal decision and is generally determined by how and when people intend to spend their payout. Decisions may also be instinctive. Some people prefer having their turn late to feel they are truly debt-free, which is not an irrational approach. To outsiders, members intending to purchase a refrigerator through this savings and credit system who do not want an early turn may not seem rational. After all, the sooner they get their refrigerator the better. The Surinamese ROSCA system therefore does not appear to follow the Western logic of individual pursuit of profit. But different principles rule the broader perspective of social capital. Most members have a deep-seated fear of debts, and an early-turn payment is considered a debt. My research also revealed that fear of debts is a common motive for joining ROSCAs. People are especially wary of debts with commercial institutions, such as department stores, because of the shame associated with them in the past. Since luxury items such as refrigerators, bicycles and sewing machines became available in Suriname, consumers have had the option of paying for their purchases in instalments. Buyers who miss payments risk having these items repossessed – a disgrace that all the neighbors will witness. If they default altogether, they may even find themselves publicly humiliated by some firms. Their photograph will be displayed in the shop, sometimes even in the front window, to inform the entire Surinamese public of their wrongdoing. Although fear of debts does not appear to be a strictly rational argument, it does motivate business practices in a society where people cherish their reputation.

Callier's explanation does not apply to ROSCA participants with a late payout turn. They receive less credit at a later stage, even though they save more over a longer period. In this case, the advantage over saving at a bank is less obvious; unlike people who bank their savings, those saving through ROSCAs receive no interest. Still, many participants prefer not to collect their payout early in the cycle. Sometimes people continue paying into the informal savings networks, even though they would get far better terms at the bank around the corner. Participation by this type of savers thus requires a separate explanation to reconcile Ardener's pronounced cultural perspective with Callier's purely economic approach. They prefer ROSCAs, because these arrangements are deeply embedded in the local culture and are familiar and trusted, whereas formal institutions are unknown and unappealing. Like the first explanation, this third subordinate rationale is based on cultural traditions, albeit only through the remote link of traditional familiarity. Solidarity in emergencies is not a factor. People join to save and are free to use the payout entirely for their benefit. These savers are as focused on personal gain as the borrowers covered in the second rationale. They are guided more by traditions, however, than by pure business rationale and would derive greater benefit from entrusting their money to a bank.

These three subordinate rationales overlook one aspect of ROSCAs. Saving through a ROSCA without an early payout turn offers a significant advantage over saving at a bank. As De Swaan has indicated, saving as a group makes people more inclined to save. Savings may be withdrawn from a bank at any time. ROSCA savers, however, voluntarily enter a collective savings commitment that deters them from impulsive consumer spending. The rationale is therefore sociological rather than purely economic. De Swaan has described this specific compelling nature of ROSCAs as 'social constraint toward self-constraint' (De Swaan 1996:12).

De Swaan uses this pair of concepts to elaborate on the central distinction between 'social constraint' and 'self-control' in Elias' civilization theory (Elias 1982:239-260). Elias argues that the focus of human impulse management in the West has shifted from external social constraint toward individual self-control. People have had to exercise greater self-restraint, as the increasing complexity of economic and political relationships has made them far more dependent on one another.

This 'civilization process' is driven by state formation. The monopoly of the central authorities on violence inhibited violence between individuals and enabled peaceful cooperation, while at the same time forcing citizens to become more restrained. This progressive self-control was strongest among the middle class, according to Elias, because of the long-term planning that the corresponding responsibilities required. As the social functions of members of the lower classes became more intertwined with society as a whole, they experienced the same change.

De Swaan argues that this shift from external to internal constraint has also affected savings habits in the West (De Swaan 1989:165). Small entrepreneurs and farmers were the first groups to save out of self-control. They independently deferred immediate gratification of their needs to have more to invest and to be better equipped to cope with setbacks later on. As a result, the urge to save was viewed initially as a typically middle-class desire. The bourgeoisie deliberately elevated itself above the working class, which was accused of lacking self-discipline. Members of the working class aiming for upward social mobility adopted the standards, values and conduct of the middle class and consequently also the desire to save to distinguish themselves from less civilized workers. Workers who did not start to save as a personal virtue devised a system in between social constraint and self-control. Doubting their own savings discipline, they submitted to social control. They voluntarily joined a mutual financial arrangement that bound them to contribute a fixed portion of their income each month. The *social constraint toward self-constraint* mechanism thus struck a balance between external constraint and self-control in workers' associations.

De Swaan also explains that the non-Western ROSCAs restrain the urge toward spontaneous consumption through social constraint and self-control. This constraint has the added benefit of protecting depositors from financial demands from those around them, whom they would otherwise have to accommodate out of solidarity. Falola (1995:170), Ardener (1995), Besson (1995:266), Philpott (1973:173), Bouman (1985 182, 184) and Hospes (1996:74) also emphasize that the constraint element of ROSCAs is particularly beneficial in this respect.[3] Unlike De Swaan, however, they do not analyse it.

Functions and motives

The literature thus provides four rationales for joining ROSCAs based on the various functions of the system. The first one is focused on mutual aid in unforeseen emergencies, based on cultural embedment through cohesive traditional solidarity.[4] The second rationale emphasizes the economic benefit of fast, inexpensive credit, an area where ROSCAs are far superior to formal institutions. The third rationale notes first of all that saving with ROSCAs is costlier than saving at a bank; those who save through the informal system nonetheless, do so because they are more familiar with informal arrangements than with formal services. Again, cultural context is a factor, although in this case in the diluted form of security in traditions. The fourth rationale primarily concerns the supportive function of reciprocal social constraint in controlling individual spending urges. These four rationales reflect an equal number of motives for participating in ROSCAs.[5]

In some respects the explanations correspond with Max Weber's types of human action (Weber 1967:12; Weber 1978:24-26) although his typology needs to be elaborated in this context. Those participating in ROSCAs out of a tradition of collective solidarity engage in 'value-rational' action according to Weber's terms. Weber believes that a certain type of conduct has a specific value, whereas the outcome of such conduct receives no consideration or is regarded as unimportant. I have labelled the value motive underlying the conduct of such ROSCA participants as the *solidarity motive.*

ROSCA participation out of cultural familiarity corresponds with Weber's notion of 'traditional' action: people act according to a custom that has become routine. I therefore describe this as participation with a *traditional motive.* Members join because they are familiar with the comfort of their traditional associations and do not weigh them against the benefits and drawbacks of the formal financial institutions.[6] Even though banks may offer a financial advantage, they do not figure within the known cultural patterns and therefore have a higher threshold.

Callier's explanation based on the theory of collective action, supplemented by Ardener's reference to the ineffective procedures of formal institutions, meets the criteria for Weber's goal-rational action reflecting goal, means and consequences. People joining ROSCAs for these reasons operate according to the *economic motive.* They join a ROSCA association out of rational self-interest, realizing that they will derive greater financial benefit this way than by operating through formal channels.

De Swaan's explanation involves a hybrid of Weber's goal-rational action and 'affective' action. People engaging in affective action are motivated by emotions and other states of mind, such as vengeance, love, hate, anger, pleasure or even ambition. 'Constraint toward self-constraint', however, concerns rational control of affections. Rather than being swept away by emotions, ROSCA participants aim to suppress these urges in favor of economic goal-rationality. In keeping with Elias' civilization theory, rational action implies impulse management here. In this case, however, actors have difficulty restraining their spending impulses and thus submit to external pressure of their own accord. I have abbreviated this complex motive as the *constraint motive.*

As will become clear, a small group of wealthy kasmoni participants mentions a fifth motive. The *nostalgia motive,* as I will call it, is a severely diluted version of the solidarity motive. These participants do not join for personal gain but are motivated exclusively by nostalgia for old traditions they have outgrown. The financial benefits matter little to them. They have advanced to the wealthy elite and aim to pay tribute to the popular kasmoni tradition. Some also feel a remote sense of solidarity with poorer kasmoni depositors. Compassion leads them to participate in the kasmoni of a less affluent acquaintance from the lower classes.

These motives reflect various views on rationality. The economic rationale is linked to the theory of collective action and the perception of the *homo economicus.* Theoretically, humans are perceived as fully goal-rational individuals guided by calculation of costs and benefits. Moreover human behavior is presumed to be reconstructed along these lines.

The constraint motive is also based in part on this perception of mankind, but the underlying psychology is more complex. Although people are capable of economic planning, their affections often prevent them from realizing their plans. As will become clear later in this chapter, Jon Elster refers to an 'imperfect rationality' here. According to De Swaan's development perspective, the ROSCA system of 'constraint toward self-control' is a transitional stage in the progression from affective to goal-rational action.

People guided by values and traditions do not act according to a strictly economic rationale. Many anthropologically-oriented critics argue, however, that this economic rationality concept is typically Western and reflects a reduced, instrumentalist perception of human behavior. They believe that the perception of what is reasonable is far broader among non-Western cultures. Even if ROSCAs do not yield economic benefits, participation in them need not be unreasonable. Informal arrangements may reinforce group cohesion and ties between individual participants.

I will circumvent this controversial discussion for the moment by offering a stipulating definition devoid of normative judgement. I use 'rationality' to refer to the goal-rationality of the economic motive, without asserting that non-economic motives are unreasonable or primitive in a broader context.

My detailed interviews with kasmoni participants have revealed that they are well aware of the functions and motives associated with the system: most mentioned one or more of these motives as their reason for participating, although their answers to my questions about their reasons were obviously far less systematic than the five categories above. The reasons mentioned by the kasmoni depositors are sometimes difficult to classify under one of the main motives I have identified. As my kasmoni interviews reveal, the different motives often overlap. People rarely act entirely rationally or entirely irrationally. 'People are [after all] guided by mixed feelings and ideas in varying measures (Goudsblom 1997:196).' Kasmoni participants may be motivated by a combination of conformist traditionalism and economic considerations. I have resolved this problem by focusing on the motive given the most emphasis by the respondent concerned.[7] Situations where the motives reported by participants appear questionable are even trickier. Some base their behavior on what appear to be business considerations, while the behavior in fact seems to arise from cultural traditions. In such cases I try to understand the interviewee better than he or she understands himself or herself by examining to what extent his conduct is goal-rational. This presumes an economic analysis of kasmoni. To distinguish truly economic motives from semi-rational ones, I will start by reviewing the system's economic benefits and drawbacks.

Kasmoni serve three economic purposes: saving, borrowing and coping with misfortunes. Participating in kasmoni is rational, if one needs these facilities, and no formal or other alternatives would serve this purpose better. What are the advantages of kasmoni over banking institutions?

First, savings: the last participant to receive cash in the kasmoni cycle has maximum use of the savings system, since this person receives his or her deposits from previous stages at the end. Compared with a savings bank, kasmoni savings have the disadvantage that participants receive no interest on their savings and are often morally obliged to pay 'cash rights' to the cash minder for services rendered. In this case kasmoni participants end up with negative interest. They pay to deposit their money, whereas banks do the opposite and pay savers for the right to store their money. This is what Herbert Simon has described as 'satisfacing' [gratifying] to relativize the rational choice theory principle that people will always maximize in the sense of pursuing optimal accumulation. In most cases, people actually appear to settle for less (Simon 1979:502-3).

One advantage of kasmoni savings is the simplicity of financial transactions. Paying the dues or receiving the total cash takes just a minute. At banks, clients often have long waits and spend a lot of time filling out forms and presenting documents. The second advantage is that the 'cashier' is usually easy to reach. She or he is often in direct proximity to members and is therefore available at virtually any moment, whereas banks have limited hours of business. In the sense that time is money, the negative interest of kasmoni savings is thus offset by the immediacy of the informal relationships. Most kasmoni participants, however, have less money than time. The ones joining kasmoni to accumulate savings are therefore not acting out of a goal-rational economic motive. They would benefit financially from bank interest. Although kasmoni savers may report economic considerations as their reason for participating, they are more likely to have joined with the traditional motive. Saving at a kasmoni is a very familiar system.

Second, credit: kasmoni give all depositors, except for the last one, faster access to a sum of money than if they had saved with a bank or at home. I have labelled this advantage as 'fast credit'. The measure of this advantage, however, diminishes with each successive turn, since the first participant receives the entire sum at the time of his first deposit, the second participant does so in the second month, while the ninth participant receives it only after contributing for nine months. The final participant receives no credit at all, as he collects his share only at the end of the cycle. Compared with bank loans, kasmoni have the advantage of being interest-free. Banks moreover have various criteria for determining creditworthiness, such as presentation of an employer's reference and several persons to vouch for the borrower. The advantage of a bank loan is that the amounts available generally exceed the standard payouts through a kasmoni, provided one satisfies the conditions for borrowing. Aside from this detail, however, participants who want the fast credit of the early payout operate based on the economic motive. Kasmoni have more to offer them than banks do.

Third, misfortune: in cases of dire need, participants are granted a payout outside their turn. Disbursement is virtually instantaneous, whereas insurance companies operate far more slowly and require more formalities, assuming that cover is available. Unlike commercial insurance companies, kasmoni are not intended to generate a profit. Frequent misfortunes might jeopardize the savings and loan system. Generally, however, kasmoni contributors rarely make use of this emergency service, and the risks are very broadly distributed. Size puts the kasmoni at a relative disadvantage: their membership is small and the deposits modest. The system is therefore not equipped to handle unexpectedly high expenses and does not cover risks. This shortcoming aside, participating in kasmoni as an emergency plan is a sound economic practice.

Kasmoni have the advantage of combining savings, credit and emergency aid. These three functions overlap and are interchangeable. All contributors will obtain satisfaction, since if one function does not meet their need, another one will compensate. To illustrate how flexible kasmoni are: in the worst case a participant may receive a payout early or late or may suffer a misfortune. If the credit function prevails against the desire of a participant, he or she may exchange with a fellow participant in favor of the savings function. In this case, the participant exchanges his or her early turn for a late one. If such an exchange is impossible, the cash minder will often accommodate the participant's savings need by keeping the amount payable until the participant claims it. This custodial service thus becomes an added function. If the cash minder is unable to hang on to the cash, the participant will accept the advantage of fast credit by changing his or her plans. If in the other extreme, participants receive a late payout counter to their plans and are unable to exchange to obtain a better turn, they can be confident of having saved a certain amount at a specific time and will adjust their plans. Moreover, they will be entitled to an earlier turn in a subsequent cycle. In most cases the cash minder compensates participants receiving unfavorable turns by giving them better turns in the next round. In the third case, that of an unexpected misfortune, participants have fast emergency credit available. Fellow participants forced to give up their turns have access to the kasmoni savings and loan function despite a minor delay. The three shortcomings discussed are in fact temporary. After all, whatever is not accomplished in the current kasmoni cycle is feasible in the next one. Participants can reduce these risks by participating in the same kasmoni with two or more contributions or by joining several kasmoni at once. Hardly anybody I interviewed was consistently dissatisfied with the allocation of payout turns.

The flexibility of kasmoni is a major advantage over formal financial institutions, which offer each of these functions through a separate counter with separate formalities or through different branches. These advantages are offset by a substantial disadvantage. The major weakness of the kasmoni is their vulnerability to fraud. Because kasmoni lack an official status, and their transactions are hardly ever recorded, embezzlers easily get away with such actions. Formal financial institutions provide additional security, although the informal social control in kasmoni is usually sufficient.

Interviews

I asked fifty-seven kasmoni participants in Suriname to describe their motive for joining the system. They mentioned all motives except for solidarity. When participants mentioned several motives at once,[8] I focused on the one they emphasized the most. Eighteen participants said they cared about the fast credit. I classify their motive as economic: they are aware that kasmoni cost less than a bank loan. The same holds true for the two participants who mentioned the emergency function: this kasmoni function offers economic benefit as well. These participants make economically rational use of kasmoni. Four participants said they joined to save money for expensive purchases; their responses to my question as to whether saving with a bank would be wiser were unsatisfactory. I have classified these participants under the traditional motive. Twenty-five other participants also stated that they contributed to kasmoni for the purpose of saving but added that the system provided them with the discipline required to save. Their motive is constraint. A small group of eight participants saved out of nostalgia.

In this article I explore the two motives mentioned the most frequently by the participants – the economic motive and the constraint motive – to provide greater insight into the kasmoni effect.[9]

Economic considerations

Eighteen of the twenty participants classified under the economic motive mentioned the fast credit available through the kasmoni as their main reason. They also mentioned the relative disadvantage of kasmoni savings compared with a savings bank. These respondents rationally considered the economic differences between the two systems. Cash minder Virginia (an interior decorator, age 63) argues that saving the intended amount at a bank account takes longer:

> Banks are counter effective, since you have to wait so long for your money. At kasmoni, the shorter waiting period leaves you with more in the end. Saving 100,000 Surinamese guilders at a bank takes an awfully long time.

Kasmoni participants are aware that saving at a bank generates interest, unlike kasmoni savings. All the same, this financial loss is acceptable, according to Angela, a thirty-six year-old administrative assistant, since the savings function is concentrated in the late turns for payouts. In her kasmoni, payout turns are determined through a raffle:

> I prefer kasmoni to banks. After all, [you get] cash, if you're lucky, since it's a raffle system, right? So you might get the first or second *anu* in a ten-month kasmoni. I'm not crazy about kasmoni where the cycles are longer than a year. The wait for the money is too long. At kasmoni you get your money faster, and you can use it as you please. At banks they make you wait. In kasmoni, though, you don't receive interest, and that can be a disadvantage.

Fast credit enables spending to be transformed into systematic planning. This advantage is very alluring. Gerard, a fifty-year old cash minder and the head of a large multinational aluminium processing plant, explained:

> Well, banks pay interest, but kasmoni are an addition to your salary. Kasmoni serve another purpose. Most savings plans are intended for old age, but kasmoni are there to help you get that fine stereo: *yongu*! Kasmoni help you count the time and plan your stereo. Even though they may not pay interest, they're a lot faster than banks. So I prefer kasmoni.

Clearly, these eighteen depositors have made a rational consideration between joining a kasmoni and saving at a bank or getting a bank loan. One participant even derived maximum benefit from the relative advantages of kasmoni and banks at the same time. After an early *anu*, he immediately deposited the interest-free kasmoni credit to a savings account at a bank to accrue interest there.

The third economic function of kasmoni is to cope with misfortunes. In emergencies, the participant affected gets an early turn, subject to the consent of the cash minder and fellow participants. The system's flexibility and low cost may rationalize participation for the sake of this emergency function. The two participants who mentioned this function are therefore classified under the economic motive as well.

In practice, however, this function is rarely invoked and usually remains dormant. In some kasmoni the cash minder does not allow for financial aid, arguing that the money is not her own. In most cases, however, cash minders and participants are compassionate in the rare instances where a fellow participant requests emergency aid. The stories reveal that in such emergencies the money is needed on the spot. Because the monthly deposits have rarely been received yet at the time the emergency occurs, the cash minder will have to advance the money herself, as fifty-six year-old Carla relates:

> You know why I do this? Something may happen at night, when the bank is closed. It happened to me. One woman in my kasmoni, it wasn't her turn yet. Her granddaughter came to me and said that her grandmother wanted to know whether I could help her with some cash, since that boy got hit by a car and died. I wondered what to do, since it wasn't her turn. My husband said: '*yepi* [help] that woman.' I gave her the kasmoni, and my husband added some from his salary. The next morning that grandmother came to settle the account. I felt I needed to help that woman, you should always help those around you.

The total amount is paid to the victim immediately in such cases, and the victim repays it by continuing to deposit his monthly contribution. Only in very serious cases, for example if a participant has lost all his worldly possessions in a fire, is the money a gift.

In the stories of all those I examined, I discovered only five incidents where the emergency function was invoked. Only two participants mentioned this insurance feature as their motive for participating. Mrs. Friede, a seventy-six year-old housewife and lottery ticket saleswoman, has never personally experienced such emergencies but considers them to be an important benefit of the kasmoni:

> What I forgot to mention is that deposits, *te den sma ben poti kasgeld* [when people used to make deposits], they were able to help in emergencies, since you couldn't just borrow money from somebody. Everybody was poor. So if somebody minded the deposits, and somebody else was sick or dying, you could ask the kasmoni organizer. He or she would help. This person would understand if you were in trouble. So the person due to receive the payout would not get it at his turn. There had been an emergency, and he would get it in the next round. The person whose turn it was heard about the emergency and would agree to help. The system helped a lot. The situation had to be a real emergency. Those who lied would not fare well. Banks are closed in the evenings and afternoons. That's the only advantage, nothing else.

Elderly people mentioned the emergency function more often than younger ones. This emergency use may have been more important in the past. It can never have dominated the system, though, since kasmoni would become so unreliable that the system would no longer function properly.

Constraint motive

Twenty-five participants mentioned the need for savings discipline. This group reports using this saving system out of personal inability to save systematically. Mr. Dorus, age 63 and a car mechanic, described this lack of will power as follows:

> Well, you can head straight for the bank [to save money on your own]. But some people are born to use the banks, and others just can't. They may picture the bank in their minds and decide to take their money there. But once they get there, they decide to spend their money instead. Joining a kasmoni averts this problem.

While some respondents justified their participation by referring to the human impulse, others mentioned external surroundings. Their intention may not have been to absolve themselves. The combination of a low income and the pressure of countless financial obligations certainly undermines opportunities to save independently and systematically. Bea, age 32 and a market woman, explained that she felt compelled to replace products sold out from her market stand with some regularity:

> Sometimes I resolve to deposit a certain amount to my bank account. But when I get to the market, I find that so many *dinges* [market goods] are missing, that I spend the money replacing them. That's why I deposit the money at a kasmoni instead of a bank.

Although lack of self-discipline is usually associated with menial occupations, some people with high administrative positions admitted their will power was weak, as the following two passages reveal. Wine (36) had a business degree from a junior college and was in charge of financial management:

> Imagine being able to make a major purchase all at once, one you could not afford with your pay check. The system forces you to save the money. Financially, you can always save at a bank, but the feeling of 'I'm stuck and need some money and will spend it' is overwhelming. The temptation is overwhelming, and that money is just waiting to be withdrawn. At kasmoni, you have to keep making your payments, even if you have had your turn, you keep paying. So the commitment is very similar to a loan. I'm always tempted to avoid depriving myself, if I have the money there.' But the kasmoni doesn't work that way, and the sense of commitment is considerable.

George (46) studied linguistics in the Netherlands, held a ministerial post in a previous government and is now an influential businessman:

> I joined because I knew the system from the past and saw it as a commitment that makes you save. And then there were my birthdays. Birthdays are important to me. I like standing in front of my house and seeing a lot of people driving up to see me. I was doing well financially at the time and did not join the kasmoni out of need. I did it to save, for my birthday, and, quite honestly, I prefer kasmoni to the bank because of the discipline.

George is also alluding to the nostalgic motive. Unlike true nostalgists, however, he also emphasizes the advantage of compulsory saving. In addition, the kasmoni satisfies a financial need related to his birthday.

Constraint motive and deferred gratification

The constraint motive merits elaboration because of its complexity. I have a personal interest in this aspect of the kasmoni based in part on my own background. Growing up in Suriname amid all the kasmoni of my aunts, I noticed how controversial the system was. Some of my uncles told their wives with immense irritation that saving through kasmoni was a sign of weakness. People were supposed to save of their own accord, at home or with a bank! My aunts ignored these reproaches and happily continued their kasmoni. In the course of my research I encountered the same objections. Non-participants disparaged the lack of will power of kasmoni members and said they felt no need for this constraint system, as they had sufficient will power to save on their own. Participants reporting the constraint motive as their reason for joining acknowledged that they lacked the self-discipline to save. Unlike the critics, however, they expressed a more favorable evaluation of kasmoni. They considered the system to be an adequate means for controlling their impulses.

How does this complex mechanism operate? Saving is a form of *deferred gratification*. People unable to muster the required self-discipline achieve their objective thanks to *social constraint toward self-constraint* in the kasmoni system. Elster labels this practice as 'imperfect rationality'.

Anthropologists, psychologists and economists wrote extensively about deferred gratification through saving in the 1960s (see e.g. Nurkse 1953; Holton 1960; Swift 1964, Firth & Yamey 1964; Veblen 1953; Renselaar 1963).[10] The practice is described as temporarily foregoing the desires of that moment to achieve a long-term objective at a later stage. This definition comprises three elements: (1) organizing in stages, (2) deferring gratification of immediate needs or short-term desires to (3) satisfy long-term needs or desires.

Breman has focused on the stages aspect. He disagrees with the view that deferring gratification of needs typified the middle class during the rise of capitalism in Europe: capital accumulation served to increase production. While this pattern appears everywhere, its manifestations vary. The objectives that lead people to defer their needs are likely to vary depending on the time and place. In other parts of the world, for example, people invest in intangible values such as power, prestige or divine mercy. Western-oriented scholars have the mistaken tendency to envisage European development as a universal civilization process, according to Breman, and consequently regard non-capitalist forms of deferred gratification of needs as irrational. On the other hand, he argues that organizing their gratification in stages is in fact attributed greater importance than the substance of their needs (Breman 1966:2-4).

Kasmoni deposits exemplify non-capitalist deferred gratification of needs. Participants saving out of constraint aim to realize their 'superior' desires by restraining their urge toward immediate gratification, without pursuing capitalist expansion. Like most Surinamese Creoles, their objective is social prestige.

Participants with economic motives have the same objective but prefer other means: they want fast credit. Borrowers satisfy their 'superior' desires immediately rather than deferring their needs. The kasmoni procedure, however, is more complicated than bank loans are. The rotating aspect means that kasmoni comprise a range of stages. The interval between deferral and gratification varies for each payout turn. Deferred gratification of needs occurs with the credit function as well as with the savings function. Given a ten-month cycle and ten individuals, only the first participant receives pure credit and therefore does not experience deferred gratification of needs. This person achieves his long-term objective instantly and is expected to repay the amount over the next nine months. The tenth participant mirrors his situation. He receives no credit at all and experiences full deferred gratification of needs. He must defer his needs for ten months before achieving his long-term objective. The other participants occupy intermediate positions. The second one obtains fast credit as well but has to make a deposit in the first round. Later participants experience successively increasing deferred gratification of needs. Depending on the payout turn, deferred gratification of needs does in fact apply, even if the participant cares about credit.

Conversely, kasmoni are purely a savings arrangement only in the tenth or final round. The sooner the turn, the less significant the deferral, until the savings element has disappeared entirely by the first turn. In practice, savings and credit overlap. Nonetheless, the economic motive and the constraint motive differ substantially. Those mentioning the constraint motive experience the organization in stages as problematic. Although they are able to prioritize their short-term and long-term needs, they report that they are unable to defer their needs of their own accord. By gratifying their 'inferior' desires against their better judgement, they never achieve their 'superior' objectives. Their reason for preferring kasmoni over individual savings is that the system compels them to defer. They manage to organize in stages thanks to the combination of voluntary and social constraint that typifies kasmoni.

As for *short-term preferences*, many Creoles believe that the spending habits of their own ethnic group are focused on immediate gratification of impulsive needs, such as good food, fashionable clothes and entertainment. Indulging in life's pleasures means that they hardly save. They run through their money before the end of the month and borrow from family, friends or acquaintances. The next month they go back to buying nice things and forget their debts altogether or leave them partially unpaid. Again, they spend their money quickly and incur new debts. They soon lapse into a vicious cycle.

All respondents automatically compared Creole spending habits to those of other ethnic groups in Suriname. They were particularly inclined to mention the contrast between Hindustanis and Creoles.

> We focus more on external objects and appreciate fine clothes, jewellery and the like. We are unwilling to eat *soso skinmofo* (frugally). Hindustanis and Javanese are better at that. They understand that most of the food is in the cooking pot. A Hindustani would never dream of pulling a fish out of a filthy gutter, frying it and eating it. But we are too arrogant to restrain ourselves.

Some Surinamese take a different view. They believe that Creoles are able to save but squander their savings:

> Creoles save but seem to do so mainly for consumptive purposes, such as celebrations, birthdays, *aanneme oso* [confirmation], nice things, furnishing their home and so on. But there are different degrees. Some people have very little, but know how to organize their lives... ummm, also at birthdays, but beyond that, so that they gradually buy an estate. I know market women who have purchased a small lot and have built a little house there. But I also know very wasteful families, especially with *sopi* [alcoholic beverages].

Most Creoles have an explanation for this Creole mindset. In their view, this is their fate, as it is God's will: 'blacks don't save, everything disappears through their stomachs. That is how God made the black people. This is not a strength of Creoles: they should save.' Others offer a semi-genetic cause: 'what a fantastic question. Perhaps carousing, *baribari* [being rowdy], eating big meals is part of the Creole nature. Whenever a music band plays here, Creoles buy the most tickets. If a thousand people show up, eight hundred are Creoles. It's the way they are, and nobody wants to change. It's in their blood, and they would need to change their state of mind.'

The third group regards these habits as a legacy from slavery: 'I heard that once and agree that it dates back three hundred years to the days of slavery. Slaves never owned anything themselves. And when they started earning their own money after slavery was abolished, they felt like *spennen* [squandering].'

Others say that Creoles do not save because wealth and material accumulation are meaningless to them. This is often regarded as a virtue:

> Look, in my view, money is not what matters most to Creoles. I think that Creoles feel that if someone robs them, they will let God handle that person: he'll get what he deserves. Friendship means far more to me. I would not stab my brother over a quarrel about money, whereas a Hindustani would. Last month I read in the paper: 'both were buried.' A Hindustani woman lay on her deathbed, and her sons were already fighting over her estate. One stabbed the other. How could anybody enjoy money that way?

Many Creoles disapprove of being too frugal and thrifty. Thrift should not prevent enjoyment of life or destroy health and affective relationships, as the many *switi tori* about other ethnic groups reveal. There is a classic story about a poor Hindustani wearing a *baba* (loincloth) shuffling through the streets of Paramaribo on his way to the bank. All of a sudden he collapses because he has not eaten in days, while carrying thousands of guilders on his person. I recorded the following account from a kasmoni member: 'I knew a Javanese woman who wanted to buy a house. She ate nothing but boiled rice with a bit of sambal for years. She bought that house but has been seriously ill ever since. So how will she enjoy her house? After saving for years, she may die tomorrow, while her children fight over her estate. Health comes first with us.'

Creoles who join kasmoni aim to distinguish themselves from the stereotype of the carefree Creole, which they project largely on Creoles from the lower classes. Those who defer their immediate needs through kasmoni spend the proceeds on *long-term objectives*, such as a refrigerator, a wardrobe, a television, a rice cooker, tuition fees and school supplies for their children, *bigi yari* (jubilee birthdays), Christian holidays or ritual celebrations, gold jewellery, tickets to travel abroad on holiday or for other reasons, repairs and/or down payments on cars, homes and pieces of land. Occasionally, somebody may even deposit money to a bank account to collect interest. Sometimes people invest kasmoni money in a business. Most of these investments are small, such as a market stand or a cottage industry.

This refutes the findings of the authors who describe kasmoni as a continuation of the Creole consumerist drive with other means. They assume that Creoles are irrational and join kasmoni mainly to celebrate and repay their debts afterwards (e.g. Buschkens 1974; Kruijer 1957). My research on how kasmoni participants spend their payout indicates the opposite. Although such consumptive spending occurs, most people are reluctant to use the kasmoni to pay for parties, particularly after the months of self-discipline that precede the payout. On the other hand, the long-term objectives are not inherently capitalist. Investments in businesses are rare and do not serve to accumulate profits. Nor do many depositors place the sum they receive in a bank account to collect interest. In most cases they spend the money on durable goods that improve their quality of life and elevate their status.

The expenditures stated reflect Creole values: a good education, their own home with a yard, economic independence and an apple for a rainy day. These achievements cultivate respect among others. The stories that participants relate about their childhood and education reveal that their parents – and especially their mothers – stressed these values. Productive accumulation of wealth, on the other hand, is not a key value, which is why kasmoni payouts are rarely used for ongoing business investments. The prevailing opinion is that accumulating riches does not bring happiness. You can't take money to your grave. Life here on earth is more important!

Kasmoni participants with the constraint motive aim to realize these long-term desires despite their inclination to indulge immediate needs. They use the combination of the kasmoni's optional and constraining traits to this end.

Imperfect rationality

The philosopher Jon Elster describes what I call constraint and self-control as imperfect rationality. He believes that philosophers and social scientists have consistently ignored this phenomenon. In general, people merely refer to the myth of Ulysses, who knew he would be unable to resist the call of the Sirens and had himself bound to the mast of his ship. Elster bases his theory of imperfect rationality on this myth and argues that people are impassioned with the following three characteristics: (1) they may be rational, in the sense that they sacrifice spontaneous gratification of needs for future gratification of needs after careful consideration; (2) in practice they often fail to act rationally and exhibit a lack of will power; (3) even when they do not act rationally, they are aware that they are being irrational and may 'have themselves bound' to protect themselves from their irrationality.[11] Elster calls this 'binding oneself' *precommitment.* He argues that binding oneself is a privileged way of resolving weakness of will, and the main technique for achieving rationality by indirect means.[12]

Elster identifies three *precommitment* strategies.[13] In this article I will discuss only the strategy that matters for kasmoni: optimal gratification is manipulated by changing the payoff structure through *public side bets.* Making a promise in public brings about this irrevocable change. Elster explains that people who want to quit smoking use this strategy. A dissatisfied smoker will pursue this strategy as follows. He will openly tell friends that he is quitting smoking. With this promise, he instantly changes the range of feasible options, as he can no longer smoke without provoking sarcasm among friends.

Elster's theory of imperfect rationality is perfect for analysing the constraint motive of participants, as well as that of other ROSCA participants who use a comparable strategy to restrain their consumption behavior. By joining a ROSCA, participants change the range of available means, as they cannot stop contributing without incurring the negative sanction of social disapproval and exclusion.

There is also a difference. Although this strategy works the same way with both decisions, the effects differ. In both cases a promise is made in public. The person making the promise deliberately submits to the control of the others to guarantee that he keeps his promise. When somebody decides to quit smoking, the external structure (i.e. the public) usually consists of a group of friends, acquaintances or family members that have not decided to quit smoking. The promise may be broken, and the only sanctions are derision and ridicule. When a ROSCA participant decides to stop wasting money, however, the public consists of fellow participants who have taken the same decision. Withdrawing from the ROSCA will lead to shame. Mutual dependence is thus far greater here and makes quitting the ROSCA in the middle of a cycle more difficult. Failure to fulfil commitments is punished through social disapproval and future exclusion from participation. Sanctions will be forthcoming from fellow participants and non-participants alike. Unlike with smokers, social control among ROSCA participants is 'organized', in the requirement to make payments at regular points in time. ROSCAs therefore offer impulsive consumers a stronger external structure than the social surroundings of nicotine addicts do.

Analysis of self-control and social constraint

The relationship between self-control or self-constraint, and social constraint in kasmoni and other ROSCAs merits deeper analysis. It shifts during the process of binding oneself in inverse proportion to the changing balance of power between short and long-term preferences. There are two characteristic moments. At a cool moment people give their long-term preferences precedence over their immediate desires. They understand that these short-term preferences might prevail again later. Before this point arises, they believe they should voluntarily commit to a social arrangement firm enough to restrain future impulses. This moment is one of self-control, since they bind themselves voluntarily.

The second moment is when the short-term preferences gain the upper hand at the point that the kasmoni deposit is due. At that point the social constraint of the group is activated. Group members need not exert actual constraint. Participants feel sufficiently obliged by the legitimate expectations that others have of them. Active constraint and possible sanctions become necessary only once the urge of participants to default on their obligation exceeds their sense of obligation to fellow participants. The ultimate outcome of this process is that the long-term preference does indeed gain the upper hand.

This scenario reveals that the initial relationship between constraint and self-control is the opposite of the composite concept 'constraint toward self-constraint' that De Swaan derives from Elias. No social constraint toward self-constraint occurs here. Instead, self-control leads to social constraint. Only at the second significant moment, when the impulsive desire threatens to supplant the long-term preference, is there social constraint toward self-control: the self-selected value will prevail only with external pressure. In the future I will therefore employ the neutral pair of concepts 'self-control – constraint'.

De Swaan relates his concept of constraint toward self-constraint to Elias' civilization theory. This constraint figured among associations of European workers at a specific stage in the civilization process. As Breman does with respect to deferred gratification of need and Elster with respect to binding oneself, De Swaan disassociates this concept from the Western civilization process (Breman 1966:11-12). Constraint toward self-control materializes everywhere, as he illustrates by referring to Alcoholics Anonymous, Weight Watchers and nicotine addicts trying to kick their addiction through compulsory social control by fellow addicts (see De Swaan 1996:21n52).

I follow this line in my analysis of constraint – self-control with ROSCAs, with the stipulation that the manifestation differs from De Swaan's examples of self-constraint among addicts.[14] Addicts and ROSCA depositors both acknowledge their undesirable urge toward impulsive behavior. Unlike ROSCA participants, however, addicts are a minority with specific compulsive behavior, which frequently affects only a limited section of their personality but is considered to be extremely harmful. Nicotine addiction, for example, derives from an irresistible need for a nicotine-like substance (see also Elster 1984: 37-38). Among ROSCA participants, however, the state of mind is believed to be far broader and non-pathological. They acknowledge a general inclination toward financially impulsive behavior, which they attempt to control through social organization.

The second major difference between addicts and ROSCA participants is that ROSCA participants, like members of European labor associations, come from specific social classes. This raises the question as to why these social groups practise the technique of social constraint toward self-control. Studies have revealed a link between social class and saving.[15] Elaborating on these ideas, De Swaan observes an intermediate form of saving among the working class in his study of European mutuals. As they have not yet internalized the self-discipline to save, workers have devised a form that mediates external and internal constraint. Geertz provides an evolutionistic analysis of the non-Western ROSCAs. He concludes: 'The rotating credit association is thus a socializing mechanism, in that broad sense in which "socialization" refers not simply to the process by which the child learns to be an adult, but the learning of *any* new patterns of behavior which are of functional importance in society' (Geertz 1962:260). In this light, ROSCAs are an educational instrument for learning to save independently. Geertz's development view is not widely appreciated. Critics argue that it is based on the ethnocentric assumption that primitivity and modernity relate to one another as irrational to rational (see Hospes, Burman & Lembete, Nelson, Sethi in: Ardener & Burman 1995).

In this article I examine constraint – self-control among kasmoni as a phenomenon in its own right that need not correspond with constraint – self-control in the sense of the Western civilization process or with the form identifiable with Alcoholics Anonymous and Weight Watchers.

Kasmoni in education

Deferring immediate gratification by setting money aside matters deeply to Creole kasmoni depositors, especially to the participants reporting the constraint motive. People with (too) many financial commitments, or who do not trust their own state of mind join kasmoni and voluntarily commit to the corresponding social obligations. As apparent from my previous discussion of the constraint motive, these participants understand the interaction between their own minds and the kasmoni constraint mechanism.

The initiative may also arise from external factors. A cash minder may start a kasmoni to provide others with financial structure. In such cases the system is often deliberately used as an educational instrument to encourage savings discipline. Many participants became acquainted with kasmoni as children thanks to a paternalist initiative, where one of their elders taught them not to spend all their money at once on the temptations of the moment. Many recall their neighbor's kiddie kasmoni, which they joined with the kids in the neighborhood. They enjoyed it and worked hard to pay their share every week. They did odd jobs for the neighbors, like raking the grounds, sweeping the house and fetching groceries to make their payments as required. Cash minder Juliette, now age 76 and previously a laundress and charwomen, started one of those educational kiddie kasmoni when her own children were young:

> I lived on an estate with other families and had nine children of my own. I watched the neighborhood children eating sweets all day and thought: I think I'll teach those kids to save. I had all the neighborhood kids – there were 21 – deposit 5 cents a week, and their mothers made sure they paid in those 5 cents.

Still others remember how while living at home as young adults, their mother would encourage them to give her some of their wages. The mothers placed this money for them in the kasmoni they had joined themselves, in some cases without informing their children. Although these young adults were not active participants, they nonetheless came to understand the value of the system. Mr. Kobi, age 69 and a tailor and former police inspector, was one of them:

> When I received my first pay packet, my mother told me: 'look, give me part to set aside for you, or you'll have a hard time keeping track of your money.' She put it in

> a kasmoni for me, but I found out only when she returned my money. I continued doing it as an adult. I felt it made for a sense of commitment and taught me to save, since I knew I had to make the payments. So I learned about this obligation from my mother.

Even today, young people deposit their money to a kasmoni at the urging of grandmothers, aunts or mothers, as apparent from the complaint by Meli, age 27 and involved in a cottage industry, that she never has any money left:

> My grandmother [who sells paraphernalia for magic rituals on the market] suggested it, since I had no idea what I did with the money from the biscuits I baked. My grandmother sold the biscuits for me, but three days later, I might take 4,000 Surinamese guilders. I would arrive home, buy things to cook, but *mi no ben luku mi skin* [paid no attention to my 'self'].[16] Then my grandmother told me: look, I'll enter you in a kasmoni, and you'll see what you do with your money.' Only now do I keep track of what happens with my money, such as how much profit I make on a bucket of biscuits, how much I spend on butter, maize and sugar... I could have brought my money to the bank, but there's no obligation there the way there is with kasmoni. At the bank I would take my money right out, which is why I do not like banks.

Adults and the elderly appreciate this discipline as well. Mr. Koso used to be a dockyard worker. After he retired, he started selling lottery tickets on the street. When leprosy prevented him from using his fingers and legs anymore, he started selling his weekly supply of lottery tickets to a small, well-known group of lottery ticket vendors. These fifteen male and female peddlers ages 40 to 70 are also members of the kasmoni he runs on the side. This connection between lottery interests and kasmoni interests enables Mr. Koso to exercise social control. He also learned about kasmoni through his mother. As a cash minder, he tries to convince the participant lottery ticket sellers of the virtues of saving:

> We lottery ticket sellers used to have a drink and chat together, since I like a pint, you know. And then I proposed the idea, I'll explain it to you. Every hour of the day, there would be somebody in need, and they would have to borrow money, and it didn't seem right. They borrowed from me, and I believe that if you sell [the participants] lottery tickets, you should not dip into the base capital. You can spend the fruits, but if you use the base, how do you carry on the business? When I noticed that, I started this kasmoni. It helped a lot, but well... everybody has problems.

Participants reporting the constraint motive thus exhibit the third characteristic that Elster associates with 'imperfect rationality'. They are aware of their own lack of will power and of how the kasmoni system compensates for this shortcoming. This external pressure is necessary for kasmoni to operate, even for participants with other motives.

The special advantages of the kasmoni described above have helped the system thrive in the Netherlands, where 280,000 inhabitants, about half the Surinamese population at the time, settled in the second half of the twentieth century.

Migration to the Netherlands

The popularity of kasmoni in Suriname derives from two advantages not offered by any other formal or informal savings and loan system: the advantages of saving through social constraint toward self-control and of fast, cheap credit. The system gives participants quick, foreseeable access to money, so that they can carry out their financial plans.

This also holds true for the Creoles from Suriname who live in the Netherlands: they are deeply involved in kasmoni transactions too. This is remarkable, since Dutch society is far more businesslike than Surinamese society, and domestic informal financial arrangements long ago made way for formal institutions. In the nineteenth century, for example, workers' mutuals were replaced by formal insurance funds (De Swaan 1989:150-161).

From the 1960s onward, Surinamese people moved in droves to the country that colonized them for three centuries. In the Netherlands they hoped to build a future for themselves through work and education. The kasmoni helped them manage in their new homeland. The payouts enabled newcomers to furnish their homes, pay for their education and fulfil their financial commitments toward relatives left behind.

The transfer to these Western surroundings did not change the nature of the kasmoni, although the system adapted to the new circumstances. Modern Dutch society, with its massive scale, anonymity and individualism made the kasmoni more vulnerable to fraud and greatly increased the rate of abuse. The tendency toward fraud grew because participants in the Netherlands had to cover the high overhead of public institutions. Since these institutions have very rigid collection procedures, kasmoni participants who are deeply in debt may have reason to default on the informal payment obligation to the kasmoni. To avert fraud, cash minders and participants impose strict rules and semi-bureaucratic procedures, such as written contracts and penalties.

Thanks in part to their more businesslike procedures, kasmoni thrive in the Netherlands as well. At present the system is used by Creoles from both lower and higher income groups, including well-integrated, second-generation Surinamese. Working-class participants mention constraint as their motive for participating. They are also more inclined to use kasmoni as an emergency fund for paying unforeseen debts. Middle-class participants refer primarily to the economic motive and thus make perfect rational use of the kasmoni arrangement.

Conclusion

Kasmoni are believed to have existed among Surinamese Creoles as far back as the period of slavery: the system helped them survive in an era when they had no access to formal bank and credit institutions. In Suriname today, kasmoni still offer major benefits, especially through their credit function and disciplinary effect. Even in the far more businesslike Dutch society, this traditional arrangement has served Surinamese immigrants well and continues to appeal to Dutch second-generation Creoles with good incomes.

Geertz has predicted that arrangements such as the ROSCAs may become self-liquidating as more modern forms of social organization emerge (Geertz 1962:263). De Swaan has observed that kasmoni will not necessarily suffer this fate. After all, unlike workers' mutuals in 19th century Europe, kasmoni are small and flexible and therefore adapt easily to new circumstances (De Swaan 1996:13).[17] Even if Geertz is right, socio-economic conditions in Suriname are unlikely to change so dramatically in the foreseeable future that kasmoni will lose their *raison d'être.* My study cannot provide grounds for conclusions about Geertz's self-liquidation hypothesis with respect to the Netherlands, because Surinamese people have not resided here long enough yet. At this time, kasmoni appear to have entered a thriving second round in their new homeland. The credit they provide is less costly than credit obtained through the formal banking system, and future generations will be able to continue to use them rationally. But this will require ongoing cohesion among the Surinamese-Creole community in the Netherlands to sustain the informal bonds of trust that are necessary for kasmoni.

Notes

1 About 100,000 Creoles live in Suriname and about the same number in the Netherlands. At the time of my fieldwork, I estimate that about one out of three participates in the kasmoni. At Creole gatherings I recorded the share of those present who contributed to kasmoni by asking at random. I also inquired how many of their family members and acquaintances participated in kasmoni.

2 See also Bijnaar 1998.

3 Ardener regards 'Captive membership', as she describes it, as a subsidiary purpose of the ROSCA: development organizations not primarily dedicated to encouraging people to save organize a rotating savings fund and plan their activities to coincide with meetings of this fund to maximize turnout of the target group and ensure optimal results. This happens in Indonesia, where sexual education campaigns coincide with ROSCA events. 'Captive membership' also occurs among prostitutes in Amsterdam from the Dominican Republic. Their pimps force them to contribute part of their income to ROSCAs set up by the pimps themselves to reduce their flight risk (personal communication from Sietske Altink, 1997). Some authors argue that the benefits of this constraint lie in the legitimate excuse that ROSCA membership gives participants to reject pressing financial obligations to friends and family (Hospes 1996; De Swaan 1996) by explaining that they have to honor a 'higher' payment commitment first. This aspect is far more important in the studies by Kane (2000) and Bähre (2002).

4 The cultural embedment of ROSCAs does not necessarily mean a state of harmony. Cultural values and institutions may result from the unilateral influence of a group with power. Within a traditional culture, tensions arising from jealousy and envy are commonplace as well.

5 These 'motives' in no way refer to individual psychological driving forces. Instead, like C. Wright Mills (1974:439-452), I am invoking Weber's sociological perception of motives: a motive is a context of meaning that seems to be an adequate ground for behavior in the view of the actor or observer. With kasmoni, these motives are associated with the system's specific functions in Creole society. Unlike Mills, however, I do not always take the motives mentioned by the actors for granted. In some cases they mention a motive that while socially desirable, proves inapplicable in their particular case. As stated by E. Goffman (1959): the interviewee engages in *impression management*, his *performance* is idealized, which means that he presents himself as being better than he is, for example by suggesting that his behavior is based on rational consideration. I then reconstruct an underlying motive that is adequate for the context concerned. In this respect I agree with Mills in that other depositors mention this implicit motive.

6 In this context the meaning of 'traditional' is restricted to cultural embedment of financial motives and is not intended in the broad sense that the scope of kasmoni is primarily cultural and non-financial. The 'traditional motive' differs from the 'solidarity motive' in this respect, where kasmoni are based mainly on general, non-financial cultural values. In my reconstruction of this last motive, I thus use Ardener metaphorically, since this author focuses largely on a goal-rational aspect. Within the traditions of mutual solidarity, ROSCAs are believed to offer objective financial advantages over formal institutions, especially by virtue of their insurance function.

7 In some analyses of open survey questions to which respondents may provide multiple answers, the first answer given is assumed to be the most important. Aarts et al. (1992), for example, in analysing what respondents consider to be the most serious problems in the Netherlands, explore only the first problem mentioned. Critics find this approach superficial, as it fails to consider the dynamics of the response process (and of the other interaction between interviewer and respondent), which means that the most important one is by no means the first one mentioned. Consider, for example, cost-benefit considerations by respondents, memory effects, differences in facility of verbal formulation, social desirability etc. Moreover, the first answer often lacks informative value and thus necessitates probing. In such cases the first answer is not always the most important one. (Courtesy of Professor C. van der Eijk.)

8 Head of a kindergarten, age 51: 'if your turn comes early, it's like an interest-free loan. There is a risk, but I am willing to accept it. It's kind of a tradition, isn't it? I don't even think about the risk. Often, if I want to do something, I am unable to muster the self-control to save. So I join, even though many people disapprove, including my husband. I want to get things for myself and for my children. He has never participated, even though he sees everything I do with kasmoni. He thinks people should have the self-discipline to save their money in a bank account. I do not save at the bank, since I have always lacked the self-discipline. Once I had a savings account, but I kept withdrawing money from it. But the kasmoni obliges me to save. So the constraint helps. And my salary is so low.'

9 Although people's justifications for their behavior may not be entirely convincing, kasmoni participants reveal remarkable insight into the various functions of the system and their own role in the process. This is particularly striking with respect to the large number of participants mentioning the constraint motive: they elaborate extensively on their imperfect rationality. Their motive does not appear dubious at all, although tradi-

tion is undoubtedly a secondary factor in their decision to participate. With the other main group, namely the participants reporting the economic motive, some doubt seems indicated: they may want to appear more rational than they are. Nonetheless, the reason they mention is perfectly adequate. At any rate, analysing the motives of the participants sheds light on the way kasmoni function.

10 Accounts of the discussion appear in Breman 1966, Schneider and Lysgaard 1953, Straus 1962.

11 In this context 'perfectly rational' does not refer to a perfect human being but to a perfect homo economicus. In human respects, perfect rationality thus means that an abstract image of mankind need not have additional normative implications. Perfect economic rationality may lead to a life of poverty from a general human perspective. In addition, the psychology of the constraint motive may make behavior that is 'imperfectly rational' in economic respects appear realistic.

12 Elster discusses five criteria for estabishing *precommitment.* Distinguishing *precommitment* from other forms of deliberate self-control requires considering the difference between the motive for binding oneself and the anticipated result of binding oneself. Without this distinction, the *precommitment* concept might be applied incorrectly to a person who invests in a business or lets wine age. Incorrectly because such persons do not intend to make an action irrevocable (motive) but do aim to enlarge future options (expected result). The desire for *precommitment* needs to be motivated by the expectation of changed behavior rather than by an unintended, predictable or not unwelcome effect: (1) the first action needs to be performed to guarantee that the second action is carried out; (2) options need to be waived for the sake of other options, and the options waived should not figure among the other options; (3) the desire to bind oneself figures within an external structure; (4) resistance against binding oneself should be less than resistance to performing the subsequent action of deferred gratification; (5) the act of binding oneself must be an act of commission and not of omission (Elster 1984:39-46). With respect to saving, these criteria indicate the following: (1) money needs to be set aside to purchase a refrigerator; (2) purchasing sweets and chips should be foregone to purchase the refrigerator, without sacrificing sweets and chips for sweets and chips; (3) the desire to set aside money needs to be realized through participation in an institutional or informal or formal savings system; (4) the urge to spend the money straight away should be weaker than the desire to save at the time of the decision to save: even though at the moment the participant actually deposits the money, the urge to spend is stronger, it is controlled in part through social pressure; (5) finally, the intention to set money aside is to be regarded as a task rather than simply as spending less money (Elster 1984:36-37).

13 (1) Manipulation of optimal gratification: (a) restricting the set of physically possible actions; (b) changing the reward structure through *public side bets.* The 'public side bets' strategy refers to an irrevocable change in the reward structure by precommitment (Elster 1984:55); (2) manipulation of the character: (a) strengthening will power; (b) changing the preference structure; (3) manipulation of information: (a) changing the belief system; (b) avoiding exposure to certain signals; (4) the fourth strategy, manipulation through rearrangement of inner space, does not constitute *precommitment,* according to Elster, because it is an intrapersonal matter. After all, *precommitment* requires a causal mechanism to drive the strategy that the individual has selected to resolve the lack of will power: by notifying your friends that you intend to quit smoking or by avoiding all tobacco shops or by going for a walk in the mountains so as to make cigarettes physically unavailable (p. 37). No such causal mechanisms apply in this fourth strategy. The corresponding mechanisms are: (a) the use of *private side bets,* thus grouping future rewards so that they stand or fall together (p. 43); somebody who fails to quit smoking will also fail in the simultaneous decision

to lose weight by dieting; (b) consistent planning. Of these strategies, 1b, changing the reward structure through *public side bets*, and 2b, changing the preference structure, are used most often in daily life, for example by people trying to quit smoking (combinations of the two occur and, according to Elster, are in fact the most efficient). The other strategies are costly, impractical, extreme or of doubtful efficacy (104-105).

14 Which are not entirely convincing as a relativization of the Western civilization model, since they remain within Western culture.

15 Empirical research by Schneider and Lysgaard (1953) indicates that at that time deferred gratification of need was linked with social class. The study among American students revealed 'impulse-following behavior' among the ones from lower social classes, meaning that they were more prone to physical violence, fairly promiscuous, not very ambitious, less concerned with good manners and inclined to spend money. 'Impulse-renunciation', on the other hand, is the behavior pattern characteristic of the middle class and as such is the counterpart to 'impulse-following'. People with this type of behavior do not get involved in fights, are sexually restrained, study longer, are more ambitious, save and keep track of their spending. They have internalized the values that correspond with this behavior and feel morally obliged to save, to plan their future and to suppress various desires and urges that conflict with these pursuits (Barber 1957:315-317).

16 'Self' means 'soul' here. In Winti, the Afro-Surinamese religion, body and soul interact continuously. Regarding Meli: if the body has been shortchanged, the same holds true for the soul.

17 The flexibility is enhanced by the main focus on the savings and loan function; the insurance function, which requires far more organization, is secondary, since in emergencies people call upon their families for help.

References

Aarts, C.W.A.M., A.G. Van der Kaap, A.M.B.Michels & J.J.A. Thomas.

1992 'Politieke problemen en strijdpunten.' In: J.J.M. Van Holsteyn & G.A.Irwin (eds), *De nederlandse kiezer 1989*, 65-122. Amsterdam: Steinmetzarchief.

Ardener, S.

1964 'A Comparative Study of Rotating Saving and Credit Associations.' *Journal of the Royal Anthropological Institute*, 94 (2):201-229. Reprinted in: S. Ardener & S. Burman (eds), *Money-Go-Rounds; The Importance of Rotating Savings and Credit Associations for Women*, Oxford-Washington: DC: Berg.

1995 'Women Making Money Go Round; ROSCAs Revisited.' In: S. Ardener & S. Burman (eds.), *Money-Go-Rounds; The Importance of Rotating Savings and Credit Associations for Women*, 1-20. Oxford-Washington DC: Berg.

Ardener, S. & S. Burmann (eds)

1995 *Money-Go-Rounds. The Importance of Rotating Savings and Credit Associations for Women.* Oxford-Washington DC: Berg.

Bähre, E.

2003 *African Migrants and Money; Informal Economic Cooperation and Ambivalence in Postapartheid South Africa.* Dissertation University of Amsterdam.

Barber, B.

1957 *Social Stratification. A Comparative Analysis of Structure and Process.* New York-Chicago-Burlingame: Harcourt, Brace & World, Inc.

Besson, J.

1995 'Women's Use of Roscas in the Caribbean: Reassessing the Literature.' In: S. Ardener & S. Burman (eds), *Money-Go-Rounds. The Importance of Rotating Savings and Credit Associations for Women*, 263-288. Oxford-Washington DC: Berg.

Bijnaar, A.

1996 'Creolen spelen kasmoni.' *Discorsi. Faculteitsblad van de Faculteit der Politieke en Sociaal-Culturele Wetenschappen* (Universiteit van Amsterdam), 26 (8):12-14.

1998a 'Wat je zaait zal je oogsten! Dwang en zelfdwang in Creools-Surinaamse onderlinges.' *Amsterdams Sociologisch Tijdschrift*, 25(3):329-370.

1998b 'Verkassing. Creoolse kasmoni in Nederland.' In: *Reizigers. Jaarboek Universiteit van Amsterdam*, 36-37, Amsterdam: Vossiuspers AUP.

1998c *Adaptations to the Practice of Kasmoni in the Post-war Period.* Paper presented at the European Social Science History Conference, Amsterdam.

2001 'Kasmoni: een spaar- en kredietsysteem in crisistijd.' *Oso. Tijdschrift voor Surinaamse Taalkunde, Letterkunde, Cultuur en Geschiedenis* 20(2):208-23.

Bouman, F.J.A.

1985 'Indigenous Savings and Credit Associations in the Third World. A Message?' *Savings and development*,1, 181-220.

1994 'ROSCAs and ASCRAs: Beyond the Financial Landscape.' In: F.J.A. Bouman & O. Hospes (eds), *Financial Landscapes Reconstructed. The Fine Art of Mapping Development*, 375-394. Boulder: Westview Press.

'ROSCA: On the Origin of the Species.' *Savings and development*, 19 (2): 116-147.

Breman, J.C.

1966 'Theoretische beschouwingen. Uitgestelde behoeftebevrediging, ondernemersgedrag en economische groei. *Mens en Maatschappij*, 41:1-20.

Burman, S. & N. Lembete

1995 'Building New Realities: African Women and ROSCAs in Urban South Africa.' In: S. Ardener, & S. Burman (eds), *Money-Go-Rounds. The Importance of rotating savings and credit associations for women*, 49-70. Oxford-Washington: Berg.

Buschkens, W. F. L.

1973 *Het familiesysteem der volkscreolen van Paramaribo.* Rijksuniversiteit Leiden.

Callier, Ph.

1990 'Informal Finance: The Rotating Saving and Credit Association – An Interpretation.' In: *Kyklos*, 43(2):273-276.

De Swaan, A.

1989 *Zorg en de staat: Welzijn, onderwijs en gezondheidszorg in Europa en de Verenigde Staten in de nieuwe tijd.* Amsterdam: Bert Bakker.

1993 'Onderlinge fondsen: toen en hier, nu en daar. Onderlinge spaar- en verzekeringsfondsen in de negentiende eeuw in Europa en Amerika, en heden ten dage in de ontwikkelingslanden en onder immigranten in de steden van het Westen.' Onderzoeksaanvraag behorend bij het projectontwerp *Transnational Society and the Social Question* binnen het programma *Prioriteiten.* Universiteit van Amsterdam.

1996a 'Onderlinge fondsen: toen en hier, nu en daar. Informele spaar- en verzekeringskassen in het negentiende-eeuwse Westen en in de tegenwoordige buiten-westerse wereld.' In: M. Van der Linden & J.Sluijs, (eds), *Onderlinge hulpfondsen. Historische en etnografische essays*, 9-22. Amsterdam: Stichting Beheer IISG.

1996b 'Rationele keuze als proces. Nut en onnut van formele theorie in de historische sociologie.' *Amsterdams Sociologisch Tijdschrift*, 593-609.

Elster, J.
1984 *Ulysses and the Sirenes. Studies in Rationality and Irrationality.* Editions de la Maison des Sciences de l' Homme, Paris-London-New York-Melbourne: Cambridge University Press.

Falola, T.
1995 'Money and Informal Credit Institutions in Colonial Western Nigeria.' In: Jane I. Guyer (eds), *Money Matters. Instability, Values and Social Payments in the Modern History of West African Communities,* 162-87. Portsmouth NH: Heinemann/Londen: James Currey.

Feddema, H.
1982 *Een incident achter de Bijlmer. De geschiedenis van een moderne wijk in aanbouw.* Amsterdam: SUA.

Firth, R. & B.S. Yamey
1964 *Capital, Saving and Credit in Peasant Societies: Studies from Asia, Oceania, the Caribbean en Middle America.* Londen: George Allen & Unwin.

Geertz, C.
1962 'The Rotating Credit Association: A "Middle Rung" in Development.' *Economic development and cultural change,* 10(3):241-263.
1973 *Interpretation of Cultures.* New York: Basic Books.

Goffman, E.
1971 *The Presentation of Self in Everyday Life.* Harmondsworth: Penguin.

Goudsblom, J.
1997 *Het regime van de tijd.* Amsterdam: Meulenhoff.

Holton, R.H.
1960 'Changing Demand and Consumption.' In: W.E. Moore & A.S. Feldman (eds), *Labor Commitment and Social Change in Developing Areas,* 201-216. New York: Social Science Research Council.

Hospes, O.
1996 'Van cliché naar clou: het aanpassingsvermogen van financiële hulpgroepen.' In: M. Van der Linden & J. Sluijs. (eds), *Onderlinge hulpfondsen. Historische en etnografische essays,* 71-80. Amsterdam: Stichting Beheer IISG.

Janssen, A.M.
1986 *Suriname. Ontwikkelingsland in het Caraïbisch Gebied.* Amsterdam: SUA.

Kane, A.
1999 *Les caméléons de la finance populaire au Sénégal et dans la diaspora.* Universiteit van Amsterdam.

Kruijer, G.J.
1957 'Landbouw-coöperatie onder de Aziatische bevolkingsgroepen van Suriname en Brits Guyana.' In: *De West-Indische Gids,* 31/32:209-235.

Nelson, N.
1995 'The Kiambu Group: A Succesful Women's ROSCA in Mathare Vale, Nairobi (1971 to 1990).' In: S. Ardener & S. Burman (eds). *Money-Go-Rounds. The Importance of Rotating Savings and Credit Associations for Women,* 49-70. Oxford-Washington: Berg.

Nurkse, R.
1953 *Problems of Capital Formation in Underdeveloped Countries.* Oxford: Blackwell.

Philpott, S.B.
1973 West Indian Migration: The Montserrat Case. Londen: Athlone Press.

Schneider, L. & S. Lysgaard
1953 'The Deferred Gratification Pattern. A Preliminary Study.' *American sociological review*, 18(1):142-149.

Sethi, R.S.
1995 'Women's ROSCAS in Contemporary Indian Society'. In: S. Ardener & S. Burman, (eds), *Money-Go-Rounds. The Importance of Rotating Savings and Credit Associations for Women*, 163-177. Oxford-Washington: Berg.

Simon, H.
1979 'Rational Decision Making.' *The American Economic Review*, 69(4):502-503.

Straus, M.A.
1962 'Deferred Gratification, Social Class and the Achievement Syndrome.' *American Sociological Review*, 27(1):326-335.

Swift, M.G.
1964 'Capital, Saving and Credit in Peasant Societies.' In: R. Firth, & B.S. Yamey, (eds), *Studies from Asia, Oceania, the Caribbean and Middle America*, 150-151. Londen: George Allen & Unwin.

Van Renselaar, A C.
1963 'Het sociaal-economische vermogen van de creolen in Suriname.' *Tijdschrift van het Koninklijke Nederlandsch Aardrijkskundig Genootschap*, 80(2):474-481.

Veblen, Th.
1953 *The Theory of the Leisure Class: An Economic Study of Institutions.* New York: The New American library.

Weber, M.
1967 *Wirtschaft und gesellschaft.* Tübingen. J.B.C. Mohr (Paul Siebeck).
1978 *Economy and Society. An Outline of Interpretive Sociology* (ed. G. Roth & C. Wittich). Berkeley-Los Angeles-Londen: University of California Press.

Wekker, G.
1994 *Ik ben een gouden munt, ik ga door vele handen, maar verlies mijn waarde niet. Subjectiviteit en sexualiteit van Creoolse volksklasse vrouwen in Paramaribo.* Amsterdam: Feministische Uitgeverij Vita.

Wright Mills, C.
1971 *Power, Politics and People. The Collected Essays of C. Wright Mills* (ed. I.L. Horowitz). Londen-Oxford-New York: Oxford University Press.

CHAPTER 4

Tontines and village cash boxes along the Tilogne-Dakar-Paris emigration route

Abdoulaye Kane

Introduction

Tontines and village cash boxes often transcend national borders, oceans and continents nowadays. Their path follows the migratory trek from the South to the North. They are set up in the major cities of Europe and America among immigrant communities from Africa, Asia, the Caribbean and the Pacific. Accordingly, tontines and village cash boxes have come a long way from being local operations in working-class neighborhoods, on markets and at workplaces in Africa. The studies thus far have tended to confine the grass-roots financial arrangements to circumscribed areas. This is perfectly understandable, given the inclination of researchers interested in the subject to describe a very limited number of tontines in detail, rather than to conduct investigations covering a broad scope comprising several areas at the same time (Lelart 1990; Pairault 1990). They rarely examine possible direct or indirect nationwide connections between these grass-roots financial arrangements and even still more rarely sub-regional or trans-national ones.

Given the opportunity, however, as I was, to conduct transversal research along an emigration route of the Senegal River people, the transnational dimension of the grass-roots financial arrangements soon becomes apparent. Tontine participants in neighborhoods in Tilogne – and to a lesser extent in Dakar – pay their dues from money sent by family members who have moved abroad and in most cases join the tontines in their host cities. Accordingly, the tontines of Senegalese immigrants in France and everywhere else infuse cash into the tontines of their countries of origin.

Other attributes of the village cash boxes further substantiate their transnational dimension. In addition to the transfer of cash from cash boxes established in the host cities (Dakar, Libreville, Paris, New York etc.) to the parent cash box in the village of origin (Tilogne), ties between these cash boxes remain very close despite the geographic distance that separates them. Together, the participants in the cash boxes develop projects and allocate the tasks among one another.

Cash-box managers meet in the village every two years on the "cultural days" to discuss the focus of their joint local development effort. They also invite each other to extraordinary General Assemblies in the host cities to coordinate their actions to help the village. The individuals running the different sections of the Tilogne village cash box thus meet occasionally in Paris or New York, where they are invited by their fellow villagers to present a project proposal or discuss a problem considered crucial for the village.

In this article we will explore the transnational nature of grass-roots financial arrangements along the Tilogne-Dakar-France emigration route. First, we will define and classify the different financial arrangements in Senegal and among the Senegalese emigrant community in France. Next, we will examine how the tontines and village cash-boxes derive from millennial practices of solidarity, mutual aid and reciprocity. Finally, we will review the transnational expansion of these financial arrangements.

Classifying grass-roots financial arrangements

Definition

We define grass-roots financial arrangements as the mass of groups or associations charging members a periodic and regular fee and either redistributing the funds raised in this manner entirely or in part to these members by turns (the tontines) or accumulating them in a fund from which financial aid is occasionally paid out to members with problems requiring collective intervention (the cash boxes).

Categorization of the grass-roots financial arrangements studied

In our research we addressed two main categories: village cash boxes and tontines. We focused on these two financial arrangements, because they are the two types of collective savings systems in Senegal. In his classification of grass-roots financial arrangements in this country, Claude Dupuy distinguishes associative collective savings from societal collective savings (Dupuy 1990). The author bases his distinction on Tonniës's classical opposition between society and community. According to this perspective, associative collective savings are based on communal principles and values. Individuals participate out of a sense of social obligation and as member of a community (the village cash boxes). Societal collective savings, however, arise from financial arrangements in which individuals participate of their own free will. In this type of arrangement, members are bound by contract rather than by obligation. These are the basic principles of the tontines.

Differentiation of grass-roots financial arrangements in Senegal

In Senegal the most common designations for tontine grass-roots financial arrangements are Natt and Tegg among the Wolof and Tegge, Tours and Piye among the Haal Pulaar. These are called Rotating Savings and Credit Associations (ROSCAs). In ROSCAs, the total amount of periodic membership dues (e.g. CFA 2,500) collected is disbursed to each member in turn. The sequence in which the total contributions in one round, know as the levée [payout], are paid out to members is determined by a raffle or is based on the respective urgency of individual needs. At the end of the distribution cycle of the levées, each member of such an arrangement will have received as much as he or she has contributed. Dues are paid exclusively in cash. This guarantees the equilibrium between the amount paid and the amount received.

Sanni diamras are another type of rotating grass-roots financial arrangements, mainly in cities. These arrangements closely resemble ROSCAs in the perfect rotation of levées among the different members. Unlike in ROSCAs, however, neither the contributions nor the levées are equal in Sanni diamras. Contributions may be provided in cash or in kind (especially as food products) and consist largely of basic staples: rice, sugar, soap, milk, cooking utensils etc. Members rarely consider 'who gives what' and 'to whom'. In practice, however, some members often feel short-changed by others with respect to the quantity of products or the total amount of money received compared to what they have contributed.

Mbotaay and Piye wudere are financial arrangements organized around family ceremonies. Mbotaay and Piye wudere are ongoing groups, unlike Natt and Sanni diamra, which cover some of the charges incurred by one of the members in organizing a family ceremony. In this kind of arrangement, proceeds or services rotate according to fate. One member may even receive an additional round from the contributions to a Mbotaay or a Piye wudere, while other members may receive nothing for a very long time.

Finally, cash boxes are an essential aspect of grass-roots financial arrangements in Senegal. In many cases they are community groups designed to protect members suffering predetermined misfortunes. The boxes accumulate periodic contributions from members in a fund used to distribute financial aid to members in trouble. They are particularly common in cities among migrants from the same village or pertaining to the same caste, the same ethnic group, the same religious brotherhood, etc. Some are called solidarity funds among co-workers. In this case, a co-worker who is deeply ill or bereaved receives predetermined financial support from the solidarity fund in the event of various circumstances.

From this perspective, the funds are explicitly intended as insurance. They arise from the ongoing desire of migrants to establish communal security networks in their host cities. This practice is exceptional among grass-roots financial arrangements, as the various articles in this book reveal. De Swaan observes in the introduction that grass-roots financial arrangements do not serve as insurance, unlike the workers' mutuals in 19th-century Europe. This is true for the tontines, which in most cases lack an explicit insurance function. Some tontines, however, include solidarity funds that have an insurance function subject to various restrictions. They substantiate the argument presented in this book by Hotze Lont, who examines the role of ROSCAs in meeting the socio-economic needs for which the formal Indonesian security system is ill equipped.

TABLE I: **Grass-roots financial arrangements in Senegal**

Redistribution	*Local designations*	*Contributions*	*Places*
Perfect rotation	Natt, Tegg (Wolof)	Money	Dakar, France
	Piye, Tegge, Tours (Pulaar)	Money	Tilogne, Dakar,
	Sanni diamra (Wolof)	Money, rice, milk	France
		Soap, utensils, etc.	Dakar
Haphazard distribution (course of fate)	Mbotaay (Wolof)	Money, fabric, jewels,	Dakar
	Piye wudere (Pulaar)	Domestic appliances, cooking utensils, etc.	Tilogne, Dakar, France
Accumulation	Village cash boxes (Pulaar)	Money	Tilogne, Dakar,
	Brotherhood funds (Dahira)	Money	FranceDakar,
	Solidarity funds (workplaces)	Money	FranceDakar

This categorization corresponds with Van der Linden's observations in this book in several respects. Van der Linden describes categories that are planned or contingent and rotating or non-rotating and reflect the various foreseeable cases in classifying grass-roots financial arrangements. The categorization in the table above is essentially based on actual cases observed at our three research sites.

Tontines

The term tontine as a reference to European tontines from the past for African solidarity systems indicates a considerable lack of awareness about this complex social phenomenon. European tontines appear to have been more longstanding, as they were closely linked with the progressive extinction of a group in which members were the same general age and had similar life expectancies. Moreover, these arrangements were based on the winner-take-all principle, where the winner was the one who survived all his peers. Natt, piye, mbotaay, sani diamra, tour, tegg and tegge, on the other hand, which are indiscriminately referred to as tontines, existed for specific periods, ranging from months to at most one or two years.

Associations or groups where the members pay dues are too easily labelled as tontines. Even the village cash boxes, for example, which are not rotating, are regarded by some researchers as tontines (Dupuy 1990). This practice has complicated classifying grass-roots financial arrangements in French-speaking Africa. In this article, we define tontines exclusively as monetary ROSCAs. Tontines are a group of individuals who agree to contribute a certain amount at periodic intervals. The total amount contributed in each round, known as the levée, is distributed to each participant in turns. A tontine from Pikine Medina Gounass, a working-class neighborhood in the suburbs of Dakar, for example, comprised 18 participants, who each agreed to contribute 500 CFA francs every fortnight. On the 15th and the 30th of the month, all participants came to the person in charge of the tontine (known as the mère-natt) to pay their contributions. At each of these gatherings, 9,000 CFA francs were raised for one of the participants drawn at random. At the end of the nine months of the tontine cycle, each of the participants had received the full levée once. The tontine ended there, unless the participants agreed to start a new cycle.

People join tontines for various reasons. Some aim to cover a future need, such as the cost of a baptism, a wedding or some other family event. Others hope to finance a revenue-generating economic activity. Still others seek to acquire material goods deemed indispensable for their socio-economic standing. All these motives, however, may be summarized as the desire among individual tontine participants to have the other members to force them to save. Constraint and self-control seem to be the chief motive of individual tontine participants. Other researchers, such as Bijnaar, reach the same conclusion regarding the tontines in Suriname and among the Surinamese community in Amsterdam (Aspha Bijnaar: this volume).

In Senegal, there are two kinds of tontines: simple or mutual tontines and tontines with an organizer.

Simple tontines

The defining characteristics of simple tontines are the personal and mutual relations between all participants. Tontines involve regular meetings, which members are required to attend or pay a predetermined fine. At the periodic meetings, contributions are collected from individual members and presented to one of the members as the levée. The gatherings may convene at a set location, such as the home of the person overseeing the tontine (the mère-natt). Alternatively, the venue may rotate, with members taking turns hosting them.

Sokhna, age 47 and married with 7 children, runs a simple tontine. Sokhna lives in Pikine Medina-Gounasse. Upon arriving to do our research in the quarter, all the women we encountered and told about our research objective advised us to speak to Sokhna, as the mère-natt or person in charge of the tontine. Sokhna's tontine comprises 23 women from the neighborhood who know one another and meet at her home for their tontine twice a month.

The gatherings start at 5.00 p.m. Fatou, age 34, serves as the tontine secretary. She is very meticulous about starting on time and records the names of late arrivals. These women are required to pay the tontine a fine of 100 CFA francs. Before the payments start, Sokhna welcomes those present and provides an update about the status of the tontine. She reports the number of participants who have received the levée thus far, the number of participants still awaiting a payout and news about the ones who failed to attend previous meetings. She then gives the floor to Fatou, who starts by requesting those who were absent from previous meetings to pay their dues in arrears, as well as a fine of 250 CFA francs. Next, she requests the contributions due at the present meeting. She calls each participant, who submits her contribution of 2,500 CFA francs to Sokhna. Sokhna holds up the money for the other participants to witness and subsequently places it in a calabash she holds between her legs.

Once all the participants have paid their dues, Sokhna retrieves a bottle containing slips of paper with the names of the participants who have not yet received the levée. She removes the slips of paper from the bottle and asks her daughter to select one at random. Sokhna hands the slip of paper to Fatou, who unfolds it and reads out the name of the levée recipient indicated on that slip of paper. Sokhna counts the money and separates the contributions received that day from the dues paid in arrears and the fines. She presents the recipient of the levée with 57,500 CFA francs amid applause from the other participants. Sokhna advises the recipient of the levée: 'use it wisely, and bear in mind that the others are waiting for their turn!' During the meeting the participants discuss various subjects. The women help each other by sharing news, practical hints, advice and lessons learned from experience.

Simple tontines, as this example demonstrates, are lively social groups. These tontines exist mainly in neighborhoods of Tilogne and Dakar and among the immigrants in France. In the neighborhoods in Dakar and Tilogne, they reflect sociability and neighborly interaction. In France, on the other hand, they tend to comprise women pertaining to the same ethnic group or from the same village or region and meet a wide variety of needs. In Dakar and Tilogne, some tontines specialize in purchasing jewellery, cooking utensils, household appliances and the like. Other tontines in Dakar enable members to make pilgrimages to Mecca, while still others are used to fund family ceremonies. In all cases, the gatherings at these simple tontines, with their instructive discussions and educational potential, reveal clearly how important social aspects are in these tontines in addition to economic and financial concerns. From this perspective, the simple tontines differ considerably from tontines with an organizer, where economic motives seem to prevail over social pursuits.

Tontines with an organizer

In tontines with an organizer, participants do not interact directly. These tontines are initiated by a single individual, who invites people to join at his discretion. This person is the organizer and the intermediary between the members of the tontine. Unlike the simple tontines, the ones with an organizer do not involve regular meetings to gather and remit the levée. The organizer comes to collect the contributions and presents the levée to the beneficiary.

The tontine run by Cheikh at the market of Tilogne is one with an organizer. Cheikh, age 37 and the father of two children, runs a tontine with 40 participants at the market in Tilogne. He owns a traditional bakery there, and the members of his tontine are fish and vegetable vendors, shopkeepers, cereal and condiment sellers, owners of large businesses and wage earners (mostly teachers). He knows the participants in his tontine personally. Each one pays Cheikh 2,500 CFA francs when his turn comes to collect the levée. Cheikh determines the sequence in which the levées are distributed to individual participants. In the event of a default on payments, he adds the missing contributions in the levée from his pocket. The tontine exists by virtue of individual agreements that Cheikh reaches with each of the participants according to the conditions described above.

The contributions to the tontine equal 2,500 CFA francs daily for each participant. Except for the wage earners, who pay their contributions monthly, Cheikh visits each participant daily to collect the dues. He goes from one market stall to another and from one shop to another to claim the daily payments and keeps the daily payments from the members for five days before determining the recipient of the levée and then discreetly invites this person to come see him to present the levée of 500,000 CFA francs, less his commission of 2,500 CFA francs. The participants never gather, neither at the start nor at the end of the tontine, and may not even know one another. The only social interactions in the tontine are the ones that the organizer arranges with each participant.

This classification of tontines according to simple tontines and tontines with an organizer corresponds with other typologies in literature about informal finance in Africa. Lelart and Lespès have identified three types of tontines in Africa: mutual tontines like the ones referred to in this article as simple tontines, commercial tontines, which are equivalent to the ones with an organizer, and auction tontines, which are common in Cameroon as well as in Benin. These tontines do not exist in Senegal, however, where they are regarded by tontine participants as conflicting with the precepts of Islam (Lelart & Lespès 1985).

Michael Rowlands refers to mutual or simple tontines as solidarity tontines and to commercial tontines and auction tontines as business tontines in his contextual of tontines in Cameroon (Rowlands 1995: 118). Margaret Niger-Thomas describes personal tontines, which are described by Lelart and Lespès as mutual tontines, by Rowlands as solidarity tontines and here as simple tontines, from impersonal tontines, which are tontines with an organizer and are described by the other authors as commercial, auction or business tontines (Niger-Thomas 1995: 10).

Our research suggests that these classifications, which are based largely on whether social or economic and financial concerns predominate, should be amended to include one that reflects the settings in which the tontines materialize. The setting is a relevant classification criterion, as the roles of tontines vary, depending on whether the tontines are based in neighborhoods, markets or workplaces.

Classification according to the sites of operation

Neighborhood tontines

Dozens of tontines emerge and grow in the quarters of Tilogne and Dakar. Most are simple tontines, although some have an organizer. Simple tontines are integral forces in neighborhood social life. Their membership consists largely of women, who use them for sociability and reciprocal socialization. The encounters that the tontines bring about therefore matter at least as much as and possibly even more than the money drawn from them. Because social aspects take precedence over economic and financial ones here, neighborhood tontines often reflect their social surroundings. Accordingly, the neighborhood tontines in Tilogne follow the precepts of social hierarchy among the Haal Pulaar, whereas the ones in Dakar reflect the city's ethnic and religious diversity.

In Tilogne and Dakar alike, neighborhood tontines generally correspond with what we have described as simple tontines, and which others call mutual tontines (Lelart 1985). While tontines with an organizer exist in the neighborhoods of Dakar, they are relatively rare. The money from these neighborhood tontines is used largely to satisfy consumer needs. Both in Dakar and in Tilogne, some neighborhood tontines are dedicated to satisfying personal needs. Participants in these tontines agree on how each one will use the money received as the levée. In several of these tontines, participants aim to obtain material objects associated with social prestige: electronic household appliances, jewellery and precious metals, fashionable clothes and shoes, furniture and entertainment devices and the like. Other tontines are dedicated to religious observance and customs, such as making a pilgrimage to Mecca or celebrating religious holidays or family ceremonies.

Market tontines

Both women and men are eligible to participate in market tontines. Unlike the neighborhood tontines, most of the tontines at the markets of Tilogne and Dakar have organizers. Members of market tontines represent a broad range of social and professional affiliations and a wide variety of economic and financial situations. The more affluent participants double or triple the deposit, while those with low incomes pool their resources to amass a single deposit and share the levée.

Most market tontines conform to the pace of operations of the participants. Contributions are collected daily and levées usually issued once every five days. Most participants reinvest the money they draw from the tontines in their businesses. They do not meet periodically and are sometimes even unaware that they belong to one and the same tontine. As stated previously, the money from the market tontines is reinvested in the business, artisanal or service operations of the participants.

Workplace tontines

Workplace tontines differ from neighborhood and market tontines in several respects. Participants all work for the same service or firm. Generally speaking, workplace tontines are simple tontines, even though the members do not meet periodically. Workplace tontines involve only one meeting, which serves to determine the number of participants, the amount of the contribution and the sequence for distributing the levées.

Workplace tontines are also adapted to their surroundings. Contributions are paid once a month, after payday. Unlike the other tontines, workplace tontines are rather formal. In fact, both the contributions and the levées are paid through transfers to the accounts of those in charge or the beneficiaries. Most workplace tontines are in Dakar. In Tilogne, the few civil servants join market tontines with an organizer. All the same, in France, when substantial numbers of immigrants pertaining to the same ethnic group are employed at the same plant, workplace tontines are a common practice. We found one at the Boulogne Renault factory near Paris.

Immigrant tontines

In France Senegalese immigrants run both tontines and solidarity cash boxes. Most of the tontine participants are women. Unlike the tontines in Tilogne and Dakar, where participants are recruited within a circumscribed setting, such as the neighborhood, the market or the workplace, the members of Senegalese immigrant tontines are often individuals living throughout the city or in some cases even in different cities. Place of origin and ethnic background are the main criteria for participating in these tontines. Among the immigrants we observed both simple tontines and tontines with an organizer.

Like in Tilogne and Dakar, participants in the simple tontines meet periodically to amass and distribute the levées. Immigrant women experience them as mutual learning contexts, where the more senior immigrants instruct the newcomers about how to handle their apartments, shop at supermarkets, deal with social services in their host country and the like. The tontines comprise women living in a city and pertaining to the same ethnic group, as well as women originating from the same Senegalese village but living in different cities in France.

Likewise, tontines with organizers in France function as they would in Tilogne and Dakar. The participants, who may include both women and men, submit their periodic contributions to the organizer, who in turn presents the predetermined beneficiary with the levées. Unlike in Tilogne and Dakar, however, the organizers do not charge for their mediation but instead accept commissions offered voluntarily by the recipients of the levée.

The solidarity cash boxes operate according to the same principles as the tontines. Unlike with the tontines, however, member contributions are not redistributed by periodic turns. Instead, they accumulate in a cash box, from which predetermined financial aid is drawn in the event of various misfortunes to help the members affected.

While tontines exist both in the countryside and in cities in Senegal, the village cash boxes we examined in our research were based near the Senegal River and brought together people from the local villages to these urban centers. And while methods of organization and operation were highly diverse in the tontines at the different research sites, they were rather homogeneous in the village cash boxes.

Village cash boxes

Village cash boxes are closely associated with migration. They were started by emigrants from the Senegal River valley in their assorted host cities to help those among them in trouble. Their members tend to be men from the same village. Everybody coming from that village is required to join the village cash box and to help raise funds for its operations. The same organizational principles appear among groups formed according to religious affiliation, such as with the Dahira arising from a brotherhood, especially among the Mourides.

Village cash boxes serve several purposes. They return the corpses of members deceased in the host cities and countries and resemble burial societies in this respect. They provide moral and financial support to members who are ill or bereaved or have suffered some other misfortune necessitating collective aid and are thus identical to mutual insurance associations. And since they fund development projects in the villages of origin, especially in social sectors such as health and education, they merit the designation Village Development Associations (VDAs).

Several studies have addressed these types of village organizations in urban environments (Gugler 1971, 1997; Meillassoux 1968; Quiminal 1991; Daum 1994; Marie 1997). In each work, the author has explored the motives that lead migrants, on the one hand, to establish mutual support systems in their respective host cities and, on the other hand, to maintain ties with their communities of origin. Gugler and Meillassoux raise economic arguments by describing how migrants may benefit from maintaining their ties both among one another in their respective host cities and with their villages of origin. Gugler and Geschiere demonstrate, for example, that democratization movements have helped the neo-citizens benefit from their identification with their villages or regions of origin. In this context, the desire to benefit from the economic, political and social opportunities inherent in the policy of indigenous peoples perpetuates their ties with their villages (Geschiere & Gugler 1998). Quiminal and Marie use moral arguments to explain the persistence of people's ties with their communities of origin after they move. Migrants help each other in the cities and help those in their villages of origin out of their obligation arising from their debt toward their community from relying on solidarity mechanisms that they have a duty to perpetuate.

These two perspectives appear indispensable to explain how migrants maintain their ties with their places of origin. The transnationalization of the village networks of migrants merits consideration as well, as this practice reveals that the adaptive abilities of these people extend beyond national and regional borders. Diversifying the centres of attention concerning migration from the valley has in fact extended the village cash boxes across continents and countries and has made them transnational. At the same time, the cash boxes drive local development in the communities of origin of their members. We have examined the Tilogne Development Association (TDA) in Tilogne, Dakar, Libreville, Paris and New York to analyse these two aspects of village cash boxes. Transnationality and a crucial role in development are found not only among the village cash boxes. Both characteristics surface among the tontines as well, although not in the same manner as with the cash boxes.

Before exploring the transnational element of grass-roots financial arrangements, however, we will attempt to explain why tontines and village cash boxes are not transitory financial arrangements to promote development by demonstrating that they derive from millennial practices of reciprocity, mutual aid and cooperation in African societies. Their presence there in non-monetary forms considerably predates modernization.

Traditional reciprocity among the current tontines and village cash boxes

Understanding the current dynamics of the tontines and village cash boxes in grass-roots African environments requires tracing their roots in millennial practices of reciprocity and sociability based largely on relationships with kin and neighbors. According to this perspective, the origins of the tontines are rural. Labor tontines and social arrangements formed to cover the expenses associated with family ceremonies were village-based. These traditional types of organizations deeply influenced the structure and operation of the monetary tontines in the cities. In this respect, the monetary tontines in the cities today may be regarded as adaptations of traditional forms of pooling monetary resources.

Exchanges of gifts and reciprocal gifts during major social events, such as marriages, religious festivals, funerals and baptisms, are central to social ties in Africa. Scholars such as Adebayo maintain that tontines date back to pre-colonial African societies. They figured within the reciprocity system that circulated labor, agricultural and artisanal products and even gold or silver jewellery instead of cash. This is why Lelart believes that labor tontines were the predecessors of the current monetary tontines. He writes:

> They [tontines] predate the use of money. In the past they provided a foundation for labor communities to make farming profitable and to repair the roofs of houses after a storm had wreaked havoc on a village. (Lelart 1985:93)

In Senegal, however, these forms of cooperation arose outside of natural disaster situations and gave rise to one cash box after another. Each time household or community projects necessitated a substantial pool of labor, labor tontines were in demand. Labor tontines were also a form of sickness insurance, as sick villagers had a labor collective available for work in the fields.

Several other authors regard these communal village solidarity mechanisms as the predecessors of the current monetary tontines (Henry et al. 1991; Essombé Edimo 1995; Mayoukou 1994). All describe the labor tontines in pre-colonial Africa and note their progressive transformation into cash tontines following the introduction of money. The studies by some historians reveal that highly complex monetary tontines already existed in some West African societies (Johnson 1970). Adebayo thus argues that monetary tontines predated the introduction of Western currencies (Adebayo 1994). He demonstrates that the monetary system of the Yoruba was highly complex and profoundly changed this society's hierarchical structure. The ROSCAs were the only form of financial intermediation during this period and were conducive to balanced social exchanges that eroded the foundations of the birth-related social hierarchy of the Yoruba.

Whatever role these pre-colonial monetary systems may have had in the rise of exchanges in West Africa, however, their operation was clearly limited by the very nature of their medium, which consisted of the cowrie shells. Transport became a problem above a certain quantity, and the lack of designated scrips in these monetary systems considerably curtailed their widespread use as methods of payment. The economic and social changes in Africa that resulted from the introduction of Western currency through colonization were entirely different from the ones accomplished through traditional monetary systems.

As Bouman emphasizes, the advent of taxation, manufactured products, education and cash crops, which coincided with the introduction of money, had a spectacular impact on virtually all aspects of social life: discontinuation of subsistence production systems, disruption of food and dress customs, reform of styles and procedures of reciprocity, adaptation of solidarity mechanisms and the like (Bouman 1995).

Over time, the reciprocity practice revolving around circulation of material goods made way for a new type of reciprocity in which money became increasingly pivotal. This progressive monetarization of reciprocity relationships surfaced in the growing mixture of gifts at family ceremonies, in the cities and countryside alike. Before money existed, exchanges and reciprocal transactions consisted largely of agricultural and artisanal products. Dowries, gifts and presents in kind could, for example, comprise heads of cattle.

The advent of money in its modern form made for more varied contributions to the organizer of a family ceremony, which henceforth included cash in addition to agricultural, artisanal and manufactured products. In the mbotaay or piye woudere arising from the socially supportive arrangements associated with organizing family ceremonies among the wolof and the haal pulaar, cash is now preferred to contributions in kind, unless these contributions are manufactured goods valued by the beneficiaries. This substantive change in reciprocal relationships arises from the practical value of money as a means of exchange and is conducive to a balanced equilibrium in this respect.

These reciprocal relations uphold gender relationships through the distribution of responsibilities in organizing ceremonies. Men arrange all religious rituals, while women are assigned to observe all customs and organize the practical aspects of the ceremonies. With a wedding for example, the men establish the alliance between the two families in the mosque according to Islamic principles and rules, while the women welcome the guests and prepare the food. In addition to these tasks, women are pivotal in the reciprocal relationships. They exchange the presents, gifts and reciprocal gifts at such ceremonies. The economic dependence of women on men means that the men are expected to remit their contributions to comply with social obligations. This essential role of Senegalese women in reciprocal relationships at family ceremonies may be one of the reasons why these women are the chief operators in mutual grass-roots financial arrangements nowadays (Kane 2002b).

Tontines might therefore be viewed as an adapted version of reciprocal relations with respect to monetarization. Such a hypothesis is all the more plausible because tontines appear to derive their organizational model, procedures and bases of trust and social control from these traditional modes of reciprocity. The principles of rotation and chance and the periodic encounters with their socialization, which remain characteristic of the mbotaay and the piye woudere, surface in the tontines. In many cases, women set up tontines dedicated exclusively to covering the costs of social events in the same manner as the mbotaay and the piye woudere.

The current grass-roots financial practices thus derive from a longstanding tradition of reciprocity and mutual aid for social events. Weddings, baptisms, funerals, religious festivals and rites of passage are special occasions at which relatives, neighbors or co-religionists manifest their solidarity by collectively assuming responsibility for the material and financial requirements of their celebration. The first major difference between these traditional forms of mutual aid and the rotating savings and credit associations is that in the former the contributions made and the services obtained by individual participants do not necessarily even out over time, whereas the latter ensure a relative balance between what people give, and what they receive by the end of the tontine cycle. The second significant difference is that traditional forms of mutual aid are based on inherent social obligations toward neighbors, whereas tontines are ruled by contractual principles and are thus deliberate acts of free will.

The roots of the tontines and the village cash boxes in millennial practices of solidarity, mutual support and reciprocity does not prevent them from being mobile and expanding and evolving transnationally. Senegalese immigrants replicate them wherever they settle in Europe and America.

Transnational nature of grass-roots financial arrangements

Many studies on grass-roots financial arrangements focus on a circumscribed, localized area and describe and analyse village, neighborhood, market or workplace tontines. The studies on grass-roots financial arrangements rarely reflect a broad regional or transnational perspective. International migration, however, has led population groups moving from the South to the North to set up tontines and communal cash boxes in their host countries that channel money to their countries of origin.

This transnational aspect comprises more than the simultaneous existence of grass-roots financial arrangements in different countries. It consists on the one hand of ongoing ties between grass-roots financial arrangements in different countries (as with the village cash boxes) and on the other hand of the flow of money transferred from the tontines of the emigrants to fund indirectly the tontines in the countries of origin.

Transnationality of the tontines

At first the tontines we examined in Tilogne did not appear at all related to any in Dakar or Paris. Upon asking the women participating in tontines in Tilogne neighborhoods how they obtained the money for their contributions – given that many do not engage in revenue-generating activities – the overwhelming majority reported that they depended on money sent from Dakar, France or some other country abroad by a relative residing there temporarily or permanently. Conversely, upon asking the participants in Senegalese tontines in France what they did with the money obtained through these arrangements, they reported sending a large share to relatives in Dakar or their home village. The obvious conclusion is that the tontines in Dakar and France indirectly generate cash for the tontines in Tilogne.

Desroche describes the flow back and forth of the tontines from North to South. 'Tontines derive from the Northern tradition of precautions, covering three centuries of adventures and misfortunes since Lorenzo Tonti devised the system. They are also a resource in the difficult circumstances of the South, where they symbolize an exogenous label attached to endogenous merchandise; this merchandise is after all diversified and contrasting, not to mention fragmented (Desroche 1990:3). This means that the European tontines of the past have little in common with the current African reality that the notion of tontines conveys in many French-speaking countries in Africa. This African reality is therefore defined by its origins and anchoring in social life, as noted above. This would also explain the persistence in Senegal of grass-roots financial arrangements alongside the formal financial channels. In Europe, on the other hand, as De Swaan explains, grass-roots mutual funds were gradually replaced by formal institutions, such as banks, insurance companies and the social security system established by European welfare states.

The presence of tontines and village cash boxes in Europe among African immigrant communities should not be interpreted as the return of these grass-roots or informal financial arrangements in their original form, as Desroche appears to suggest. African tontines in France and elsewhere are intended to replicate social ties on the one hand between the immigrants themselves and on the other hand between these emigrants and their country of origin. This is undoubtedly why Senegalese immigrants join tontines, despite the convenience of banks and insurance companies in their host society. The subtle return of the tontines in major European cities among immigrant groups from Africa (Kane 2002a; Almedom 1995; Summerfield 1995), Asia (Srinivasan 1995; Light & Deng 1995) and South America and the Caribbean (Bijnaar 2002) indicates an incipient transnationalization of informal financial arrangements driven by globalization.

The transnational nature of tontines is closely linked to migration. Despite the convenience of banks in the host countries of the waves of international migrants, immigrant groups there organize informal financial arrangements. Senegalese immigrants in France have several other reasons for joining tontines besides replicating the social ties noted above. One is that the overwhelming majority of the tontine members are illiterate women who do not work outside their home. They pay their tontine contributions from the monthly allowance that their husbands give them to compensate them for being confined to their household. Most immigrant women have no real income and can neither read nor write in French. Accordingly, they have great difficulty dealing with banks and find banking procedures far too complex.

Lack of legal residence status may be another reason for joining immigrant tontines. Illegal immigrants have difficulty opening bank accounts and are therefore forced to meet their financing needs through informal financial arrangements. This is the case among polygamous families in France. As the French authorities do not recognize polygamy, only one of a polygamous man's two, three or even four wives is eligible for a residence permit. The others are illegal aliens and have no option other than the tontines to save and to obtain credit.

The essentially mono-ethnic composition of immigrant tontines attests to the importance of the identity aspect. In addition to their purely financial role, tontines have an important socio-cultural function and serve as vehicles for sociability by enabling immigrant women to adapt more easily to the way of life in their host society. In the 1960s and 70s, these Senegalese women organized tontines to escape their state of isolation during their early years in France (Kane 2001a).

Studies on tontines among immigrants reveal that they operate in almost the same manner as the ones in their countries of origin. They are organized according to the same logic as the Senegalese enclaves established in French cities. In the Paris suburbs of Mantes la Jolie and Mureaux, the Haal Pulaar communities are reminiscent of life in the North of Senegal, despite being situated in Ile de France. All the same, tontines satisfy the socio-economic needs of Senegalese immigrants in France. When Senegalese immigrants started to arrive in France, the tontines were essentially, as I mentioned above, socializing networks intended to help the immigrants (especially the women) adapt to their host society.

In addition to these social considerations, the replication of tontines in the host countries accommodates the desire to amass savings to transfer these monies to the countries of origin. Understanding the transnational nature of the tontines requires exploring how participants use their *levées* in immigrant circles. The Senegalese immigrants in France report that they send the bulk of the monies they raise through tontines to their country of origin. Some support needy family members, friends or neighbors, while others invest their money in real estate.

Fatim, age 42 and a member of a tontine in Boulogne, explained how she sent the entire sum she drew from her tontine (8,000 French francs) to her brother to pay for his visa to the United States. Penda, age 33 and a member of a tontine in Compiègne, sent over half the money she obtained from her tontine (20,000 French francs) to a younger brother to finance a Groupement d'Intérêt Economique [Economic interest group] (GIE) specialized in fabric imports and exports. Her brother purchases fabric from Mali (bazin fabric dyed by Malian women) and sends it to Penda, who resells it in France. Penda has joined a second tontine that specializes in purchasing and building houses in Dakar. The 40,000 French franc levée is enough to buy a plot of land in the suburbs of Dakar. She hopes to continue participating in this tontine in the future to build a little house over time.

In the examples described above, the money raised in the tontines is ultimately transferred to Senegal. The cash is transferred through informal channels. The best-known methods include sending the money with a trusted person returning to the country and the procedure referred to as the 'Fax' transfer system. Immigrants returning to Senegal bring along millions of francs in commissions for friends, relatives and neighbors to give to their families left behind in Senegal. The Fax is an informal transfer system devised by a few immigrant businessmen or associations with counterparts in Dakar and in the valley. They offer immigrants a rapid and safe transfer system that is less costly than the official channels. The immigrants give the money to be transferred to the person who runs the Fax in Paris. This individual faxes his counterparts in Dakar and in the village the list of recipients of money transfers and the amounts due to each person. Transfer costs are 30 French francs for amounts from 100 to 50,000 French francs, 50 French francs for amounts from 50,000 to 100,000 French francs, 70 French francs for amounts from 100,000 to 200,000 French francs and 100 French francs for amounts over 200,000 French francs. The money raised through the tontines is sent through these informal transfer channels and infuses fresh cash into the tontines of the Senegal River valley.

The recipients of money transfers participate in local tontines and thus use the money toward their contributions to these local tontines. This is the case in the tontines in the Tilogne neighborhood where the majority of women report drawing their contributions from money orders sent by their husbands or close relatives living abroad. In the second case, the immigrants send the money to a trusted individual, who arranges to purchase a plot of land and possibly to build a house. This trusted person organizes the tontines, where the emigrant's money is reinvested for a while.

In addition to these aspects, tontines facilitate travel between the host country and the country of origin for their participants. Some tontines are even dedicated exclusively toward trips their participants' trips back to their country of origin. The Haal Pulaar women's tontine in Compiègne is dedicated to helping participants go on holiday. The 25 members each contribute 200 French francs a month. They accumulate the contributions in a cash box, from which they draw financial aid for their members who decide to travel to Senegal on vacation. The financial aid provided for participants returning to Senegal on holiday equals eight thousand French francs. Participants who do not return to Senegal in a five-year period are entitled to the same 8,000 French francs provided to those who do go back there. Women who return frequently are entitled to financial aid every three years. Tontines of this type operate in Trappe, Mureaux, Creil, Boulogne and Orléans. Such tontines facilitate the mobility of their members between their host countries and their countries of origin and thus drive the transnational flow of human beings between rich and poor countries.

The transnational nature of village cash boxes: the Tilogne Development Association

The transnational element distinguishes village cash boxes such as the Tilogne Development Association from other grass-roots financial arrangements. Most studies about these associations overlook this aspect by consistently focusing on relations between immigrants in a given host country with their village of origin (Quiminal 1991; Daum 1994; Delville 1991). These studies do not take into account that the migrants from the valley are spread across continents and countries and have set up similar organizations to pursue the same objectives almost everywhere. Their dispersion in several countries, their preservation of close ties with the village and their belief that integration is impossible in the host countries are relevant criteria for establishing the rise of village Diasporas among the Haal Pulaar immigrants in France and elsewhere (Koser et al. 2003; Cohen 1997; Van Hear 1998; Kane 2002b).

Three major characteristics of the Tilogne Development Association justify describing them as transnational. The first is the presence of this village association in various countries, with the most dynamic sections in Senegal, Gabon, France and the United States. In each of these countries, the association is registered with the relevant authorities.

The second characteristic is the common goal of participating in realizing communal projects in the village of origin. Each section is free to pursue this fundamental objective alongside other, autonomous targets. TDA sections in France,

Gabon and the United States, for example, protect their members from various risks in their respective host cities.

The third and final characteristic concerns the joint effort among the sections to coordinate local development activities through regular correspondence, phone calls, faxes or e-mails. They team up to organize 'culture days' in Tilogne, where the directors of the different sections meet and discuss actions to be taken and ways to finance them. The last cultural days were organized in August 2002. On 23 January 1998 the directors of the TDA sections in Tilogne, Libreville and the United States were invited to attend the annual general assembly of TDA France. At this event the different sections decided to set up a coordination committee, comprising a representative from each section.

The distribution of tasks among the different sections appears based on the opportunities available to individuals by virtue of their current place of residence. The sections abroad, i.e. in Paris, New York and Libreville, thus provide the financial backing for the projects. The Dakar section deals with the central authorities, for example by requesting teachers or sanitation staff to operationalize the infrastructures set up by the village cash box or to negotiate with the customs authorities to get equipment sent by the TDA sections abroad released from the harbour or airport, while the local section supplies labor at the time of construction and manages and maintains the communal equipment obtained in this manner.

The TDAs comprise five main poles around which the actions of the villagers and their worldwide Diaspora are organized. Two of these poles are in Senegal: one in the village and the other in Dakar. The numbers of people from Tilogne in other African countries have led sections to be established in Libreville, in Ouagadougou and elsewhere. Based on this same principle of concentrations of people from Tilogne, sections have been established in countries in Europe and America as well, including one in Paris and another in New York.

The village of Tilogne is large enough to rely exclusively on its residents to set up a transnational village network consisting of the different TDA sections across the cities or countries with a substantial Tilogne Diaspora. Smaller villages form joint transnational unions or federations, such as the liaison association for the development of the Agnam, which comprises nine neighboring villages.

The diagram below conveys the relations between the different sections of the village mutuals across the major cities where a substantial number of people from Tilogne have settled. The transnational scope of the TDA revolves around these five poles. The local pole is the association comprising the villagers residing in Tilogne. They are the true beneficiaries of the projects carried out by the Diaspora. The Dakar pole mediates the transit between the local section and the foreign sections of the mutual. Finally, the foreign poles in Africa, Europe and the United States are the financial backers and fund village projects.

The arrows in the diagram depict the two types of movements. The first one symbolizes the transfers of money, medication and equipment from the migration destinations to the village of origin. The various sections send money, medication and equipment to the village. In the past, the TDA section in France was by far the

DIAGRAM: **Transnational scope of the Tilogne Development Association**

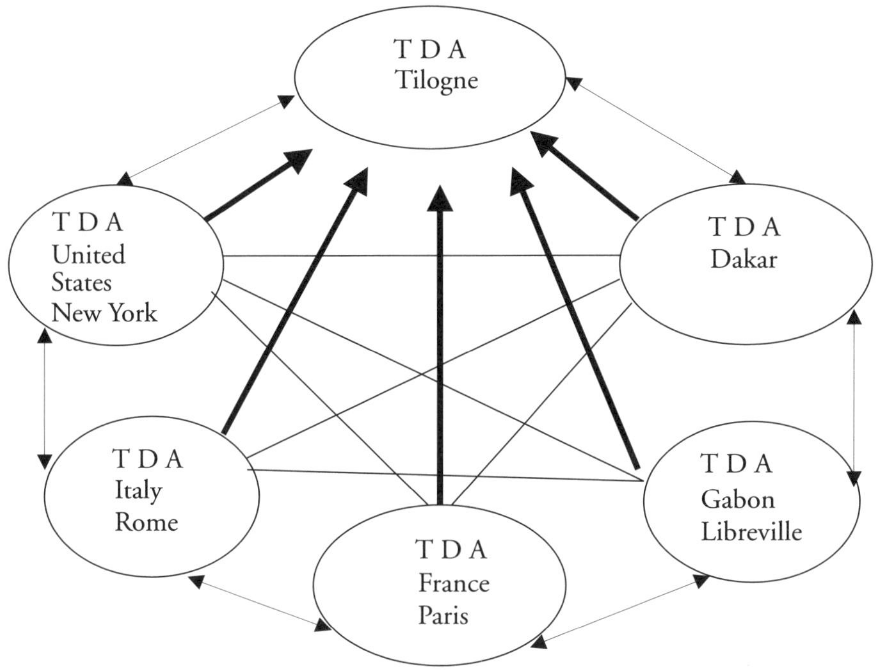

most involved in this type of transfer. Recently, however, the TDA section in New York has transferred more money than the TDA section in France. This process highlights the different trends in immigration dynamics in France and the United States. Since the Schengen agreements restricted the flow of migration from countries outside the European Union, very few young people from Tilogne have arrived in France. As a result, the TDA section in France is losing its pool for recruiting new members. As the entire system is based on intergenerational solidarity, serious financial problems are anticipated for TDA France in the near future. At the same time, however, increasing numbers of young people from Tilogne are bound for the United States, where the immigration policy, though restrictive, offers more opportunities. This incessant movement of young adults leaving the village and arriving in the United States has made the TDA section there more dynamic compared to the one in France.

The second type of movement comprises the flow of information between the different sections through the different vehicles of communication, which are most frequently letters, telephones, faxes and recently e-mails. Since 1999, the local section has had a computer connected to the Internet to facilitate communication with the different TDA sections abroad. Use of these new information technologies has enabled these networks of migrants to communicate far more directly with their places of origin. In the 1980s Tilogne had only five telephone lines. By the late 1990s the village had over one hundred. Telephones are considered above all to be a practical medium between migrants and their families. Henceforth, migrants, even when they are thousands of kilometres away from home, are able to take decisions, solve problems, mediate family disputes, arbitrate and the like, as if they were with their families. New information technologies have brought migrants closer to their communities of origin and have thus considerably reduced the likelihood that they will integrate in their host societies.

This transnational nature of village associations is not exclusive to Tilogne. In fact, nearly all villages in the Senegal River valley have the same form of transnational organization (Daum 1994). The Association pour le Développement d'Ourosogui [Ourosogui development association] (ADO) and the Association Liaison pour le Développement des Agnam [liaison association for the development of the Agnam] (ALDA) have the same transnational characteristics (Abdoul Hameth Ba 1998: 99). Tracking the itineraries of the migrants, the village associations branch out across the cities of Africa, Europe and America. Aside from the mutual aid system intended to provide the people coming from these villages with social protection from the misfortunes and uncertainties of life in the cities, the practice of maintaining ties with the villages of origin raises questions about the underlying motives. In other words, while mutual aid between emigrants is easy to explain, the persistence of communal links across a transnational area is difficult to understand.

Geschiere associates the endurance of ties between migrants and their villages with the benefits that the neo-citizens derive from their identification with respect to their place of origin. Claims of indigenous peoples enable certain neo-citizens to become involved in national politics. The contribution from migrants through the execution of development projects in their village is therefore not motivated solely by altruism but also derives from the presence of counterparts in terms of power and prestige.

Alain Marie advances another explanation based on his social debt theory. He believes that migrants arrive in their host cities heavily indebted to the communal solidarity mechanisms they used along their emigration path. Already upon leaving their village, they receive moral and financial support from their extended family. When they arrive in the city, they are taken in hand by family members who have settled there. They receive money to travel abroad from an elder brother, an uncle or a father who is in Europe or in other African countries. All this aid is a joint investment in a member of the community in the hope that his success will carry over to the family and the village. Migrants are thus obliged to preserve the link to repay all those who have helped him along his journey.

Conclusion

The transnational nature of grass-roots financial arrangements reveals the adaptive capacity of informal transnational networks. Globalization affects not only multinational firms and the market economy but extends to the informal and grass-roots sector as well. The dispersion of Senegalese emigrants across different continents and countries coincides with replication in the host societies of customs and socio-economic and cultural conduct specific to Senegalese society, leading in turn to the establishment of Senegalese enclaves in the heart of Western cities such as Paris and New York. The replication of tontines and village cash boxes figures within this logic. Thanks to new communication technologies, tontines and cash boxes enable their participants to be both here and there at the same time.

References

Adebayo, A.G.
1994 'Money, Credit and Banking in Precolonial Africa. The Yoruba Experience.' *Anthropos*, 89:379-400.
Ardener, S.
1953 'The Social and Economic significance of the Contribution Club among the Southern Ibo.' West African Institute of Social and economic Research, Annual Conference Sociology Section, Ibadan: 128-142.
1964 'The Comparative Study of Rotating Credit Associations.' *Journal of the Royal Anthropological Institute*, 94(2):201-229.
Ardener, S. & S. Burman
1995 *Money-Go-Rounds. The Importance of Rotating Savings and Credit Associations for Women.* Oxford/Washington D.C.: Berg.
Ba, A.H.
1998 'Incidence des réseaux migratoires sur les pays de départ: le cas de la migration sénégalaise.' In: S. Barouh (ed.), *Dynamiques migratoires et rencontres ethniques*, 89-102. Paris: l'Harmattan.
Bijnaar, A.
2002 *Kasmoni. Spaarzame levensgenieters in Suriname en Nederland.* PhD thesis, University of Amsterdam.
Bop, C.
1995 'Les femmes chefs de famille à Dakar.' *Africa Development*, 20(4):51-67.
Bouman, F.J.A.
1994 'ROSCA and ASCRA: Beyond the Financial Landscape.' In: *Financial Landscapes Reconstructed*, Boulder: Westview Press, 375-394.
1995 'ROSCA: On the Origin of the Species.' *Savings and Development*, 2, XIX:117-145.
Bouman, F.J.A. & K. Harteveld
1976 'The Djanggi, a Traditional Form of Saving and Credit in West Cameroon.' *Sociologia Ruralis*, 16(1-2):103-118.
Bouman, F.J.A. & O. Hospes.
1994 *Financial Landscapes Reconstructed. The Fine Art of Mapping Development.* Boulder: Westview Press.
Daum, C.
1994 'Ici et là-bas, immigration et développement: les associations des émigrés ouest-africains en France.' Migrations et Société, CIEMS, *Migrations et Développement*, 6, 32, March–April: 99-110.

Delville, P.L.

1991 *La rizière et la valise: irrigation, migrations et stratégies paysannes dans la moyenne vallée du fleuve Sénégal.* Paris: Syros-Alternatives.

De Swaan, A.

1994 *Sous l'aile protectrice de l'Etat.* Paris: Presse Universitaires Françaises.

De Swaan, A. (ed.)

1994 *Social Policy beyond Borders. The Social Question in Transnational Perspective,* Amsterdam: Amsterdam University Press.

Diarra, H.

1998 'Associations d'immigrés et développement: le point sur deux décennies d'intervention.' *Hommes et Migrations,* 1214, July-August:74-84.

Diatta, M.A. & N. Mbow

1999 'Releasing the Development Potential of Return Migration: The Case of Senegal.' *International Migration Quarterly Review,* 37(1):241-266.

Dromain, M.

1990 'L'épargne ignorée et negligée. Les resultats d'une enquête sur les tontines in Sénégal.' In: M. Lelart (ed.), *La tontine. Pratique informelle d'épargne et de crédit dans les pays en voie de développement,* 161-162. Paris/Montrouge: John Libbey Eurotext.

Dupuy, C.

1990 'Les comportements d'épargne dans la société africaine: études sénégalaises.' In: M. Lelart (ed.), *La tontine. Pratique informelle d'épargne et de crédit dans les pays en voie de développement,* 31-51. Paris/Montrouge: John Libbey Eurotext.

Dupuy, C. & J.M. Servet

1987 'Pratiques informelles d'épargne et de prêt: exemples sénégalais.' *Economie et Humanisme,* 294, March-April: 40-54.

Essombé Edimo, J.R.

1995 *Quel avenir pour l'Afrique? Financement et développement*: Paris: Editions Nouvelles du Sud.

Evers Rosander, E.

1997 'Le Dahira de Mam Diarra Bousso à Mbacké. Analyse d'une association religieuse de femmes sénégalaise.' In: E. Evers Rosander (ed.), *Transformation des identités féminines,* 160-174. Uppsala: Nordiska Afrikainstitutet.

Geertz, C.

1962 'The Rotating Credit Association: a "Middle Rung" in Development.' *Economic Development and Cultural Change,* 10(3):241-63.

Geschiere, P. & J. Gugler

1998 'The Urban-Rural Connection: Changing Issues of Belonging and Identification.' *Africa,* 68(3):309-319.

Gugler, J.

1971 'Life in a Dual System: Eastern Nigerians in Town.' *Cahiers d'Etudes Africaines,* 11(3):400-421.

1997 'Life in Dual System Revisited: Urban-Rural Ties in Enugu, Nigeria, 1961-87.' *World Development,* 19(5):399-409.

Henry, A., et al.

1991 *Tontines et banques au Cameroun, Les principes de la Société des amis* 7. Paris: Karthala.

Jaussaud, E.

1998 'Les associations d'immigrés et l'émergence d'une économie de développement local.' *Economie Solidaire et Migrations,* 10, 56, March-April: 77-85.

Johnson, M.
1970 'The Cowrie Currencies of West Africa.' *The Journal of African History*, 11:17-49, 331-353.
Kane, A.
2001a *Les caméléons de la finance populaire au Sénégal et dans la Diaspora. Dynamique des tontines et des caisses villageoises entre Thilogne.* Dakar et Paris, PhD thesis, University of Amsterdam.
2001b 'Diaspora villageoise et développement local en Afrique: le cas de Thilogne Association Développement.' *Hommes et Migrations*, 1229, January-February:96-107.
2002a 'Financial Arrangements Across Borders: Women's Predominant Participation in Popular Finance, from Thilogne and Dakar to Paris. A Senegalese Case Study.' In: B. Lemire et al. (eds), *Women and Credit. Researching the Past, Refiguring the Future*, 295-317. Oxford: Berg.
2002b 'Senegal's Village Diaspora and the People Left Behind.' In: D.Bryceson & U. Vuorela (eds.), *The Transnational Family: New European Frontiers and Global Networks*, 245-263. Oxford: Berg.
Lelart, M.
1985 'L'épargne informelle en Afrique.' *Revue des etudes comparatives*, 14(2):53-78.
Lelart, M. & J.L. Lespès
1985 'Les tontines africaines: une expérience originale d'épargne et de crédit.' *Revue de l'economie sociale*, July-September:157-159.
Mayoukou, C.
1994 *Le système des tontines en Afrique: un système bancaire informel.* Paris: L'Harmattan.
Meillassoux, C.
1968 *Urbanization of an African Community. Voluntary Associations in Bamako.* University of Washington Press.
Nagarajan, G. et al.
1993 'Financial Intermediation through ROSCAs: Peri-Urban Banjul, The Gambia.' Report to USAID/The Gambia, Colombus, Ohio State University.
Naïr, S.
1998 'La politique de codéveloppement liés aux flux migratoires.' *Migrants et solidarité Nord-Sud*, 1214, July-August: 47-57.
Niger-Thomas, M.
1995 'Women's Access to and Control of Credit in Cameroon: The Mamfe Case.' In: S. Ardener & S. Burman (eds), *Money-Go-Rounds. The Importance of Rotating Savings and Credit Associations for Women*, 95-110. Oxford: Berg.
Nzemen, M.
1993 *Tontines et développement ou le défi financier de l'Afrique.* Yaoundé : Presses Universitaires du Cameroun.
Quiminal, C.
1990 'Du foyer au village: l'initiative retrouvée.' *Hommes et migrations*, 1131, April: 19-24.
1991 *Gens d'ici, gens d'ailleurs.* Paris: Christian Bourgeois.
Rowlands, M.
1995 'Looking at Financial Landscapes: A Contextual of ROSCAs in Cameroon.' In: S. Ardener & S. Burman (eds), *Money-Go-Rounds. The Importance of Rotating Savings and Credit Associations for Women*, 111-123. Oxford: Berg.

Servet, J.M.
1990 'Les tontines, formes d'activités informelles et d'initiatives collectives privées en Afrique'. In: M. Lelart (ed.), *La tontine. Pratique informelle d'épargne et de crédit dans les pays en voie de développement*, 53-80. Paris/Montrouge: John Libbey Eurotext.

Van der Linden, M. (ed.)
1996 *Social Security Mutualism. The Comparative History of Mutual Benefit Societies.* Bern: Peter Lang.

Yaya, W.
1969 *Les Toucouleur du Fouta Tooro: stratification sociale et structure familiale.* Dakar: IFAN.

CHAPTER 5

Social security in financial self-help organizations

An Indonesian example[1]

Hotze Lont

Introduction

The Western welfare state has long been considered an exemplary model of social security policies in developing countries. With these models coming under increasing pressure, however, there has been growing disappointment with the achievements of state-based social security in many of these areas. Social insurance and protection schemes are often limited to small sections of the population (civil servants), the benefits provided are not only negligible, but corruption and bureaucracy make them very difficult to obtain.[2]

An increasing awareness of the limited role of state social security in developing countries has led to a search for alternative private institutions that can serve a similar purpose. Financial self-help organizations (SHOs) are often among the first private institutions identified as real or potential social security instruments. Von Benda-Beckmann et al. (1988:16), Bouman (1994b:375; 1995a:118-127; 1995b:372), Van Ginneken (1999:20-26), Midgley (1994:225), and Woodman (1988:81) perceive financial SHOs as having a social security function, or they identify these organizations as social security institutions. Bouman (1994b:375) provides examples of special purpose SHOs that insure against 'illness, accident, death, and other possible mishaps' as well as financing for 'rites of passage, life cycle events, spiritual and religious ceremonies and education.' Also Van Ginneken (1999:21-2) and Midgley (1994:225) point to such functions as marriage and survivor's benefits. The same authors not only view special purpose SHOs as providing a form of social security, but they see this as true of financial SHOs in general. Van Ginneken (1999:21) states that ROSCAs (Rotating Credit and Service Associations)[3] are 'above all a way of encouraging savings and can be perceived as a form of social insurance' (see also Calomiris & Rajaraman 1998). In this role it is up to the participants themselves to allocate specific sums to cope with adversities and deficiencies. Lydon (1992:21) claims for ROSCAs that 'the range of social benefits procured through participation… has increased to encompass everything from security deposits against a possible famine, to safeguards for women in the event of separation or divorce.'

Such general statements may romanticize financial SHOs by exaggerating the solidarity between participants and obscuring institutional limitations. The many examples the above authors provide for instances in which financial self-help organizations help people cope with adversities and deficiencies do not indicate whether this form of protection is equally available to all participants in all types of such organizations. Much remains unclear about how financial self-help organizations are regulated, what kinds of problems emerge, and what their limitations are. An exception is Gerdes (1975), who studied to what extent different Ethiopian financial SHOs 'provide protection against various recognizable threats to income and security.' He details the differences between various types of financial arrangements, as well as the actual financial practices that are in place.[4]

This chapter aims to investigate how financial self-help organizations provide protection against adversities and deficiencies using the concrete social setting of urban Indonesia as an example. After providing a perspective on social security in developing countries, there is a short description of the research area and a typology of local financial self-help organizations. This is followed by an analytical model for assessing systematically the multiple mechanisms through which financial self-help organizations can provide protection: 1) the direct allocation of specific sums, 2) the use of social capital to improve access to economic capital, and 3) the use of economic capital to improve access to other forms of economic capital. The chapter ends with an assessment of the relative importance of financial self-help organizations with respect to other coping mechanisms, comparing them to similar organizations in India, South Africa, Senegal, and Surinam.

Social security in developing countries

There is growing scholarly interest in social security in developing countries (Hirtz 1994). According to Schmidt (1994:83), the origin of the term 'social security' is the 1935 Social Security Act in the United States, and its use is still usually associated with state support. It is in this context that Marshall (1975:106) defined social security as: 'Arrangements for providing cash benefits, by social insurance, family allowances in respect of children, and the various grants made subject to means test which we can refer to collectively as "assistance"', which is a definition that refers directly to the role of the state. But directly applying this concept to Third World societies, as attempted for instance by Galjart (1994), can be problematic. In contemporary developing countries, most people will have to rely on non-state mechanisms to cope with adversities and deficiencies. Thus a broader definition of social security is necessary for it to be relevant to ordinary people in Indonesia, a definition that not only includes the state, but all other arrangements that have similar manifest or latent functions.

Recent studies have focused on a variety of institutions, arrangements, and strategies that offer protection against the hazards of life and provide functions similar to those of the welfare state's social security system. Burgess and Stern (1991:43) argue that social security can be found in any form of public action by the state, community, or household. Van Ginneken (1999:5) defines social security in a broader sense as: 'The provision of benefits to households and individuals through public or collective arrangements to protect against low or declining living standards arising from a number of basic risks and needs.' Although Drèze and Sen (1991:5) have a slightly broader focus, they also allow for individual relations in their definition, as they include the use of social means to prevent deprivation and vulnerability to deprivation in their concept of social security. A similar approach is used by F. & K. von Benda-Beckmann (1996:1), who state that 'the field of social security covers all arrangements through which people unable to acquire food, shelter, care and education for themselves, are taken care of' (see also Hirtz 1995). Here, however, our basic assumption is that the concept of social security is applicable only when the consequences of individual adversities and deficiencies are, to a certain extent, also borne by others. Social security thus refers to those social relations, arrangements, and institutions where risks are shared. Accordingly, social security arrangements can be conceived as social care arrangements for coping with individual deficiencies and adversities, whether in the form of assistance or insurance (De Swaan 1989:153).

This broader view of social security in developing countries provides several important lessons, three of which are central in my analysis of social security. The first is that few people want to, or can, rely on a single source of social security, and hence they decide to commit to a multiplicity of relations, institutions, and arrangements. These multiple sources can only be analysed in connection with one another, as a 'layered fabric of social security' (F. & K. von Benda-Beckmann 1994:19). Moreover, the 'different social security structures operating at different scales of social organization and space may merge' (F. and K. von Benda-Beckmann 1994:20). The various arrangements that play a role have their own normative bases, which results in different notions of need and, hence, care provided. Each applies different procedures and conditions, making them not equally useful for specific contingencies. Engagement in a variety of social security arrangements not only allows people to achieve broader protection but, as we will see, it is a strategy that may even strengthen the separate elements.

Second (and implied by the previous point), an analysis of social security requires that the active role of the individuals involved also be considered. Whether people will benefit from social security arrangements depends very much on their personal abilities and their resources, their position within a community, their activities in the past, and what they can do in the future. It is important not to differentiate sharply between those who give support and those who receive it. After all, the receiver of today can be the giver of tomorrow. Furthermore, an active recipient of care is also able to assess and choose between alternative coping strategies to achieve a perceived optimum.

An appreciation of the active role of individuals also focuses on the individual coping strategies that people use alongside or in place of social security arrangements. Such strategies may often be more relevant to attempts to diminish vulnerability than are social security arrangements. We can see an example of this in the story of Karto, an Indonesian pedicab driver. Several years ago he had to undergo surgery in a hospital for a broken pelvis. He received around Rp 50,000 from the municipal social department and neighborhood contributions. To pay the remaining Rp 300,000 of the hospital bill he preferred to sell his pedicab rather than beg for more money from neighbors or relatives. When he recovered he immediately purchased another pedicab, on credit, so he could again earn money – and equally important to Karto, so he could sell the pedicab if he were again confronted with an urgent need. It would be short-sighted for a researcher not to take the sale of the pedicab into account, even though it did not involve help from others. After all, the pedicab was much more relevant to Karto's socio-economic security than his neighbors or the state was.

The third lesson (also related to the two previous points), is that more insights can be gained by using actual problems rather than via institutions that have been set up to deal with such problems. An institutional approach often fails to acknowledge the importance of arrangements that are not normatively defined as social security arrangements; it also neglects to direct attention to the role of social actors (F. & K. Von Benda-Beckmann 1994:11-5). It is better to follow the sequence of Platteau's analysis (1991:123): 'Collective risks or specific risks may threaten from time to time the livelihood of either many or a few inhabitants. To face these uncertainties, villagers must adopt a range of coping strategies to reduce risks, to share and pool them, or to adjust to their consequences once they have materialized.'[5]

The myriad uncertainties, insecurities, and risks can best be described if a distinction is made between adversities and deficiencies, as De Swaan did (1989). Deficiencies refer to insufficient access to resources for meeting specific needs. Adversities are damaging events that could not reasonably be foreseen. These concepts are closely related to what Drèze and Sen (1991:10) refer to as deprivation and vulnerability. Marshall's definition of social security (see above) also reflects this basic distinction. The occurrence of adversities and deficiencies prevents people from attending to their basic needs. At a certain moment people may be unable to gain access to food, medicine, old age care, or education because they are too poor or have been struck by adversity. But this study is not limited to the poor. Although adversities are more pressing if the people who experience them already live in a condition of deficiency, people of all classes are confronted by adversities. Furthermore, while some occupations may be paid well, the rates of payment may fluctuate enormously.[6] It is only reasonable that the consequences of adversity should be different for a wealthy factory owner than for one of his workers. Nevertheless, they are both vulnerable, and in some respects the factory owner may have even more at stake.

Bujung, a place where money flows

Research was conducted in Bujung, an urban neighborhood on the outskirts of Yogyakarta, a provincial capital on the island of Java. Bujung has around 5,000 inhabitants, and like many neighborhoods in urban Yogyakarta, the area is divided into different social and topographical spaces (see Guinness 1986:103-108). The elevated, upper section, of the neighborhood is mainly occupied by people belonging to the lower middle class: teachers and other lower echelon civil servants, traders, and skilled laborers. Lowly or unskilled laborers, small traders, and pedicab drivers live in the lower section, which is located along the two rivers that border the neighborhood. Although both sections need to work together in a compulsory neighborhood organization (RT and RW),[7] for the rest they keep to themselves. Within the confines of their own sections, neighbors tend to have rather close relationships with one another. They spend many hours together on the streets, in their houses, and during the frequent meetings of various social organizations.[8] In Bujung, occupational multiplicity is the norm. Generally more than one household member contributes to the household income and each may be engaged in more than one income earning activity. Some of these activities earn daily incomes, while others are paid weekly, monthly, or even annually.

In the monetary economy of Bujung, adversities and deficiencies concern temporary or permanent financial gaps, that is, income does not cover expenditures. Many jobs provide highly uncertain incomes. Pedicab drivers and traders are good examples of this type of daily variation in income. Construction workers may go many days without a job. Even civil servants, who do earn a regular basic income, depend heavily on infrequent bonuses. As a result, almost all households in Bujung are confronted by more or less fluctuating incomes. Expenditures fluctuate as well, and may be unevenly spread over time. Households spend a relatively stable amount of money on daily food, but some expenditures are monthly or annual, for example, housing and education. What is especially irregular are expenses for family ceremonies, hospital treatment, and luxury goods. Consequently, irregular financial cycles are a fact of life. Cycles of income and expenditure often do not neatly coincide, which inevitably results in financial gaps that have to be met one way or another. For almost any household in Bujung that does not have abundant wealth, these financial gaps create serious insecurities.

Bujung's financial self-help organizations come in many forms. For example, there is a basic distinction between ROSCAs (*arisan*) and ASCRAs (*simpan pinjam*). The ROSCA is an arrangement whereby all participants regularly contribute to a collective fund, a kitty, which is subsequently disbursed to all members in turn. The sequence of disbursement is generally determined on the basis of a lottery, but sometimes through bidding. The ASCRA is an arrangement whereby all participants contribute to a fund that can be used by all participants to take out loans. The loans are repaid with interest, accumulating additional capital in the loan fund.[9]

Five local types of financial SHOs can be distinguished, primarily on the basis of the size of contribution and the relative importance of social as opposed to financial activities. The first cluster is comprised of 'social SHOs,' which manage small ROSCAs, ASCRAs, and several special funds, including a funeral fund. This is the largest category of financial SHOs. The Bujungese participate in hundreds of these organizations, within and beyond the neighborhood. Participation is often obligatory, so that in our survey at least one member in all households joined such a social SHO. The second cluster is that of the 'private ROSCAs,' entailing a simple ROSCA arrangement. Such SHOs have no meetings, and the social aspect remains limited to a few minutes of chatting before and after the lottery. The financial contributions do not greatly exceed those in the social SHOs, but they result in larger sums. There are a few dozen private ROSCAs in Bujung. The third cluster is that of the 'open ASCRAs,' of which there are a few dozen in Bujung. These organizations have both an ASCRA and a funeral fund, and operate more publicly than private ROSCAs. The two remaining clusters are the 'market ROSCAs' and the 'credit cooperatives.' The market ROSCA is a more commercial form of the private ROSCA, and operates in the markets. Credit cooperatives are a more commercial version of open ASCRAs, often having a formal legal status. Default is rare for any of these organizations.

Financial SHOs provide monetary sums in the form of kitties and loans. Social SHOs may provide amounts ranging from Rp 10,000 to Rp 50,000. Private ROSCAs range from Rp 30,000 to Rp 400,000, and open ASCRAs between Rp 50,000 and Rp 600,000. Both market ROSCAs and credit cooperatives may provide Rp 300,000 to Rp 3,000,000 to participants. For comparison's sake, during my fieldwork, a laborer's daily wage was between Rp 5,000 and Rp 10,000. Most civil servants earned between Rp 300,000 and Rp 500,000 per month. Almost all households join one or more of the social SHOs, and somewhat more than half of them join one or more of the SHOs in the other categories. Women predominate in the private ROSCAs and market ROSCAs, but participation is mixed in the other categories (although men and women often have their own groups).

Participation in financial SHOs is widespread in Bujung. Members of a single household generally join a number of different financial SHOs.[10] The categories seldom represented in financial SHOs include children, the elderly, temporary migrant laborers, and those who live on the margins of the neighborhood. The latter category includes both poor scavengers and the wealthy Chinese who live along the main road. Of the households that do participate, somewhat more than half join financial self-help organizations that include high contributions and large loans: private ROSCAs, market ROSCAs, open ASCRAs, and credit cooperatives.[11] One often-mentioned reason for not participating in these more expensive organizations is the fear of being unable to meet their financial obligations. Others feel that they can save enough on their own. The following sections describe how those who do participate may or may not derive protection from their organizations.

Direct protection from financial self-help organizations

Financial self-help organizations can provide protection against financial need in two ways. First, as a means of insurance. This exists in most of Bujung's social SHOs and open ASCRAs. Such organizations have emergency funds that are built up from regular contributions paid by all participants. The main problem with these arrangements is that they are usually limited to disbursements for death, and only exceptionally for illness. There is no coverage for crises in housing, education, and unemployment, despite the urgent need. Moreover, the disbursements are comparatively small, most are limited to Rp 10,000. At best, the sum may be as high as Rp 60,000, but funeral costs can easily be ten times that amount.[12]

Second, ROSCAs and ASCRAs may fill financial needs by direct payments from a kitty or by issuing a loan. But participants can only determine to a very limited extent just when they can receive these sums. Most ROSCAs distribute the kitties as a lottery, and it is almost impossible to convince the winner of the kitty to exchange with someone who is in urgent need. ROSCA organizers explained that most participants are so eager to receive their winnings that no one is willing to surrender the kitty. 'Everybody needs the money!'[13] While ASCRAs do not formally allow for taking out a loan when needed, many organizers (supported by a majority of the participants) aim to lend as much as possible to maximize the annual dividend, encouraging all participants without debt to take out new loans, even if they do not need them.[14] As a result, everybody is almost continuously indebted to the ASCRA, and only those who have just repaid their old loan are able to take out a new one.

There are various ways to gain access to the funds, however. For instance, it is possible to take out a loan under someone else's name who is free of debt. A participant explained: 'I allowed Priyanto to borrow in my name. He needed an operation at the hospital, and I feel I cannot refuse him the loan. I have known him for a long time, so there will probably be no problem with repayment.' The true borrower pays the monthly installments on the loan, even though the borrower in name only remains formally responsible. This way the named borrower enables the actual borrower to take out a second loan from the ASCRA, although it is formally prohibited. Organizers of ASCRAs regularly stress that loans should be used for personal purposes only and should not be transferred to others. Secondary borrowing is therefore generally done in secret, and is facilitated by those who participate in the societies primarily to socialize. They do not need to borrow money themselves.

One drawback is that participants must wait to borrow money until the day of the next meeting, which takes place once a month. This makes it difficult to meet urgent necessities directly from ROSCA or ASCRA money. In our survey only one respondent mentioned participating in a ROSCA mainly as protection against adversities, whereas 118 respondents mentioned money and personal savings as reasons for participating.[15] Only one respondent mentioned ROSCAs as the solution for 'the most difficult problem their household had ever experienced,' whereas borrowing money was mentioned most frequently. Financial self-help organizations were mentioned only twelve times as a source for paying a recent hospital bill; gifts (113), savings (73), and loans (29) were much more common ways to pay such emergency expenses. These sums are principally viewed as ways to pay for non-urgent needs, such as home improvements or building a new house. For urgent, pressing needs (such as hospital costs, school fees, and wedding gifts), it is more difficult to call on such self-help loans.

As a consequence, participants who wish to use financial self-help organizations for urgent needs must do so indirectly. They can either use the social capital they have built up during their participation in ROSCAs or ASCRAs, or they can allocate their economic capital so that it provides indirect protection. Although in actual fact this distinction does not describe two separate modes of operation, it does explain how social capital produced in financial SHOs can be used to mobilize economic capital outside these organizations, as well as how economic capital produced in financial SHOs can be used to mobilize other forms of economic capital and social capital outside these organizations.

Managing relations: coping based on social capital

Participation in financial self-help organizations can indirectly provide access to loans or gifts from neighbors, relatives, acquaintances, colleagues – anyone who participates or is connected to the organization. Through participation in a financial SHO, others get to know who you are and that you are able to deal with money in a responsible way. Building up such contacts (for possible later support) can be understood as the production of social capital in financial SHOs.

In recent years the concept of social capital has become increasingly popular in the social sciences, and there are now many interpretations and applications (Woolcock 1998). Here we use a narrow interpretation, similar to Bourdieu, who focused 'on the benefits accruing to individuals by virtue of participation in groups and on the deliberate construction of sociability for the purpose of creating this resource' (Portes 1998:4). In this interpretation Portes takes the concept of social capital as 'decomposable into two elements: first, the social relationship itself that allows individuals to claim access to resources possessed by their associates, and second, the amount and quality of those resources' (ibid.:4-5). In other words, people are able to mobilize (financial) resources if they have meaningful relationships with others who have these resources available, and participation in a financial SHO can be one of the ways to achieve such relationships.

Reciprocity

We need to understand that the exchange of support between relatives and friends (in the broad meaning of the word, including colleagues, acquaintances, and neighbors) is in itself problematic and not self-evident in the context of Bujung.

The Bujungese do not help everybody they know, not even everybody they like. They want to make sure that they will receive something in return, and for that both parties have to trust each other. The practice of helping others is firmly rooted in the norm of reciprocity, a classical theme in anthropology (Gouldner 1973:200).

Reciprocity is the practice whereby 'gifts are given in order to evoke an obligation to give back a gift, which in return will evoke a similar obligation – a never ending chain of gifts and obligations' (Kopytoff 1988: 69). In that sense gifts involve a type of debt, not unlike debts generated by credit transactions. Gouldner (1973:242) explains that reciprocal relations are based on the norm of reciprocity, which entails that 'people should help those who have helped them, and people should not injure those who have helped them.' What is typical of this kind of reciprocity – generalized reciprocity, to use Sahlins' term (1972:193-5) – is that normally the debt is never settled completely. The debtor returns the favor but usually gives a little bit more than he has received. In that way the original creditor becomes the debtor and the debtor the creditor. When this type of exchange has occurred a number of times, the parties may not clearly remember who is indebted to whom, but both feel a responsibility to help the other if they can when the other is in need of help.

Reciprocity mediates risk and trust. The fact that two people engage in a reciprocal relationship shows that they trust each other, that they are willing to take a risk, willing to commit themselves to each other, and that each is capable of fulfilling his obligations towards the other. In this way it is both an exchange of obligations and an exchange of information between both parties. The existence of the norm of reciprocity explains how the act of supporting others might very well be in a person's own interest, and may create a safety network through which support can be mobilized (Rowlands 1995:119;Vel 1994:159-63). Gouldner (1973:201) emphasized that this principle not only applies to arrangements between two individuals, but can also be embedded in a context of normative social relations. There are situations in which A is obliged to help B because B once helped C, which leads to A feeling strongly affiliated to C.[16]

As beautiful as the theory may sound, most Bujungese are very careful when investing in reciprocal relations with others. Except for a small circle of close relatives and intimate friends, people are seldom prepared to give substantial gifts or interest-free loans. They rarely give more than a few thousand rupiah to buy groceries or repay a tenacious moneylender. Such sums solve urgent problems, but their usefulness is clearly limited to small financial needs.

The problem with establishing a reciprocal relationship is that it is never possible to be completely certain that support is properly reciprocated. There is a realistic[17] risk that the other is 'fishing' for money, intending to run away as soon as he has acquired enough. There are many stories circulating in Bujung about people who built up debts from many of their neighbors and then ran away. In some cases the debtor may not even run but remains in the community, ignoring the polite forms of social pressure exercised by his neighbors. If in these transactions favors are not quickly returned, one way or another, support relations can easily turn into a serious quarrel. Jadiyo told me:

> Some years ago my wife lent Rp 75,000 to Asman's wife.... We thought: 'she is a civil servant and has a fixed income, so there is no problem.' It was decided that the money should be repaid on payday, say the tenth of the month. On the tenth my wife went to their house, and Asman's wife said that there was no money. There was no problem, we waited for the next month. That month my wife went back again. Again there was no money, but Bu Asman paid the interest, no more. The third month my wife went back again and knocked on the door for the third time. The door was opened, Asman's wife saw that it was my wife and immediately slammed the door shut again. My wife was mad as hell, and therefore Asman's wife was also angry with my wife.... It was all very embarrassing.

Many Bujungese warned me never to lend any money to anyone, asserting that they themselves never lent money to anyone, but also recalled in disgust the occasions when they had been stupid enough to lend a neighbor some money. As one man said: 'You should only lend money to someone you can trust, but you cannot trust anyone who asks for a loan.' The only reason why some people still lend money to acquaintances is that they give in to those who boldly beg for money, and because they are afraid to look stingy.

A notable exception is *sumbangan*, the financial gifts and gifts in kind that are given in cases of death and illness and at certain ceremonial occasions. Each gift is small, but together they can form substantial sums. All people in a circle of friends and neighbors are expected to give *sumbangan*, and social control is very effective. It is also an investment in a reciprocal group rather than a relationship. This increases the likelihood that such gifts are properly reciprocated by at least part of the group.[18]

The role of financial SHOs

It would be an error to assume that because the arrangements entered into in financial self-help organizations also form a continuous chain of credit and debt, all participants are automatically linked in reciprocal relationships. As we have seen from the unwillingness to exchange opportunities to collect on kitties, joint participation in a ROSCA does not imply a sense of solidarity. Because payments and repayments are stipulated precisely, there is no reason to assume that a generalized reciprocity exists among the participants. No participant of Bujung's ROSCAs and ASCRAs would dream of claiming support from others solely based on joint membership. Nonetheless, joint participation in a financial self-help organization does have a certain relevance.

Some types of financial self-help organizations facilitate social capital more than others. Expanding and strengthening social networks is only possible if participants know each other or have some interaction with each other. Market

ROSCAs and credit cooperatives do not lend themselves to this as easily as do other organizational forms. Private ROSCAs do not usually have official meetings, but at least the participants see each other when the lotteries take place. The significance of social networks in financial self-help organizations is greatest with open ASCRAs and social SHOs, which have elaborate monthly meetings.

Meetings of financial self-help organizations are an important form of social interaction.[19] As one man said: 'wherever there is an activity, there are bound to be ROSCAs or ASCRAs.' The meeting is an occasion to show your face. As one of the participants said: 'By attending these meetings you can make friends. People will know who you are and where you live.' If a self-help organization is organized among members of an existing social network, it is usually expected that people will join it, as do all the others, to confirm the importance of existing social ties. Whether it is a descent group, a group of pedicab drivers, or a neighborhood group, if that group decides to organize a ROSCA or ASCRA, all members of that group must join the arrangement to show that they care. A participant in a financial SHO shows his concern for his fellow participants and shows that he is financially trustworthy. The norm of reciprocity dictates that such an act needs to be rewarded. Exchanges among participants in ROSCAs and ASCRAs take place in a more or less controlled environment, however, which is closely monitored by the organizers and the other participants. Thus reciprocity is more safely established and at the same time is also less powerful. The smaller the risks taken, the smaller the reward, so participants in ROSCAs and ASCRAs cannot hope to gain as much in return as if they had invested in a personal relationship.

Participation in financial self-help organizations is a basic requirement for obtaining material and non-material support from not-so-intimate fellow participants. An upper section electrician explains what kind of support he expects:

> There is an advantage to joining ROSCAs and being active in neighborhood life. Only if a person is exceptionally active in the organization of a self-help organization or participates in many of them, or indeed if he is very active in any other social activity within the community, is he or she likely to receive special attention in times of need. [A normal degree of participation] ensures that when you need help, you do not need to ask people but they will come by themselves. It would be embarrassing if I had to ask.

If a person decides not to participate in a ROSCA or ASCRA, it sends the message that he is not interested in others. It means that he effectively excludes himself from establishing reciprocal relationships with many members of the group. Not only are all the important issues of the neighborhood section, working group, or group of friends discussed at the meeting, but because of its regularity the meeting also becomes the basis for social interactions within the group. Depending on the kind of group and the socio-economic circumstances of the individual, the gradual exclusion from such a group can have real consequences. Bu Joyo is a woman who never attended the ROSCA in her RT. When she had the *slametan* (ceremonial meal) to celebrate the thirty-fifth day of her baby daughter, she not only had to ask for help but she also had to pay those who came to help. Jadiyo, a lower section shop attendant who is not so eager to attend the meetings of the ROSCA RT, said that he increasingly felt like an outsider in his own neighborhood. He explained that the attitude of his neighbors changed towards him because he did not attend the meetings.

Managing money: coping based on indirect allocations

Financial self-help organizations can be useful coping mechanisms in another way: their capital sums can improve access to other forms of economic capital. These sums can provide collateral for loans and provide a good beginning for savings and investment. Credit and savings can offer protection against financial needs, while investment is an attempt to enhance normal living conditions and lessen vulnerability.[20]

Although most of the literature views economic capital as closely related to social capital, it does not receive the same attention. Bourdieu (1989:122) and Portes (1998:7), for example, only have very brief descriptions of economic capital. Scholars like De Haan (2000:344) and Ellis (2000:8) are somewhat more expansive, distinguishing natural capital, physical capital, and financial capital, but their distinction is rather general and lacks context. Economic capital deserves much closer attention, especially the different types of assets and money, the different purposes they are used for, the various special obligations they entail, as well as their specific qualities.[21]

Financial SHOs are unrivalled as a means for acquiring significant amounts of money. The sums that are built up in ROSCAs and ASCRAs are well protected because access to them is difficult, meeting the preference for limited liquidity (Bouman 1994a:117). Neither the participant nor anyone else is able to use the accumulated savings. Not only is it difficult to touch money contributed to a financial self-help organization, but participants feel an obligation to save and contribute on a regular basis. Participants who fail to save regularly are scorned and embarrassed. De Swaan (1996:12) describes this as social constraint toward self-constraint, which causes the participant to become an exemplary saver, able to defer gratification.

Informants frequently mentioned this mechanism as the primary reason to participate in self-help organizations: 'Without ROSCAs I cannot save. If I save in the house I spend my money too easily.' Ratih, a small trader: 'Guyub Rukun [a small ASCRA] is very good for me because if I tried to save at home I would be unable to save. The money is too easily taken. I can spend it on all sorts of things, from presents for people who marry or to enjoy myself. For a loan of Rp 600,000 I only have to save Rp 2,000 per day from the profit of my shop.' Suwarsih, the organizer of a ROSCA says: 'I like my ROSCA because it is impossible to save money in the house. Whenever my husband has had a good day as a *tukang ojek* (motorcycle taxi), I may try to save money in the house, but when a few days later there is no money coming in and the children are screaming, I am bound to take money from those savings. It is better not to have any money in the house.' Bu Karto, a participant in another ROSCA, says that she likes to join ROSCAs because it is only a little bit each day, and that is not so difficult (*tidak terasa*). The street trader Surono adds: 'The advantage of ROSCAs is that it becomes a fixed expenditure. You can count on it. Every month there is the electricity bill and the water bill. The same way we know that on certain dates we have to spend money on the ROSCA. When we try to save on our own, we would miss all the social contacts, and we would also not be able to save as much as we save now.'

Collateral for loans

The Bujungese have a wide array of options for obtaining loans, and each option has different characteristics, qualities, and disadvantages. The bank gives relatively large, cheap loans, but requires sufficient collateral. Employers can pay wages in advance and do not deduct interest payments. As we have seen, relatives and neighbors, if they are prepared to do so, provide loans that are interest-free but leave the borrower morally indebted. Pawnshops provide loans based on pawned assets, which are lost if the borrower is unable to repay at the stipulated time. Moneylenders generally do not ask any questions, but demand a very high interest rate. And finally, small neighborhood shops (where prices are higher than at the market) may be willing to provide goods on credit, but only for regular customers. For filling sudden financial needs, availability is an important factor. Loans from moneylenders are quite readily available, while bank loans can take a great deal of time. Loans from employers are widely preferred, but their credit is usually limited to a month's wage, and many Bujungese have already used that option. Loans from relatives and friends are inexpensive but difficult to get and often small.

Accumulated sums from financial SHOs are useful for borrowing because they can serve as collateral for loans. This leads to a widespread system throughout Bujung called '*gali lobang tutup lobang*.' The expression means 'dig a hole, fill a hole,' and refers to the practice of taking on new loans to repay old ones. In principle, the practice of repaying loans with loans can create a long chain of indebtedness. A loan from a neighbor is repaid with a loan from a brother, which in turn is repaid by a loan from a moneylender, a pawnshop, or the bank.[22] Agus, a furniture maker, explains:

> When we are talking about *gali lobang tutup lobang*, it means that when you have a loan with a friend, you have set a date to return it. Suppose that at that date you do not have the money, then you ask for postponement (*semaya*). You can not ask for postponement all the time because that person will become angry. Three times is the maximum. To solve this problem you can take out a loan with another friend, with whom you start on friendly terms. This can go on forever, but you have to have a lot of friends for it, more than two.

Using accumulated sums in ROSCAs and ASCRAs as collateral for loans from other sources are part of this practice. The borrower indicates to a lender, who may be a friend or a professional moneylender, that he is likely to receive a loan or kitty in the near future. He promises the lender that he will repay the loan immediately as soon as his winning is paid. Nugroho suggested that this was his primary motivation for joining a ROSCA: 'We joined a ROSCA of Rp 6,000 per day. That will give us 5.1 million rupiah within two years time. This ROSCA can be useful for collateral. When we need money we can show a friend who has money that we joined this ROSCA. When we receive the kitty we can use it to repay the loan.' This way the participants of ROSCAs and ASCRAs have access to their money when they need it, but before they are actually entitled to it.

A chain of debts can get out of control, creating a spiraling debt cycle (Rahman 1999:78), and the Bujungese are very much aware of that. In Bujung, the story of Harjo is often recalled. He was a pedicab driver who liked drinking and gambling. Harjo had debts all the time, but he was always able to repay them sooner or later. One day Harjo had the opportunity to buy his house at a cheap price. He took the offer and borrowed money to pay for the house. The loan was a little too high for Harjo, and he had problems with repaying it. Later Harjo fell ill. The stories claim it was the stress of having the large loan that made him sick. Harjo had to stop working, and he could not repay his debts. When his condition became serious, there was no money to bring him to the hospital, and so he died. Whether the story is entirely true or not, it serves as a reminder not to be too careless about *gali lobang tutup lobang*.

Nonetheless, the practice of repaying loans with loans can have positive aspects, as it helps people cope with financial difficulties. It also makes it possible to keep the loans current. This is very important because of the pressure to pay a loan when it is due. Expensive loans can also be burdensome, such as those from a moneylender or bank. They can also become very urgent if money has been owed for a long time (especially to a close relative like a brother). Whenever the borrower meets his brother, he may feel embarrassed that he has not repaid the loan, especially if his brother's wife is in the hospital and he knows his brother needs money for an operation. If money is not readily available, many Bujungese prefer to replace urgent loans with loans that are less urgent and less onerous in order to obtain a few weeks respite. Inability to repay loans can create tension, conflict, and loss of reputation, and it can also mean the loss of goods that served as collateral for the loan.

The availability of collateral not only reassures lenders, but also provides borrowers with more confidence that the transaction will take place as planned. Most borrowers worry that they are not able to repay a loan from a friend. They are embarrassed if they fail to repay, (i.e., violating the norm of reciprocity). Setro, a dishwasher, says: 'When you borrow money from someone, you do not want to be indebted for too long, and you do not want to have too many debts with too many different people. Then you will get dizzy. Therefore, it is often good to borrow from an ASCRA to close a previous loan.' If it is a loan from a professional moneylender, borrowers worry about the high interest payment. Without their expectation of receiving accumulated sums from their financial self-help organizations, many borrowers would not dare engage in such credit relations.

Participating in as many financial self-help organizations as possible can facilitate the use of these sums as collateral. Their quality as collateral depends partly on how soon the windfall arrives. The more frequently a participant can obtain new windfalls, the greater are his chances to secure a loan. In addition, if someone participates in a number of financial self-help organizations, the security of a loan no longer depends on any single windfall.

Providing a good start to saving

The second form of indirect allocation is converting it to savings, and here, too, there are several options. Apart from participation in financial self-help organizations, the Bujungese also save at home and in the bank. Savings at home can be in the form of cash or property, such as gold, building materials, chickens, pedicabs, televisions, and other durable goods. Each form of savings has specific advantages and disadvantages. Bank savings yield interest, but the bank requires relatively large deposits, and the money can only be accessed during business hours. Cash savings are easy to access when needed but easily spent on trivial matters. This latter problem is considerably less with savings in the form of property. This type of savings is also less subject to sudden inflation, and can be used before conversion to cash. On the other hand, it may be necessary to accumulate a substantial amount of money before such assets can be purchased.

With savings it is a matter of finding the right balance between liquidity and the lack of it. While money needs to be available for an emergency, it should not be readily available when someone asks to borrow some or when the snack seller passes by. To keep savings safe, they need to be set aside one way or another, and they should have a distinct status, not confused with daily shopping money or pocket money, and spent for such purposes. The best way is to keep it in a separate place, such as a moneybox or a savings account, or to keep it in a different form (i.e., in the form of property).

If participants receive a sum from their financial self-help organization before they actually need it, they can try to protect themselves against possible future adversities and deficiencies by placing such sums in a personal security fund to be drawn upon in times of financial need. They can also use the sum to expand household income. Ratmi explains: 'We have a bank account where we bring our extras. When the big sums from the ROSCA come in we usually bring it to the bank first, before we spend it on the expenditure we planned.' Some people decide to deposit the money from an ASCRA loan in their savings account, and then pay their installments from regular income. In the same way people also deposit the kitties from ROSCAs in the bank or use the money to buy gold. Larger amounts are much easier to retain than smaller ones, and depositing it in the bank or converting it to gold makes it even more difficult to get at. In many cases those savings become earmarked as special purpose money: to pay school fees or for 'unexpected needs.'

Investment

The third option is to invest the sums received to improve household income so that the family is less vulnerable to adversities and deficiencies. This can be effective, but for most people in Bujung the ability to invest in enterprises is very limited. Most entrepreneurial activities require a substantial one-time investment; it is fairly difficult to make sequential investments that expand revenues. One reason for this is that expanding production often requires additional workers. Most entrepreneurs in Bujung are careful not to hire anyone to work in their business except spouses and children. Regular employees are more expensive, are considered less trustworthy, and require constant control. Moreover, they are likely to ask for loans or prepayment of wages. Many business owners in Bujung do not want to employ anyone in their business, because 'a worker will be more of a burden than a help.'

Another reason for this reluctance to hire outsiders is that expanding production also requires more customers. When discussing investment with a food-stall owner on the main street, the owner said: 'Well, I could build another level on top of my stall, but that does not mean that I would sell more. Now, every day I prepare nine kilos of rice. Some days I sell all of those nine kilos and other days there are some leftovers. There is a lot of competition here. With more seats I would not sell more food. It is better to use the money for a sewing course for my daughter.'[23] Few of the (aspiring) small-scale entrepreneurs of Bujung are willing to take the risk of taking out a loan to invest in business. Most small-scale businesses in Bujung have been started with the owner's own capital, obtained from an inheritance or some form of *rezeki,*[24] or with a 'soft' loan from a friend or relative. Moreover, since loans from most ASCRAs have strict terms of repayment, they are not attractive for small business investors.

Relation to other coping mechanisms

Participation in financial SHOs produces social and economic capital.[25] Both forms of capital can be used to cope with adversities and deficiencies that lead to financial difficulties in the household budget, difficulties that are an inherent consequence of the fluctuating financial cycles that most Bujung households have to live with. The production and mobilization of social and economic capital involves activities by alert individuals who have an eye for what can and what cannot be achieved and are able to take advantage of the situation.

The social capital produced through financial SHOs can take the form of personal contacts with other participants and of a favorable reputation in social and financial affairs. These can make it more likely for a person to obtain support in times of need and serve as a kind of 'human collateral' for risky loans. But the financial benefits available in Bujung that are based on social capital are limited. The Bujungese are reluctant to engage in reciprocal relationships; they fear that investments in these relationships will not bring any returns. The social capital produced in financial SHOs leads to little more than a broader access to small short-term loans and to non-material or practical support. For these reasons, most people in Bujung focus on coping strategies based on direct investment in economic capital rather than in social capital. It is much more certain and much less troublesome to invest excess income in personal assets, to deposit it in the bank or invest it rather than give it to neighbors, relatives, or friends.

The main advantage of ROSCA and ASCRA kitties and loans is that they impose limited liquidity and self-restraint. Savings accumulating in financial SHOs are thus protected against financial erosion because the saver has no intermediate access to his money. Nevertheless, these 'protections' are also the largest disadvantage of financial self-help organizations. The sums are so inaccessible that it is difficult to activate them when adversities and deficiencies occur. Participants of ROSCAs and ASCRAs often have to wait several months before they have access to the much-needed sums. That is why financial SHOs only play an indirect (but important) role in helping to cope with adversities and deficiencies.

The financial landscape of urban Yogyakarta contains many different financial practices. Though each of these practices has specific characteristics, most are more readily accessible for coping with sudden financial need. Mobilization of household savings in cash and property, as well as loans or gifts from employers, relatives, friends, pawnshops, and moneylenders are much more important in this regard. They are the sources for coping with medical costs, school fees, and other prohibitive expenses.

This does not mean that financial self-help organizations are irrelevant for coping with insecurities. Without participation in financial self-help organizations, many of the most commonly used coping mechanisms would be unavailable. A remarkable example of this is the way in which secondary lending from ASCRAs can facilitate a reciprocal relationship. Bu Bantoro, an elderly blind woman, belongs to an ASCRA named UKK.[26] Living with her children, she cannot do much with loans from UKK. Instead she lends part of the loans she is entitled to to neighboring women who come to visit her. She also gives some of the UKK loans to her children who provide her with food and shelter.

The financial sums from ROSCAs and ASCRAs allow people to repay large loans from relatives, friends, and moneylenders. In many cases the expected sums are explicitly claimed as security for such emergency loans. The contribution of financial self-help organizations to household savings is probably even more significant. ROSCAs and ASCRAs create a collective pressure to save, making it more difficult to get at the contributions. This enables people to save relatively large amounts of money. Without ROSCAs and ASCRAs, few people would be able to convert their small incomes into jewelry and other assets, or to make deposits to their bank accounts. In short, the 'problem,' or disadvantage, of a lack of liquidity is solved by using financial self-help organizations in strategic combinations with other savings techniques and sources of credit. Each source of money open to the Bujungese can only be tapped in a limited way, at particular moments, and against certain costs. These different sources of capital, however, allow people to combine the various resources in a useful way and adapt to their specific limitations.[27]

Comparison with other countries

A comparison of the situation in Bujung with research findings by Bähre, Kane, Bijnaar, and Smets reveals a number of differences and similarities.[28] The two African examples stand out in the area of direct provision of help through insurance. Bähre reports that almost everyone in the South African Xhosa slum where he worked participated in burial societies. These societies usually provided more than half the cost of a funeral. Kane, too, found high participation rates in burial societies in Senegal, with relatively high provision of benefits. Furthermore, among Senegalese migrants in France he also found arrangements that insured against illness, accidents, police fines, and visits back to Senegal (Kane 2001:174-180). This contrasts with what Bijnaar found for the Creoles in Surinam: there were some funeral funds, but only very small, almost symbolic, disbursements. In the poor slums of the Indian cities of Sangli and Hyderabad, Smets found no insurance funds whatsoever among the financial self-help organizations.

In all research areas participants are limited in their capacity to influence the time when the sums from ROSCAs or ASCRAs will be disbursed. Unlike Bujung, in the South African example people hardly ever exchanged their turn at funds in ROSCAs, although secondary lending in ASCRAs where borrowing is mandatory is somewhat more common. Exchanging turns is occasionally pursued in the Indian example, but not often successfully, because this is an issue that may stir up conflicts between participants. Only among Surinamese migrants in The Netherlands is it usual for needy ROSCA participants to ask for priority in distributing a kitty, mainly because of urgent debts to companies or service providers. Although organizers are reluctant to do so, in extreme cases they are prepared to give priority to one of their participants (Bijnaar 2002:179-80).

As for mobilization of social capital as an indirect means of protection, Bähre, Bijnaar, and Smets mention instances where ROSCA participants received material support from other participants when struck by adversity. Bähre (1999:14) gives the example of a participant whose shack burned down, and fellow participants provided blankets, pots and pans, and other household items. In Surinam this support is only provided by the organizer, because the participants tend not to know each other. Smets remarks that in India support from fellow participants is not always provided, but depends very much on the nature of the relationships among participants, the history of the organization, and the social context. In all these examples (including Bujung), support cannot automatically be expected from other participants simply because of shared membership. Participation in financial self-help organizations may only strengthen the social capital that already exists, and is rooted in other relationships of friendship or kinship.

When economic capital from financial self-help organizations is indirect, loans from ROSCAs and ASCRAs are used to repay debts as explicit or implicit collateral for loans, not only in Bujung, but in other countries as well. This is quite common in India and among Surinamese immigrants in The Netherlands, and probably takes place in Surinam itself and in South Africa, although it is less common there. As far as using these sums to provide a good start for savings, it is common in all cases to use these sums to purchase assets of various kinds. Kane (2001:77) found that 47 per cent of the sums from neighborhood ROSCAs in Dakar are used for consumption purposes. The researchers doubted if those assets are mobilized to cope with adversities or deficiencies, because when assets are sold or pawned to deal with an immediate need, this cannot be planned for beforehand – as occasionally happens in Bujung. Bähre adds that the items purchased by South African Xhosa in Cape Town are not really in demand by buyers or pawnshops.

Altogether, the general picture that emerged in Bujung applies to other places as well. Financial SHOs provide protection through the strategic ways participants manage to accumulate and exchange social and economic capital by combining those resources with other relationships and arrangements. The insurance function, though more important in Sub-Saharan Africa, remains rather limited. In South Africa insurance does not go beyond funerals, and the associations of Senegalese migrants in France seems to be exceptional.

Explanations for the absence of insurance and assistance in financial self-help organizations

Why is the commitment to insurance and assistance in financial self-help organizations in developing countries not very strong? Given the extent of the adversities or deficiencies experienced by their participants, there is certainly a potential need. Many social SHOs and open ASCRAs (and some credit cooperatives) maintain small funeral funds. A few organizations even have a health fund. But these efforts are very limited: they do not begin to meet the need. Compared to Senegal and South Africa, they are especially small in Bujung. There, as in most other places, nothing is done for the disabled, the aged, fire, unemployment, housing, or education. There is also a need for a special fund to meet the costs and burdens of ceremonial festivities. But none of this is organized, and each individual household must find its own way to deal with these costs by themselves. Why?

It is not simply that Indonesian financial self-help organizations are not ready to take on these burdens, or that perhaps in the course of time they will develop insurance and assistance arrangements. Such an evolutionary perception of institutional development does not seem plausible. Over the past decades, despite massive social and economic change, there are no indications that such a development is emerging, and there is no reason to assume automatically that this will happen in the future. What must be taken into account are the actual circumstances in which these institutions are situated.

In a recent article Das Gupta (1993:61-62) gives a number of preliminary suggestions to explain why Indian mutual associations did not focus on security and insurance. While these may be true for the Indian situation that Das Gupta describes, they fail to explain the absence of large funeral funds in Indonesia. His first explanation, a lack of experience with insurance, does not play an important role, because the Indonesians have long experience with smaller funeral funds. Das Gupta also points to the high mobility of Indian laborers, who continuously move from one place to another. This cannot explain the reluctance to engage in long-term insurance arrangements in Bujung, where the population is not so mobile. Das Gupta also assumes a lack of time, energy, and money, the latter also being the reason given by the people in Bujung themselves. Considering that Indonesians invest much time, energy, and money in ROSCA and ASCRA arrangements, this explanation is not very convincing. A lack of actuarial skills (suggested by De Swaan 1996:13), may well be an impediment to assistance arrangements targeted at disability and old age, but does not explain the limited development of funeral funds. Funeral funds are relatively easy to manage, and the average number of deaths in a given period is not too difficult to estimate. Even if a shortage of funds should occur, it could be solved simply with a loan from a linked ASCRA. This leads us to conclude that there must be a more fundamental reason for the absence of insurance and assistance.

The availability of alternative forms of protection might be considered a prohibiting factor. De Swaan (1996:13) suggests that the prevalence of ROSCAs and ASCRAs in many developing countries can be explained by the presence of sufficient alternatives to obtain insurance outside of the self-help organizations – and the absence of such alternatives for savings. This may play a role in developing countries. Relatives, friends, and neighbors do offer help when there is death or illness, and those Indonesians who are entitled to a pension have less reason to join local pension schemes. Nevertheless, it is not at all evident that these alternatives are so much better than what the financial self-help organizations offer. Furthermore, the abundance of alternative forms of saving and credit has not prevented the establishment of ROSCAs and ASCRAs.

What clearly plays a role is the nature of the adversities and deficiencies for which insurance and assistance are sought. Some of these cases are too difficult to deal with through local insurance and assistance arrangements. A well-known problem is the covariate risk. If a large number of the participants are likely to suffer from adversities or deficiencies at the same time, there is little scope for effective protection. This is true for the un(der)employment, which is most often associated with a period of recession, as in the recent economic crisis. A similar problem occurs with provisions for old age. When the average age of existing members in a self-help organization increases, it becomes more difficult to attract younger members to supply the funds for members who have become inactive (De Swaan 1996:13). This problem can be solved by substituting a single sum upon retirement for regular pension payments, an option that only requires a simple savings fund with each participant providing for his own retirement[29] – although such an arrangement provides only limited protection. Quite another problem is that of adversities that occur irregularly: it is difficult to establish a disability fund if there are no claims for many years. The same is true for fire, which also rarely happens in a small community. With such adversities it is impossible to estimate the amount of money that needs to be reserved, a problem that can only be overcome by insuring the risk at a higher level.[30]

A third problem is that many risks and needs are not equally relevant for everyone. Social security arrangements cannot be set up for any arbitrary group of people; they need to be based on existing social networks of people with similar needs, whether in a neighborhood setting, family, or work. Homogeneous background does not imply homogeneous needs. It is clear that a specialized housing scheme is difficult to establish when some members of a social group are more in need of a (better) house than others are. And finally, there are some risks that are considered to be the victim's fault, which makes it difficult to judge whether someone is really entitled to support. For example, if someone is penniless or unemployed, it is difficult to determine whether he was unlucky or just lazy and irresponsible. We have seen that even illness is looked upon with suspicion. A related problem is that some risks are voluntarily entered into. If someone chooses to organize an extravagant marriage celebration or sends his children to tertiary education and then has financial problems, it is only reasonable that his neighbors will not be prepared to step in with immediate assistance.

But admitting the reasonableness of this, it is still feasible to establish larger funds for funeral payments. There is even some scope for arrangements targeted at illness, housing, and ceremonial festivities. For such arrangements to function properly, however, there needs to be a sufficient degree of trust. This is one of the points made by De Swaan (1996:14), who emphasizes the need for trustworthy treasurers. Historically this was a role taken on by owners of bars and clergymen who, for different reasons, were seen as reliable guardians of money (Van der Linden 1996:31). As we have seen, there are also a number of people in Bujung who inspire confidence, a fundamental requirement for organizers of ROSCAs and ASCRAs. There is a significant difference, however, between trusting people to be controllers and trusting them to be guardians of money. Emergency funds, unlike ROSCAs and ASCRAs, work with full funds between meetings of the organization, and these funds must be kept in custody. During meetings, participants can quite effectively check on the work of the treasurer, but what he does with the money between meetings is not so easy to discover. The funds can be misused by dishonest treasurers. Indonesians are very used to people taking something for themselves when they get an opportunity, and this is an important reason for keeping contributions to emergency funds at minimum amounts.

But is trust so much greater in Senegal and South Africa (the research areas where Bähre and Kane found much more effective funeral funds)? Certainly in the violent conflict-ridden community in Cape Town this is not the case. Perhaps the key is located in the funeral costs. In both South Africa and Senegal the dead are supposed to be buried in their places of origin, which involves very high transportation costs. In Bujung, on the other hand, the dead are buried quickly, and brought to a graveyard that is never far away. Costs of funeral ceremonies are also high, but nothing like in South Africa, where a funeral may cost as much as half a year's household income. In such a context people are perhaps forced to overcome the problem of trust because of the prohibitive cost of funerals; they must take a risk that the Bujungese are not willing to accept.

Another barrier in Bujung is the difficult relationship between the upper and the lower sections (Lont 2002:27-66). There is more hostility than solidarity between the different sections of the neighborhood. Isolated initiatives to bridge this gap merely reinforced the existing divide,[31] a social cleavage that pretty much precludes the establishment of an insurance and assistance program at the level of the neighborhood, which would substantially redistribute resources from the not-so-poor to the poor. If such a program were possible, the advantage of scale could help to deal with some of the problems of risk management outlined above.

Finally, we can also take into account Platteau's suggestion (1997) that the notion of insurance is unacceptable in societies governed by the principle of balanced reciprocity. Arrangements in which some people benefit more than others because they were 'lucky enough' to experience adversity can be perceived as fundamentally unfair in such a cultural framework. Platteau bases his argument on observations of traditional rural communities in Sub-Saharan Africa, but the idea can be recognized to a certain degree in the Indonesian context as well, at least for receiving equal shares. In ASCRAs and ROSCAs participants are always very insistent on receiving their fair share (the proportionality principle, which requires that each should contribute and benefit equally). Each ASCRA participant should take out the same amount of credit, so that each pays the same amount of interest. During the economic crisis many Bujungese insisted that each household receive the same amount of rice, whether rich or poor. Along the same lines, it could be argued that collective insurance and assistance arrangements are too impersonal. They deprive people of opportunities to express or create a social relationship through a personal gesture of help. The dominant set of norms and values with regard to support may very well be another strong barrier to establishing insurance funds at the community level.[32]

Conclusion

An analytical model that regards financial self-help organizations as instruments for the accumulation and exchange of economic and social capital can help assess their social security function. But attributing a true social security function to financial self-help organizations may be somewhat premature. Bujung's organizations hardly provide immediate and direct security to their participants. Direct insurance arrangements are a form of collective action that is very difficult to achieve.

Instead, the social security function of financial self-help organizations has several different forms (with various advantages and disadvantages), which varies considerably from one type of organization to another. The evidence also suggests that the protection provided by financial SHOs is closely linked to social networks and to other financial arrangements, which participants themselves must combine in a strategic and purposeful way. Hence, the social security function of financial self-help organizations should be studied in context rather than assumed *a priori*.

Notes

1 This research was financed by the Royal Netherlands Academy of Arts and Sciences (KNAW). I also wish to thank Juliette Koning for substantial comments on an earlier version.
2 Ahmad et al. (1991), F. von Benda-Beckmann et al. (1988), F. and K. von Benda-Beckmann (1994), Dixon & Scheurell (1995), Van Ginneken (1999), Meereboer (1994a; 1994b) and Midgley (1984) situate this problem as a field of research.
3 ROSCA stands for Rotating Savings and Credit Association, a particular type of financial self-help organization whereby participants contribute to a kitty, which is given to each participant in turn.
4 The issue of financial self-help organizations and social security has become all the more timely because of the recently growing interest in 'microinsurance,' a direct spinoff of microfinance. Its growing popularity can be seen from the several workshops that have been organized recently, among others, by CARE and MBP-DAI, ICWC and UNCDF, and the ILO. See also 'The Microfinance Newsletter' (Credit and Development Forum, Dhaka), No.7, 2000, and the theme issue of 'Small Enterprise Development,' Vol.12, No.1, 2001.
5 This chapter focuses on some of the institutions intended to provide protection against contingencies, but in data collection the contingencies themselves formed an equally important starting point.
6 This is true for some coolies and pedicab drivers whose circumstances are discussed below.
7 RT stands for Rukun Tetangga, a neighborhood group comprised of around 40 households. Five or six RTs together make one RW (Rukun Warga).
8 For vivid descriptions of neighborhood life in Yogyakarta, see Guinness (1986) and Sullivan (1992).
9 The full names of these institutions are Rotating Savings and Credit Associations (ROSCAs) and Accumulating Savings and Credit Associations (ASCRAs). See also Ardener (1995) and Bouman (1995b). In daily conversation, the term *arisan* is used not only for the ROSCA itself, but also to refer to the organization that hosts the ROSCA, often together with other types of financial arrangements.
10 Most people in Bujung, including those who participate in financial self-help organizations, also have bank accounts. Only a small proportion, especially the larger entrepreneurs and formal sector workers, are able to obtain credit through their banks.
11 Although it may be supposed that participation in high contribution SHOs is limited to the wealthier inhabitants of Bujung, those who live in the upper section, this is not the case. On average, the people from the lower section invest a larger part of their income in financial SHOs.

12 These insurance arrangements are also seldom mentioned in the literature on financial self-help organizations in Java. Exceptions are Kakisina et al. (1991:13), Bouman and Moll (1992:214), and Patma-Mingoen (1980:94). Kakisina et al. share my observation that these funds are relatively small. Bouman and Moll, however, describe a self-help organization of pedicab drivers in the center of Yogyakarta in which the emergency fund is the central arrangement.

13 An exception took place in a lower section ROSCA RT. Here it was decided that two participants, who were unable to work because of illness, could take precedence in the lottery of the ROSCA. If surrendering a kitty were possible anywhere, it would be in a ROSCA RT, where the kitties are small and participants frequently meet outside the meetings as well. In general, however, it is not true that '[I]f one is the victim of a sudden misfortune... one can always persuade the other members to take the pool out of turn,' as Geertz (1962:427) states for Modjokuto. Bouman (1995b:378) also mentions this to be a widespread practice in ROSCAs in general; other Indonesian observations can be found in Murray (1991:79) and Mai (1992:7). It remains difficult to determine why this practice is absent in Bujung, but it is possible that these observers were misled by an ideology of solidarity on the part of their informants.

14 This can be called the proportionality principle. All participants are expected to make the same contributions to the annual dividend so that nobody benefits more than anyone else.

15 More precisely, we asked respondents about the umbrella they had set aside for a rainy day, in reference to the well-known proverb '*Sedia payung sebelum hujan.*' The survey was held among 156 households equally divided over the upper and lower sections of the neighborhood.

16 See also Portes (1998:7-9) who mentions internalized norms, calculation, and social pressure as possible forms of motivation for others to make resources available on the basis of social capital.

17 I mean realistic in the sense that this risk is perceived to be realistic by most Bujungese.

18 Another sphere where reciprocal exchange seems to be much less problematic is that of non-material favors. If you help others, people come to visit you when you are ill, when your mother is dying, when your son is being circumcized, etc.

19 Financial SHOs are not the only meaningful form of interaction. In and around Bujung there are many ways to come into contact with other people. It is possible to stay on the streets and alleys to chat, to engage in voluntary community work to build sewers, bridges, and pavements, and to attend each other's ritual ceremonies.

20 See Drèze and Sen (1991:3-4) on protection and promotion.

21 Studies that thoroughly discuss the implications of different types of money include Carsten (1989), Shipton (1989), and Zelizer (1989).

22 Place in the sequence is largely determined by the seniority or urgency of a loan (see Hospes 1997:9).

23 Of course, investments in education for children also serve a similar final purpose.

24 The word *rezeki* has a connotation of luck, and is used to refer to a windfall, sudden income that is relatively large and unexpected.

25 This chapter focuses on the usefulness of the different forms of capital produced in financial SHOs but not on those required for financial SHOs. Economic and social capital is obviously also required to participate in financial self-help organizations, to pay the contributions and to become eligible as a participant. The different forms of protection against adversities and deficiencies described in this chapter are naturally only an option for those who (can) participate in financial self-help organizations.

26 The emergence and development of UKK is described in detail in Lont (2002:103-131).

27 This juggling with social and economic capital, with financial mechanisms and arrangements involves decision making. The decisions that people make can to a certain extent be explained in terms of the social-economic circumstances of life in Bujung. Still, different people make different decisions, and in fact it is possible to speak of a repertoire of options (compare Vel 1994:6-14). Differences can be explained in terms of social networks and social background. An actively religious civil servant, born and raised in Bujung, has different options than a non-religious unskilled laborer who recently moved to the city.

28 This section is based on Bähre (1999; 2000; 2002), Kane (2001), Bijnaar (1998; 2002), Smets (1992; 2000; 2002) and on personal communications with these four researchers.

29 A similar solution applies to an education fund where there would be a covariate need for funds because most school fees have to be paid in the same month each year.

30 We should keep in mind that the limited ability to cope with these aspects of risk management also disrupted the mutual associations in nineteenth-century Europe (see Van der Linden 1996:30-32).

31 See Lont (2002:171).

32 In their evaluation of a health insurance program in Guinea Conakry, Criel and Waelkens (2001) recently refuted Platteau's view. The program officers were able to explain the rationale of insurance to participants. The possibility remains that introduction of an insurance principle that contradicts the principle of general reciprocity is more easily introduced by an outside agency than by a local initiative.

References

Ahmad, E. et al.(eds)
1991 *Social Security in Developing Countries.* Oxford: Clarendon Press.

Alexander, J.
1987 *Trade, Traders and Trading in Rural Java.* Oxford: Oxford University Press.

Ardener, S.
1995 'Women Making Money Go Round: ROSCAs revisited.' In: S. Ardener and S. Burman (eds), *Money-Go-Rounds*, 1-19. Oxford: Berg.

Bähre, E.
1999 'Financial Self-help Groups in South-Africa; An Overview.' *Werk in Uitvoering* 64, Amsterdam: ASSR.
2002 *Money and Violence; Financial Mutuals Among the Xhosa in Cape Town, South Africa.* PhD thesis, University of Amsterdam.

Bijnaar, A.
1998 'Wat je zaait zal je oogsten! Dwang en zelfdwang in Creools-Surinaamse onderlinges.' *Amsterdams Sociologisch Tijdschrift*, 25(3):329-70.
2002 *Kasmoni: spaarzame levensgenieters in Suriname en Nederland.* PhD-thesis, University of Amsterdam.

Bouman, F.J.A.
1994a 'Informal Rural Finance; An Aladdin's Lamp of Information.' In: F.J.A. Bouman & O. Hospes (eds), *Financial Landscapes Reconstructed*, 105-22. Boulder: Westview Press.
1994b 'ROSCA and ASCRA; Beyond the Financial Landscape.' In: F.J.A. Bouman & O. Hospes (eds), *Financial Landscapes Reconstructed*, 375-94. Boulder: Westview Press.
1995a 'ROSCA: On the Origin of the Species.' *Savings and Development*, 19(2):117-48.

1995b 'Rotating and Accumulating Savings and Credit Associations; A Development Perspective.' *World Development*, 23(3):371-84.

Bouman, F.J.A. & H.A.J. Moll
1992 'Informal Finance in Indonesia.' In: D.W. Adams & D.A. Fitchett (eds), *Informal Finance in Low-income Countries*, 209-23. Boulder: Westview Press.

Burgess, R. & N. Stern
1991 'Social Security in Developing Countries; What, Why, Who, and How?' In: E. Ahmad et al. (eds), *Social Security in Developing Countries*, 41-80. Oxford: Clarendon Press.

Calomiris, C.W. & I. Rajaraman
1998 'The Role of ROSCAs; Lumpy Durables or Event Insurance?' *Journal of Development Economics*, 56:207-216.

Carsten, J.
1989 'Cooking Money; Gender and the Symbolic Transformation of Means of Exchange in a Malay Fishing Community.' In: J. Parry & M. Bloch (eds), *Money and the Morality of Exchange*, 117-141. Cambridge: Cambridge University Press.

Criel, B. & M.P. Waelkens
2001 'The Social Perception of a Mutual Health Organization in Guinea-Conakry (West Africa).' Paper, Conference on Livelihood, Savings and Debt, Wageningen, 14-16 May.

Das Gupta, R.
1993 'Social Security and Mutual Assistance in India; A Preliminary Account.' *International Social Security Review*, 46(3):53-68.

De Haan, L.J.
2000 'Globalization, Localization and Sustainable Livelihood.' *Sociologia Ruralis*, 40:339-65.

De Swaan, A.
1989 *Zorg en de staat; Welzijn, onderwijs en gezondheidszorg in Europa en de Verenigde Staten in de nieuwe tijd*. Amsterdam: Bert Bakker.
1996 'Onderlinge fondsen; Toen en hier nu en daar.' In: M. Van der Linden & J. Sluijs (eds), *Onderlinge Hulpfondsen*, 9-22. Amsterdam: IISG.

Dixon, J. & R. P. Scheurell (eds)
1995 *Social Security Programs; A Cross-cultural Comparative Perspective*. Westport, Connecticut: Greenwood Press.

Dreze, J. & A. Sen
1991 Public Action for Social Security; Foundations and Strategy.' In: Ehtisham Ahmad et al. (eds), *Social security in developing countries*, 3-40. Oxford: Clarendon Press.

Ellis, F.
2000 *Rural Livelihoods and Diversity in Developing Countries*. Oxford: Oxford University Press.

Galjart, B.
1994 'Social Security in Development Countries; Political and Economic Aspects.' In: M.-T. Meereboer (ed), *Social (In)Security and Poverty as Global Issues; Pre-conference Reader*, 19-26. The Hague: DVL/OS.

Geertz, C.
1962 'The Rotating Credit Association; a "middle rung" in development.' *Economic Development and Cultural Change*, 10(3):241-63.

Gerdes, V.
1975 'Precursors of Modern Social Security in Indigenous African Institutions.' *The Journal of Modern African Studies*, 13:209-28.

Gouldner, A.W.
1973 *For Sociology. Renewal and Critique in Sociology Today.* London: Allen Lane.
Guinness, P.
1986 *Harmony and Hierarchy in a Javanese Kampung.* Singapore: Oxford University Press.
Hirtz, F.
1994 'Issues and Authors in the Field of Social Security in the Third World; An Introduction.' *Focaal,* 22/23:231-6.
1995 *Managing Insecurity; State Social Policy and Family Networks in the Rural Philippines.* Saarbrucken: Verlag fur Entwicklungspolitik.
Hospes, O.
1997 'New Studies on Informal Finance; Exploring the State-of-the-art and the Art of the State.' *Savings and Development,* 21(1):5-18.
Kakisina, S. et al.
1991 'A Study of Arisans in the Regency of Boyolali.' Fakultas Ekonomi, Universitas Kristen Satya Wacana, Salatiga.
Kane, A.
2001 *Les caméléons de la finance populaire au Sénégal et dans la diaspora; Dynamique des tontines et des caisses villageoises entre Thilogne, Dakar et La France.* PhD-thesis University of Amsterdam.
Kopytoff, I.
1988 The Cultural Biography of Things; Commoditization as a Process.' In: Arjun Appadurai (ed.), *The Social Life of Things,* 64-91. Cambridge: Cambridge University Press.
Lont, H.
2002 *Juggling Money in Yogyakarta; Financial Self-help Organizations and the Quest for Security.* PhD-thesis, University of Amsterdam.
Lydon, G.
1992 'Banking à l'Africaine; Prevalence and Popularity of Rotating Savings and Credit Associations.' African Studies Thesis, McGill University
Mai, U.
1992 'Credit, Consensus, and Power; The Local Association as a Modern Institution of Socialization.' SDRC working paper, No. 167, University of Bielefeld.
Marshall, T.H.
1975 *Social Policy in the Twentieth Century.* London: Hutchinson. [New Edition].
Meereboer, M.T. (ed.)
1994a *Social (In)Security and Poverty as Global Issues. Pre-conference Reader.* The Hague: DVL/OS.
1994b *Social (In)Security and Poverty as Global Issues.* The Hague: DVL/OS.
Midgley, J.
1984 *Social Security, Inequality and the Third World.* Chichester: John Wiley & sons.
1994 'Social Security Policy in Developing Countries; Integrating State and Traditional Systems.' *Focaal,* 22/23:219-29.
Murray, A.J.
1991 *No Money, No Honey; a Study of Street Traders and Prostitutes in Jakarta.* Singapore: Oxford University Press.
Patma-Mingoen, H.K.
1980 Economische samenwerkingsvormen onder boeren in een West-Javaans dorp. MA-thesis, Leiden University.

Platteau, J.-P.
1991 'Traditional Systems of Social Security and Hunger Insurance; Past Achievements and Modern Challenges.' In: E. Ahmad et al. (eds), *Social Security in Developing Countries*, 112-63. Oxford: Clarendon Press.
1997 'Mutual Insurance as an Elusive Concept in Traditional Rural Communities.' *Journal of Development Studies*, 33(6):764-796.
Portes, A.
1998 'Social Capital; Its Origins and Applications in Modern Sociology.' *Annual Review of Sociology*, 24:1-24.
Rahman, A.
1999 'Micro-Credit Initiatives for Equitable and Sustainable Development; Who Pays?' *World Development*, 27:67-82.
Rowlands, M.
1995 'Looking at Financial Landscapes; A Contextual Analysis of ROSCA's in Cameroon.' In: S. Ardener & S. Burman (eds), *Money-Go-Rounds*, 111-124. Oxford: Berg.
Sahlins, M.
1972 *Stone Age Economics.* London: Tavistock Publications.
Schmidt, S.
1994 'Social Security in Developing Countries; Basic Tenets and Fields of State Intervention.' In: M.-T. Meereboer (ed), *Social (In)Security and Poverty as Global Issues. Pre-conference Reader*, 82-103. The Hague: DVL/OS.
Shipton, P.
1989 *Bitter Money; Cultural Economy and Some African Meanings of Forbidden Commodities.* [American Ethnological Society Monograph Series, Number 1.]
Smets, P.
1992 *My Stomach is my Bishi; Savings and Credit Associations in Sangli, India.* Amsterdam: Free University. [Urban Research Working Papers, No.30.]
2000 'ROSCAs as a Source of Housing Finance for the Poor; An Analysis of Self-help Practices from Hyderabad, India.' *Community Development Journal*, 35-1:16-30.
2002 *Housing Finance and the Urban Poor; Building and Financing Low-income Housing in Hyderabad, India.* PhD-thesis, Free University, Amsterdam.
Sullivan, J.
1992 *Local Government and Community in Java; An Urban Case-study.* Singapore: Oxford University Press.
Van der Linden, M.
1996 'De historische logica van onderlinge arbeidersverzekeringen.' In: M. Van der Linden & J. Sluijs (eds), *Onderlinge hulpfondsen*, 23-44. Amsterdam: IISG.
Van Ginneken, W.
1999 *Social Security for the Excluded Majority. Case Studies of Developing Countries.* Geneva, ILO.
Vel, J.A.C.
1994 *The Uma-economy; Indigenous Economics and Development Work in Lawonda, Sumba (Eastern Indonesia).* PhD-thesis, Wageningen Agricultural University.
Von Benda-Beckmann, F. et al.
1988a 'Introduction; Between Kinship and the State.' In: F. Von Benda-Beckmann et al. (eds), *Between Kinship and the State*, 7-20. Dordrecht: Foris Publications.
1988b *Between Kinship and the State; Social Security and Law in Developing Countries.* Dordrecht: Foris Publications.

Von Benda-Beckmann, F.& K.
1994 'Coping with Insecurity.' *Focaal*, 22/23:7-31.
1996 'Where Structures Merge.' Unpublished paper.
Woodman, G.R.
1988 'The Decline of Folk-Law Social Security in Common-Law Africa.' In: F. von Benda-Beckmann et al. (eds), *Between Kinship and the State*, 69-88. Dordrecht: Foris Publications.
Woolcock, M.
1998 'Social Capital and Economic Development; Towards a Theoretical Synthesis and Policy Framework.' *Theory and Society*, 27(2):151-208.
Zelizer, V.
1989 'The Social Meaning of Money; "Special Monies".' *American Journal of Sociology*, 95(2):342-377.

CHAPTER 6

Changing financial mutuals in urban India

Practice, functions, trust and development trajectories

Peer Smets[1]

One of the characteristics of financial mutuals is their (relatively) short cycle, which offers participants and organizers the possibility of adjusting their rules and regulations for the start of a new cycle. Simultaneously, organizational set ups, membership, functions and trust relations can change according to the needs and wishes of the organizers within the context where they operate. On the basis of my case studies, this paper will focus on changing financial mutuals in urban India. Moreover, it will search for development trajectories and confront these findings with development trajectories of financial mutuals as seen by others.

Introduction

Financial mutuals are organizations in which individuals, groups of individuals or families join to create their own organizational set-up for pooling finance for a specific predetermined purpose. Financial mutuals are a global phenomenon and are known under different names in different regions and countries. It is assumed that financial mutuals expand in number and type on a global scale. Nowadays they are widespread in the so-called developing countries (see e.g. Ardener 1964; Bouman 1995; De Swaan in this volume), but also in western countries, among migrants (see e.g. Bijnaar in this volume, Smets & Broekman 1996; Srinivasan 1995; Summerfield 1995). This paper restricts itself to India, where these mutuals are known as *bishis, bishi mandals, chit funds, chitties,* and *committees.*

In rural and urban India, financial mutuals are widespread. In general, there is a notion of popularity, but figures lack. One exception is my earlier research in Sangli, where we asked people waiting for buses and shopping in the central markets of Sangli about their knowledge of and participation in *bishis* (N= 326). It appeared that 95% of these interviewed persons were familiar with the working of *bishis* and 58% were participating in at least one *bishi* at the time of interviewing. From those interviewed, 69% of the women and only 52% of the men participated

(Smets 1992:11-12). Such popularity may give an indication of the demand for '(1) a simple and convenient outlet for savings; and (2) a convenient meeting point between deficit and surplus units, which provide attractive yields to the surplus units.' (Shanmugam 1991: 220). In order to understand the phenomenon of financial mutuals, it is necessary to look into different types of financial mutuals: savings associations, rotating savings and credit associations, and accumulating savings and credit associations.

In a savings association, for which Smets (1996) had earlier introduced the acronym SAVA, members regularly pay a fixed or variable amount to a common fund that accumulates over time, but no credit will be provided from the kitty. It will grow for a non-fixed or predetermined period, after which all participants will receive back their deposits, in kind or cash, possibly enlarged by interest payments (cf. Adams 1992:13; Schrieder & Cuevas 1992:46).

In a rotating savings and credit association (ROSCA), people regularly deposit money in a common fund, which is allocated entirely or partially to each participant in turn. The order of rotation may be decided by drawing lots, auction, seniority, voting, negotiation, consensus, bribery or decision of the organizer (see e.g. Ardener 1964; Bouman 1978:38; Nayar 1986; Smets 1992:13-23).

Contrary to a ROSCA, in an accumulating savings and credit association (ASCRA), the pooled savings are not directly redistributed, but accumulate in a fund for a specific time. The pooled money can be used to provide credit to its members only, or also to non-members. In order to cope with emergency cases, community development or joint investments a part of the fund can be kept separate (Bouman 1994:376).

Financial mutuals are managed in either an authoritarian or democratic way. In an authoritarian financial mutual, decisions and responsibility are in the hands of the organizer(s) and in a democratic financial mutual the participants themselves have to take care of its management and maintenance.

The organizational and management options cannot be seen independent of their participants. Financial mutuals 'do not behave; rather it is people who construct and reconstruct their own form of the association.' (Hospes 1995:127) In other words, 'it is people that count: people make rules, adapt rules and compare rules and resources of different saving and credit arrangements.' (ibid.:130) People' s roles as developers, initiators, managers and evaluators of these associations determine how their function, organizational set up, operation and management develop over time.

Origin and development patterns of financial mutuals

This section will focus on the origin and development options of financial mutuals as could be traced in the literature dealing with financial mutuals. The origin of financial mutuals can be found in reciprocal exchange systems of gifts and labor, and in grain, rice and vegetable banks (Adams & Canavesi 1989:222;

Radhakrishnan et al. 1975:5; Radhakrishna & Galab 1997:10-11). Another explanation could be that financial mutuals have also evolved from the need for financial assistance. Common kitties were created for social events connected with life cycle events, such as marriages and funerals. Other people join in another mutual to deposit finance for times of insecurity and emergency or for investments in the improvement of their living environment. Furthermore, a person in need of cash may request friends and neighbors to lend him some money, which he will repay with a number of invitations for social gatherings where drinks and food are paid by the borrower. By doing so an association emerges (Schrader 1991:2).

Bähre illustrates how people develop sufficient trust in each other to set up a financial mutual together. Six men in Cape Town decided to help each other to be in time to catch the train to their work. They agreed that a person who is late had to buy a packet of McIntosh sweets. Through this mechanism of social control the trust developed, which eventually formed the basis for the establishment of a ROSCA. In this ROSCA a part of the men's weekly earnings was pooled and handed over to one of the six participants at a time. When more members joined, parties were organized and credit provided (Bähre 1996:20).

After having focused on the origin of financial mutuals, an overview of development trajectories of financial mutuals will be provided. On the basis of Robertson's study on institutional transformations in sharecropping arrangements, Lont (2002:182) distinguishes phylogenetic and ontogenetic development of financial mutuals. Phylogenetic development focuses on modifications in the characteristics of institutions in society. Ontogenetic development refers to changes of individual financial mutuals 'during their time of existence'. Attention may hereby be paid to for example changing rules, the organizational set up, financial arrangements and membership from cycle to cycle.

An example of a phylogenetic development perspective is Geertz's view on financial mutuals. Geertz (1962:259-263) ascribes to financial mutuals (ROSCAs) an instrumental role that helps people in traditional societies to survive in a so-called 'modern' society. ROSCAs form a platform where people can learn new norms and values, which enable participation in more rationalized and less personal kinds of organizations such as banks. Here, traditional rituals keep the ROSCA participants together and create an atmosphere in which more 'rational' behavior patterns can be learned. Over time, the 'traditional' elements which enforce solidarity will diminish and be replaced by the more formalistic, impersonal, single-purpose relations required for the development of institutions based upon 'the financial probity of members and leaders and the legal enforceability of obligations, and in the development of more complex patterns of organization and commercial calculation.' (ibid.:261). In other words, ROSCAs form 'a link between the largely unmonetized economy of the past and the largely monetized economy of the future.' (ibid.:245). Geertz suggests that ROSCAs are 'perhaps self-liquidating, being replaced ultimately by banks, cooperatives, and other economically more rational types of credit institutions.' (ibid.:263). The ROSCA

> is merely one of a whole family of such intermediate 'socializing' institutions which spring up in societies undergoing social and cultural change, not only in economic, but in the political, religious, stratifactory, familial, and other aspects of the social system as well. (ibid.:263)

These institutions are seen as 'middle rungs between traditional society and more modern forms of social organization' (ibid.). This suggests that ASCRAs and SAVAs, which are not included in Geertz's analysis, can be seen as such middle rungs. ASCRAs can also be seen as a kind of credit co-operatives that evolve from ROSCAs. By making use of Geertz's development trajectory from simple to more complex financial mutuals it may be suggested that they develop along the line SAVA-ROSCA-ASCRA. Here, the assumption is made that saving is easier for an association to deal with, but when savings and credit are combined, more advanced organizational arrangements are required. Especially when the organizational set-up becomes more complex and the number of participants increases, there is a tendency that the management is in the hands of a few and is characterized by an authoritarian style.

The development trajectory of Geertz is criticized by, for example, Ardener (1964) and Hospes (1995:129). Geertz's view is rejected because he denies the diversity of regions and financial mutuals by treating countries as homogeneous economic units. Moreover, Geertz's analysis does not have an explanation for the existence of different types of financial mutuals in one area at the same time. Another criticism is the limited use of Geertz's dual classifications such as rational-irrational, economic-non economic, and modern-traditional (Ardener 1964:222).

However, Hospes (1995) does not reject the development trajectory of Geertz completely. He merely recognizes that financial mutuals are influenced by the economic conditions of the environment in which they operate. In addition, Hospes states that Geertz overemphasizes the economic function of mutual funds. It is people that count. Financial mutuals are 'flexible forms of co-operation that restructure social relations in changing contexts.' (Hospes 1995:129)

How people count also depends on the legal context in which financial mutuals operate. For example, Seibel and Schrader show how the initiative of an organizer of Nepalese ROSCAs, called *dhikuti*, in combination with an adjustment of the legislation has taken care of the transformation of these ROSCAs into regular credit institutions. This indicates that financial mutuals in the informal sector[2] can develop into formal organizations (Seibel & Schrader 1999:52-53). This suggests that a legalization of informal financial activities can help their development and will benefit the formal economy and market. De Soto (2001) argues that it offers the possibility of channeling informal capital into the formal economy. However, many citizens have little choice other than to live and work entirely or partly outside of the judicial system. When they possess property, they are often unable to transform this property into a deed or derive capital from it. Moreover, they cannot establish 'profitable contracts with strangers, cannot get credit, insurance or utility services. They are dependent on immediate family and neighbors.' (55)

I agree that it is people that count and make their financial mutual, which is context dependent. This has led to a kaleidoscope of financial mutuals, for which structural patterns of development will be searched for. There is little insight in how financial mutuals develop over time, because of their cyclical character. Financial mutuals may mushroom and disappear when a cycle is finished. After each cycle rules and regulations, and even the members may change. Due to the generally short-term cyclical character written records are rather scarce if available at all. When some written records are available, they tend to be cashbooks. Additional information has to be gathered by interviewing those who have been participating in and/or organizing financial mutuals and by studying secondary sources too. In addition, there is another methodological problem. How can ontogenetic development patterns be extrapolated to phylogenetic development trajectories? One way of dealing with this is to search for ontological development patterns, and to then test them over a longer period of time, maybe a hundred years or more. For the time being we have to restrict ourselves to ontogenetic development patterns.

To obtain insight in the ontogenetic development of financial mutuals, the next section shows how a semi-nomadic tribe organizes and manages their financial mutuals and how these mutuals develop over time, ultimately resulting in the establishment of an informal financial center. This informal financial center offers the possibility for citizens living in and outside the Mandula settlement to save and borrow at a fixed time. During the monthly activities, the organizers of the financial mutuals offer their services at many places in the street or inside houses.

The development of an informal financial service center

Before focusing on the development of a financial service center in one of the slum areas in the city of Hyderabad, the focus will be put on their initiators, the Mandula. Originally, the semi-nomadic tribe[3] of the Mandula could be traced in especially Telegana, Guntur and the coastal districts of the Indian state of Andhra Pradesh. For six months, they would wander in small groups of fifteen to twenty families from one place to another to hunt together and sell herbal medicines and talismans. To increase their income they might also sell things like goats, or beads, mirrors, vermilion keys, locks and other fancy articles in villages. Normally, the Mandula would settle on the outskirts of a village for about three to four days. Once their business activities were completed they would leave for another village. Sold goods could be paid for in kind or money, but buying on credit was also possible. In such a situation, the Mandula would come back to the village to collect their payments just after the harvest. This relationship between the peasants and the Mandula has been strengthening over time. When they left for another village, the Mandula carried their belongings, including their huts, on donkeys. However, after half a year of trekking, they would settle in a base camp (GAP 1977:20; Raghaviah 1968:237).

In such a base camp, individual groups called bands would gather. Each band is a peer group, which is divided in clans. Its leader in the traditional council represents each clan, known as *gotra* or *interperu*. In the base camp, the traditional leader called *kapu* would settle disputes. He should belong to the *interperu Vontedhu* and his assistant (*ghata puri)* to the *interperu Adapally*. Moreover, marriages took place and new alliances for certain territories were formed (personal communication Raju Ramachandra of the Tribal Research Institute, Hyderabad).

All *interperus* would meet once a year at the Sivaratri festival, where Mandula offered goats, pigs and rice to various deities (Thurston & Rangachari 1975:448). The Mandula also prayed in front of the Hindu Gods, but under all circumstances and on any special occasion they worshipped the deities *Bangaru Maisamma* and *Pochamma* (Ranga Raju 1969:77).

In 1962, about 20 Mandula families settled in Hyderabad. While being settled in Hyderabad, the occupation practices of the Mandula settlers diversified. Some people still practice hunting and prepare medicines. In the past, men and women of different *interperus* went hunting together, but the share of the catch regularly led to disputes among the *interperus*. Since the 1990s, women have found their own economic activities and have been selling items such as fancy goods and kitchen utensils. Furthermore, men have become employed as businessmen, laborers and government employees.

A new couple is supposed to form its own economic unit with its own shelter. Moreover, the new couple is encouraged to join a financial mutual. When they obtain finance from the kitty, the money should be passed on to the groom's parents, who will monitor its expenditure. Here, the first priority is the repayment of the debts made for the marriage and/or the construction of shelter. In general, it is the male head of the household, who as the financial manager of the household budget, takes out credit. The huts people build resemble those they used to build when they still led a semi-nomadic life. Later on, plots were bought at what were at that moment the outskirts of the city of Hyderabad. In 1970, the first hut dwellers constructed a house here with mud-plastered walls and an asbestos roof.

Possessions and debts are hereditary. When the father dies the men of the community and a few leaders join to discuss the division of the property and debts. Women, except the widow concerned, do not attend such meetings. The division of the property will take place in front of her. At this meeting it is also decided which son has to take care of his mother. After her death the widow's small share in the inheritance will be given to the son who took care of her when she was still alive. The widow's share is much smaller than the share the sons get. However, the sons are responsible for the repayment of outstanding debts. If the sons are still too young, the widow may repay only a small amount. Until the son is grown up no interest will be charged for the loan, as long as it was obtained from within the Mandula community. If a woman takes out a loan, the debt will be transferred to her sons when she dies.

The Mandula community in Hyderabad has its own leaders. Originally the *kapu* came from the *Vontedhu*, who was assisted by the *gata puri*, an *Adapally*. In the 1970s, a new generation of leaders arose and dominated the operation and maintenance of the community through a neighborhood committee. These leaders belong to the *interperus Adapally, Vontedhu* and *Yarva.* It was again in the 1990s that a new generation of leaders of *Adapally* and *Vontedhu,* settled disputes within the community. Police assistance will be avoided. The Mandula have their own systems of fines and punishments for each offence of norms and values. For robbery and beating somebody a fine of Rs.2,000[4] and Rs.1,000 respectively will be charged. Fighting while being drunk can be fined with Rs.200-300. In general, this fining system has a preventive nature.

The role of the traditional leaders was taken over by the neighborhood committee initiated by the Urban Community Development Department of the Municipal Corporation of Hyderabad, where again *Adapally* and *Vontedhu* dominate.

From financial self-help towards a financial service center

In the 1960s, the Mandula who settled in Hyderabad pooled money to repay credit that had been taken out for the construction of a community center. This pooling mechanism was the basis for a SAVA, where money was saved in a common fund for a specific purpose. This financial mutual was locally called *Sangam Chittie.* Later on, this association developed into a savings and credit association. In the meantime, other financial mutuals were organized in which the Mandula and non-community members could join together.

Below the development of the financial mutual *Sangam Chittie* will be discussed, followed by the description of the financial center developed in the settlement.

Sangam Chittie

The *Sangam Chittie* was started in 1969. Each adult was asked to pay 50 paise (= Rs. 0.5) per month to repay the credit of Rs. 5,000 that was taken out for the construction of a community hall. After a period of three years, the loan was repaid, but the payments into the financial mutual continued. In the meantime, the *kapu,* who organized these financial arrangements, built his own house and many suspected him of cheating. Some blamed him for selling land illegally, while others accused him of confiscating money from the common fund. Despite many suspicions, it was hard to judge the trustworthiness of these accusations.

The collection of the monthly contributions continued and had become Rs. 1. This money was pooled in a common fund for the construction of a temple. By 1986, Rs. 25,000 had been collected and the construction of the temple had started, but this amount was not sufficient. An additional sum of Rs. 25 was collected from each house. This house-to-house collection was so successful that Rs. 2,000 could remain in the common fund after construction of the temple. The payment of contributions stopped because the common need was over and so was the motivation for saving together. The collection of savings was replaced by fines charged for deviant behavior in the Mandula community and a kind of marriage fee. For each marriage, Rs. 1,000 had to be contributed to the common fund instead of a festive meal for the community members. However, in reality food continued to be served to guests during wedding ceremonies.

Loans were provided from the kitty to the participants. Nowadays, a part of the fund is also used for festivals such as Independence Day and Republic Day, the cleaning of the local Pochama temple (Rs. 40 per month) and newspapers for the community hall. Moreover, partial payments are made from *Sangam Chittie* for the payment of the salary of the garbage collector in their neighborhood. However, due to the allocation of a part of the fund for community purposes, the amount of loans provided has temporarily dropped. When the size of the kitty inclined again, the total number of borrowers increased also.

TABLE 1 **Interest charged (auction amount) in Sangam Chitti (1992-1993)**

no.	*J(92)*	*J*	*A*	*S*	*O*	*N*	*D*	*J(93)*	*F*	*M*	*A*	*M*	*J*	*J*	*A*	*S*	*O*	*N*	*D*
1	53	63	40	27	27	30	31	20	16	24	30	30	22	24	30	22	27	10	19
2	53	63	41	26	30	30	31	20	20	26	31	29	24	25	29	27	28	12	21
3	53	64	42	26	30	31	31	20	21	30	30	30	23	26	30	23	28	13	20
4	54	66	41	26	30	31	31	20	20	30	30	30	24	28	30	22	29	14	20
5	54	68	42	26	30	31	31	20	21	31	29	30	23	26	30	22	28	15	20
6	55	68	41	26	30	32	31	20	22	31	30	30	24	26	30	22	28	14	24
7	56	69	41	26	30	31	31	19	21	30	30	30	22	25	29	20	28	13	24
8	56	69	41	27	28	31	31	18	21	31	31	31	22	27	30	14	27	13	25
9	56	70	33	25	22	30	31	18	21	30	31	30	23	25	29	17	28	14	24
10	52	70	32	24	21	31	31	18	20	30	32	31	23	26	29	13	25	14	24
11	58	69	28	25	20	35	30	18	20	30	30	31	24	24	28	10	26	13	25
12	58	72	19	25	23	77	30	16	20	30	30	31	22	24	30	12	26	13	25
13	58	74	12	24	23	77	30	12	21	30	30	30	23	24	28	11	25	13	26
14	59	70	20	25	25	77	30	10	20	31	30	30	23	23	28	11	24	13	25
15	59	74	42	26	22	77	24	10	21	30	31	32	23	24	26	13	24	13	26
16	62	74	42	27	30	77	22	10	21	30	30	31	21	25	26	15	25	13	27
17	60	74	42	25	30	77	16	10	22	30	31	30	22	25	27	11	27	15	26
18	-	-	42	24	30	-	11	11	23	30	31	31	22	25	26	11	26	15	27
19	-	-	-	-	-	-	16	15	22	30	33	31	23	26	26	11	28	17	30
20	-	-	-	-	-	-	16	15	22	30	34	33	21	26	29	12	30	18	40
21	-	-	-	-	-	-	16	14	20	30	?	33	20	27	30	10	27	18	40
22	-	-	-	-	-	-	20	18	26	31	?	31	19	30	30	12	-	-	-
23	-	-	-	-	-	-	31	-	26	33	30	30	22	30	30	10	-	-	-
24	-	-	-	-	-	-	-	-	-	-	26	31	24	18	30	9	-	-	-
25	-	-	-	-	-	-	-	-	-	-	-	34	24	-	-	10	-	-	-
26	-	-	-	-	-	-	-	-	-	-	-	-	24	-	-	24	-	-	-
27	-	-	-	-	-	-	-	-	-	-	-	-	24	-	-	-	-	-	-
28	-	-	-	-	-	-	-	-	-	-	-	-	21	-	-	-	-	-	-
29	-	-	-	-	-	-	-	-	-	-	-	-	18	-	-	-	-	-	-

? = this information was not readable due to serious cuts in the documents available; J=January; F=February; M=March; A=April; M=May; J=June; J=July; A=August;S=September;O=October; D=December. J92=June 1992; J93= January 1993

In December 1993, a group of five persons was supposed to be responsible for the management of the *Sangam Chittie*, but in reality, one single group member ran it. The *Sangam Chittie* had hundred-and-twenty members and new members from the Mandula community were still welcome. Each new participant had to pay Rs. 50 as an entrance fee. The fund grew to such an extent that twenty-one loans of Rs. 300 could be provided. The purpose of this credit was not fixed. Moreover, the loan including interest had to be repaid at the following month's meeting. The credit bore an interest rate, which was decided by bidding. The highest bidder obtained the loan. Table 1 presents an overview of the auction amounts at the monthly meetings from June 1992 till December 1993.

Table 1 also shows that the average number of loans in 1993 was higher than that in the second part of 1992. Furthermore, the auction amount increased when demand was high. This occurred in June, July and November 1992, and December 1993 in particular. In December 1993, the interest for the first loan was Rs. 19; for the second loan it was Rs. 21, etceteras. The interest rates were especially high for the last loans because several people were desperate to obtain a loan. The following example will give an impression of how the bidding activities are very gender sensitive. The description below shows that this financial mutual is male-dominated, reflecting Mandula culture where the men dominate financial affairs and the public domain.

> A female participant tried to bid on the loans of Rs. 300 through the window with bars. The men in the community hall ignored her. After several unsuccessful attempts she decided to go into the community hall and made a bid on the last loan. She needed the credit urgently and finally received it at an interest rate of Rs. 40. When she was handed over the money, she was disappointed that she had to pay such a high price for it. In the meantime, several men obtained more than one loan, which caused fights with several women, who were in need of a loan as well. One man claimed that the additional loans were meant for their wives and daughters.

In order to ensure repayment of the loans, several measures were taken. Firstly, a guarantor was required, who had to be a participant of *Sangam Chittie* and could not borrow from the kitty himself during the period the loan he was guaranteeing was not repaid. Secondly, in case of delay of repayment of the credit taken, a penalty was charged. The size of the penalty equaled the largest auction amount during the meeting that month. In December 1993, it was Rs. 40.

The financial service center

Apart from *Sangam Chittie*, other financial mutuals have been organized since the 1970s. Initially they were intended only for the Mandula, but later on these *chit funds* were also accessible for non-community members.

Some of these *chit funds* resembled the *Sangam Chittie* in that they were of the ASCRA type. In each of the *chit funds* eighteen people participated. They deposited a fixed amount of either Rs. 20, 25, 30 or 50, depending on the association in which they participated. The loans had a one-month term and the interest was determined by means of auction. Furthermore, the organizers are paid a commission of 2% of the total fund.

The other *chit funds* were auction ROSCAs. How the auction ROSCAs operated can best be illustrated by an example of a *chit fund* with a cycle of seventeen months. Such a *chit fund* had seventeen members, who all had to pay a monthly contribution of Rs. 300 to the kitty. From the collected amount of Rs. 5,100 an amount of Rs. 100 had to be deducted as commission for the organizers. On the remaining amount of Rs. 5,000 the participants bided. With each bid the remaining sum in the kitty became smaller. In other words, the person accepting the highest discount received the fund. However, the maximum deduction permitted was Rs. 1,500. If the auction amount reached that level and several participants were still aiming at getting the fund, a lottery had to take place in order to determine the allocation of the kitty. A maximum auction amount was introduced to avoid excessive auction amounts in order to bypass big losses for the person who desperately wanted the fund.

There were four groups of four, five, seven, and ten associations respectively. These four groups of organizers belong to the *interperu* as shown in Table 2. Among one group of organizers a non-Mandula from another neighborhood was included.

TABLE 2 **Chit funds and their organizers**

Chit funds	*Interperu of the organizers*
Group 1	Adapally (son of ghata puri/ assistant of kapu)
	Oraganti
	Yarva
Group 2	Vontedhu
	Vontedhu (son of kapu, traditional leader)
	Yerakula (non-Mandula, from outside neighborhood)
group 3	Adapally
	Adapally
	Vontedhu
group 4	Singajogi
	Singajogi
	Yarva

All *chit fund* groups meet on the seventh of each month from 1 to 4 p.m. From noon onwards, the four groups of *chit fund* organizers gathered at different places in their neighborhood. Three groups (number 1, 3 and 4 in Table 2) sat on carpets and mats in the open air and one group (number 2) went inside a house. Each group had a big steel box for depositing the money collected. *Chit fund* participants went to their group and paid their contributions to the kitty of their financial mutual. Till 1.30 p.m. money was collected by the organizers and the amounts were written down in cashbooks. Then the bidding activities would take place. The *chit funds* of the same organizers were linked to each other. In fact, in one group there were seven *chit funds*. Here, all the contributions collected were pooled and divided into seven amounts, which had to be auctioned one after another. All the participants of the seven *chit funds* had to try to obtain the kitty seven times during a meeting, but only once during a cycle.

During the *chit fund* gatherings, tea was served to all the participants. The costs of this had to be borne by the organizers. One organizer, who mentioned the auction amounts, which were increased by Rs. 10 each time, led the auctions. The winner of the kitty was noted down and only after all the bidding activities had taken place in a group, payments took place. The winners of the fund had to bring forward a guarantor before they received the fund. Both the winner and the guarantor had to sign a revenue stamp paper. In the case of default, the guarantor was asked to put pressure on the defaulter; otherwise goods had to be taken from the guarantor's house. If there was a small delay in payments the guarantor could advance the contribution. Finally, the auction amounts had to be divided among all participants. The non-receivers of the kitty wait in the neighborhood till they can obtain their share in the auction amounts.

Some people were not allowed to participate in the auction because their credibility was not proven. For new members it was crucial that they were considered credible. New participants for the *chit fund* were selected on the basis of their occupation, the size and regularity of their income and possession of their own house. In general, a person was only accepted as a member if he was living in his own house. This minimized the risk of default. Such persons would not run away after having received the kitty (cf. Smets 2000:21). This fits the idea of Hechter (1987:110) that only people 'who are not likely to leave the community' will be accepted as participants. If the participant was a tenant or a squatter, the leader of the neighborhood concerned was asked about the credibility of the participant. Tenants who participated in a *chit fund* could only bid on the fund during the last few sessions. In one ROSCA a solution was found for a tenant who wanted to receive the fund earlier. She had to pay the outstanding payments for the complete cycle before the fund could be released. Despite complaints of the beneficiaries, the organizers were quite strict to prevent cases of default.

The management skills were learned from the older generation of leaders. One organizer said the following about the management skills needed:

> When there is faith, managing a *chit fund* is a good business. When you organize a *chit fund* you have to move along with the people. Running a *chit fund* is not a joke.

The organizers were paid for the management of the auction ROSCAs, but they had to provide insurance services to their *chit fund* members for which purpose Rs. 100 from the kitty of each auction ROSCA was deducted. One of these insurance functions encompasses the compulsion of the organizers to pay the amount due if participants died or were hospitalized. In a particular case one person had only paid four monthly contributions and the organizers took on the financial obligations. Only when the kitty was received, was the original participant given back his payments, while the organizers kept the remaining amount.

Another insurance function refers to the moneylending activities by the *chit fund* organizers or others. Participation in a financial mutual can serve as collateral for taking out a loan. The expected lump sum from the financial mutual will be used for the repayment of the loan obtained (Smets 2002:21-22).

The size of the loan provided was less than the kitty minus an amount slightly above the maximum auction amount of Rs.1500. When the kitty was, for example, Rs.10,000 the loan had to be a maximum of Rs.8,000. The interest rate was 2% per month. The repayment of the loan took place when the borrower had received the kitty. Other organizers even lent money to non-members, but only if, as required, they were well known. Moreover, they had to live in a house of their own, and a guarantor was required. The working capital could come from the *chit funds*, but could also be borrowed from, for example, other *chit fund* organizers. If the money was borrowed the interest rate for lending was 2.5 to 4% per month.

Government initiated community-based loan scheme

In 1991, the Municipal Corporation of Hyderabad introduced community-based loan schemes in several slums in Hyderabad. These schemes promoted a revolving fund for the community concerned to create an alternative for 'unscrupulous' moneylenders and encourage the participants to save. The beneficiaries were supposed to contribute part of the fund, before the British funding agency ODA (Overseas Development Administration, nowadays called the Department for Institutional Development or DFID) could add four times the contributions pooled in the fund. The total amount of money was deposited in a joint account, which was in the name of the community development officer of the Municipal Corporation of Hyderabad and one of the members of the neighborhood committee. This neighborhood committee member stressed that the loan scheme comes from ODA and not from the Indian Government. He said:

> The government has not done anything for us. It is ODA, which has brought the water connections, sewerage, the construction of the community hall, television, youth club materials and so on.

For the establishment of the loan scheme, it was expected that 100 households would each pay Rs.50, but in reality five members of the neighborhood committee felt responsible and paid each Rs. 1,000. This was done because they felt that the slum dwellers had already sufficiently contributed to common purposes. The pooled sum of Rs. 5,000 was supplemented with Rs. 18,000 from ODA. The leaders of the Mandula community considered the ODA contributions a gift. They said that the Municipal Corporation of Hyderabad would never come to collect the seed money. From the common fund, loans were to be given for employment purposes only, such as the purchase of trading materials. However, borrowers preferred to allocate the loan according to their own preferences rather than spending it for the predetermined productive purpose. Each borrower was to bring forward a guarantor to obtain credit. Initially men could receive a loan of Rs.1,000 and women a loan of Rs. 500. The women received a smaller loan, because they were assumed to be only involved in part-time business. From March 1993 onwards, the women could also obtain larger loans. The access to the community-based loan scheme was restricted to members of the Mandula community. Consequently, non-Mandula living in the same neighborhood were excluded. One of the non-Mandula describes this as follows:

> I am not allowed to partake in the scheme, because it is reserved for Mandula only. He told me that he is even lucky that opposite his house some Mandula are living. Otherwise there had been no road of ODA in front of his house.

A loan of Rs.1,000 had to be repaid in ten monthly installments of Rs. 100. In addition to this amount, interest had to be paid. The interest for the first month was Rs. 20, for the second month Rs.18, for the third month Rs. 16, et cetera. In the last month the interest was reduced to Rs. 2. This equaled a monthly deduction of Rs. 2.

If sufficient money was available in the kitty, the community development officer of the Municipal Corporation and the members of the neighborhood committee sat together and decided by mutual agreement who would obtain the loans. If there were too many loan applications, some people were asked to postpone their loan demand till the following month. If this was not possible all applicants could obtain a smaller amount. However, loans were not provided to members of the same family in the same month. Another selection criterion for the disbursement of the loans was the income level; the poor were given the first priority.

At or around the ninth of every month, a meeting would take place from 10.30-11.30 a.m.. At this meeting, the loan installments were repaid and loans were given if sufficient money was available in the common pool of the community-based loan scheme. Table 3 provides an overview of the loans provided. It appears that from April 1992 onwards loans were provided (bi)monthly, while it may be safely concluded that before April 1992 it was of a more irregular nature. Later on, loans were even sometimes released biweekly. The shorter terms in between the release of loans are an indication that the loan fund was growing.

The following is a description of what happened at one of the monthly meetings.

> The organizer had spread a carpet onto the floor of the community hall and was sitting on it. People were coming in one at a time to pay their installments for the community-based loan scheme. The organizer shouted that the members were not coming quick enough and wanted to speed up the procedures. The people either paid Rs.50 or Rs.100 for the repayment of loans of Rs.500 and Rs.1000 respectively and the interest concerned. Every payment was noted down in a cashbook. Then a lady entered the room and asked how many months she still had to pay to clear her

TABLE 3 **Financial transactions of the community-based loan scheme**

	Loans in Rs					*Total loan amount*
Date	*400*	*500*	*800*	*900*	*1000*	
13-07-1991	-	19	-	-	13	22,500
18-10-1991	-	16	-	-	-	8000
20-01-1992	-	1	-	-	10	10,500
23-04-1992	-	9	-	-	9	13,500
12-05-1992	-	10	-	-	1	6000
15-06-1992	-	9	-	-	-	4500
13-07-1992	-	10	-	-	-	5000
14-09-1992	-	1	-	1	3	4400
12-11-1992	-	2	-	-	4	5000
20-12-1992	-		1	-	4	4800
13-01-1993	2	7	-	-	1	5300
09-02-1993	-	8	1	-	1	5800
09-03-1993	-	8	-	-	2	6000
15-03-1993	-	-	-	-	5	5000
17-05-1993	-	1	-	-	4	4500
23-06-1993	-	5	-	-	2	4500
12-07-1993	-	-	-	-	7	7000
20-07-1993	-	-	-	-	5	5000
19-08-1993	-	1	-	-	5	5500
13-10-1993	-	1	-	-	7	7500
16-11-1993	-	-	-	-	6	6000

> debt. The organizer looked in the cashbook and told her that there were only two months left. Most women stayed outside the community hall and paid their installments to somebody at the door or window, who handed over the money to the organizer. Only a few women entered the community hall, as the community hall was mainly male territory. At one point boys were sent into the slum to call the participants who still had not come to pay their installment. Around 12.00 a.m. six people had still not paid. In the meantime, about Rs. 5,000 was collected, which was brought to the bank.[5] Loans were not given, because the fund had to grow to be able to provide more loans at the same meeting. It was expected that loans could be provided next month. However, loans had to be given a couple of days later to the beneficiaries by cheque. For this purpose, the participants had to open an account with the bank near the slum.

If the loan is not repaid, the guarantor is required to put pressure on the defaulter. Such a guarantor has to go to the person to ask for payment of the debts. This can be illustrated by one of the participants who told me:

> The borrower, who had taken out the loan, was required to pay his installment at the ninth of each month between 10-11 a.m., but he complained that he did not have any money to repay. Together with ten other people the guarantor went to the defaulter's house to ask him to repay his debt. The borrower refused. Then the guarantor took some utensils from his house and brought them to the community hall. He told the borrower that he could get them back once the outstanding installment had been paid. Within one hour the money was brought to the organizer and the utensils were returned.

Only when the borrower paid the installment a few days later the guarantor was willing to advance the money.

In short, the example of the Mandula community's involvement in trading and financial experience could be used for managing financial mutuals. Within the settled community in Hyderabad, one sees a change from pooling money to SAVA and ASCRA respectively. Later on, financial mutuals are employed on a more commercial basis. In these mutuals non-Mandula's were also welcomed. In other words, the development trajectory starts from simple to more complex financial mutuals. Below, the paper will discuss several aspects of the financial mutuals, which will be compared with findings from other case studies.

Financial and social functions of mutuals

The Mandula while wandering around were used to deal with finance; they delivered goods to villagers on credit and payments could be collected later on. After settling down in Hyderabad, the establishment of a SAVA helped them to survive in a new environment by enabling the construction of community facilities. During this period, traditional leaders ruled the Mandula community and the neighborhood committee. In the meantime, members of the Mandula community have become increasingly economic and financial independent on the traditional leaders. Simultaneously, the SAVA changed into an ASCRA when the need for financing community facilities was felt less. The *kapu* reflects to it as follows:

> My father was also a traditional headman. In the city, I have lost control over the people, because they have become economic independent. Nowadays, there is a challenge between traditional and modern leadership. The traditional council has no power in the city. The young people are not respecting the traditions. They have become economic independent. The traditional leadership is challenged at all levels.

From the mid 1980s onwards, other ASCRAs and auction ROSCAs have been established. The establishment of the ASCRAs offers the possibility of providing loans for personal purposes, which was given a higher priority. Private initiative by organizing and managing *chit funds* arose also outside the *interperus* of the traditional leaders. Other members of the local Mandula community partake in the financial mutuals and benefit in one way or another, but women less then men.

The leaders of the Mandula community have the power to rule the community, but the ordinary Mandula spread gossip when they think the leaders concerned benefit too much. This becomes especially manifest when leaders build large houses for themselves. This happened with the traditional *kapu* in the beginning of the establishment of the settlement, but also in the 1990s when a leader started constructing his own house. Gossip was spread about the leader concerned. How could they invest so much money for their own benefit? To understand the meaning of the spreading of these rumors, I will first focus on the concept of gossip.

> Gossip [...] is almost by definition a story told about an absent third party; once launched, it becomes an anonymous tale with no author but many retailers [...] Behind every piece of gossip that is not merely news is an implicit statement of a rule or norm that has been broken. It is in fact only the violation of expected behavior that makes an event worth gossiping about. The rule or norm in question is often only formulated or brought to consciousness by the violation itself. (Scott 1985:282)

Scott considers gossip a weapon of the weak, which enables them to employ weak social sanctions to those who step outside the established normative setting. For the Mandula, it indicates that the leaders may make profit, as long as it is not too excessive.

Concerning the organizational set up of these financial mutuals, their development in the Mandula settlement shows that a SAVA can be replaced by an ASCRA, but later on ASCRAs and ROSCAs developed simultaneously. Consequently, a development along the line *SAVA → ROSCA → ASCRA* is not applicable. It is more a matter of which kind of financial mutual people develop in order to meet their needs in a changing environment. When the needs of the people change, another type of financial mutual may be required. It is people who initiate, organize, manage and evaluate their financial mutuals. It is not the development from a traditional towards a more rational society, but a changing environment – for the case study described the process of consolidation of a new settlement – which defines people's needs. Such an environment does not necessarily develop according to the sequence *traditional → modern and non-rational → rational.* It is traditional elements that still play a role in the financial mutuals. Moreover, the operation and management of the financial mutuals demonstrate rational behavior.

Such rational behavior is also manifest in other cases. For example, people participate in a financial mutual because banks, credit unions and housing finance corporations are not always accessible for them. In addition, it is possible that clients opt for the cheapest finance they can obtain; for example when financial mutuals offer cheaper credit compared with the formal financial sector as the Economic Research Group (1993:14) of the newspaper *Deccan Chronicle* illustrates for housing finance. The auction ROSCA, where members compete by offering the highest discount on the common fund offers cheaper finance but with a shorter term compared with the housing finance offered by private housing finance institutions. This shows that certain financial mutuals can be very efficient and effective in their operation and maintenance (see also Smets 2000).

When there is much competition among the financial mutuals, efficiency and effectiveness of financial mutuals increases. Such developments can take place when the local economy boosts. Simultaneously, there tends to be a shift from a social to a more economic/financial function of financial mutuals (Bouman 1989:68; Seibel & Shrestha 1988:183). If the local economy commercializes and monetizes, the number of financial mutuals often increases in size, spread and the amount of finance (e.g. Radhakrishnan et al.1975:4-6; Seibel & Shrestha 1988:183), especially when the formal banking sector cannot cope with the growing amount of money being in circulation (Bouman 1995). Moreover, the lower income sections of society have to benefit from the economic development.

In addition to a financial and insurance function of financial mutuals, they can also have a socializing function. Participants may gather while depositing their contribution, allocating and disbursing the fund or part of it. At such moments food and/or refreshments may be served. For Hyderabad, different views appear. Anderson (1966:338) states that the *chit funds* have no or only a minimal socializing function. Here, the financial function dominates. However, Smets traced *chit funds* among middle and high-income women in Hyderabad and Sangli, which have a very important social function and where finance plays a minor role. Here, the social function dominates and pleasure, instead of finance, is the main drive, as shown in the Sangli example (Smets 1998) below.

> In the Indian city of Sangli, one woman motivated some other women to join in a *bishi mandal* to develop a new friendship. In January 1983, this led to the start of a *bishi mandal*, in short *bishi*, with twelve well to do married Gujarati women.
>
> This particular *bishi* has a cycle of 11 months. In 1990, they started the seventh cycle in which the participants met monthly. The start of the new cycle always corresponds with the celebration of the second day of the Hindu festival of *Makar Sankranti*[6], on which the women give each other small presents. The woman at whose house this function is held is the secretary for the following cycle.
>
> In September 1990, I joined a meeting at the house of one of the *bishi* participants. When some female members arrived, they said hello to the host woman, who was busy in the kitchen. Other women quickly went into the living room to meet their friends who were already seated. The host woman and her female family members served several snacks. In the meantime, the *bishi* participants showed each other their new *sarees* (Indian clothing for women) and ornaments. When the tea was served the women exchanged news about television programs, new movies in the cinema, functions in the temple and new books. Furthermore, their children were favorite topics to talk about. The women seemed very willing to talk to one another and to give moral support to those women who face difficulties at home.

> At the meeting the hostess wrote the names of all the participants on pieces of paper. A small child was asked to take one of the lots; the woman whose name was drawn was to be the hostess for the next meeting. She fixed a date and invited all other participants.
>
> The women pointed out the alternatives to me if a woman is not in the position to receive all the women at her home. Then, the host can invite all *bishi* participants for a dinner in a restaurant. In such a situation, the hostess has to bear the costs of the dinner.
>
> One woman proudly said that her husband had just bought a new car. This news encouraged the other women to ask for a party with snacks or a dinner at the house of the couple concerned. One woman added that a visit to the cinema would also be appreciated. The secretary who wanted to collect all the contributions interrupted the discussion. Every participant paid a monthly contribution of Rs. 100, which was noted down in a notebook. The total fund of Rs. 1100 was handed over to the hostess. At this moment one woman proudly showed me the ring she had bought from the *bishi* fund.
>
> Some women had to pay a penalty of Rs. 2 for non-attendance during the last meeting. They said that they had not been able to come because of, for example, unexpected visitors. Penalties would not be charged if a woman was absent at a *bishi* meeting due to illness or a funeral in her family. The size of the penalty for not appearing at the Hindu festival of *Makar Sankranti* was as much as Rs. 5. The secretary collected all penalties and noted them down. At the end of the cycle this money is used for a visit to the cinema. At the end of the meeting the hostess gave a demonstration of the preparation of the snacks she had prepared.
>
> In December, the last month of the *bishi* cycle, the women usually organize a gathering for the participants and their family members, including the men. During the other meetings men are not allowed.
>
> In addition to the *bishi* meetings, the women join for a picnic three times a year. At one of these picnics their children are also present. The women also meet at special funerals and functions. This happens, for example, at weddings and the Hindu festival of *Narali Purnima*[7], which is celebrated by eating sweet rice and worshiping the light of the full moon.

Participation in a financial mutual as described above generates pleasure and thus leads to an improvement of the material, socio-cultural or psychological wellbeing of the participants.

The socio-cultural wellbeing may be affected by the participation in a specific ROSCA directly or indirectly. The participants have to play their expected roles in the ROSCA, which creates a strong group feeling. Indirectly, by having the opportunity to obtain a lump sum at once, the prestige and respect of a participant outside the lottery ROSCA may increase. This happens, for example, when the fund is spent on prestigious goods or (religious) festivals, which can, moreover, strengthen ties between community members.

The psychological wellbeing of participants can be improved by releasing the participants from the strains of daily life. For the women the gatherings are a welcome change from their daily housekeeping and they give the women self-confidence. To strengthen a common group feeling, the women tell each other jokes and exchange fantasies. They talk to each other about problems and frictions they face in daily life. For example, a woman may complain about the drinking habits of her husband, or his visits to prostitutes. Thus the ROSCA meeting functions as an outlet for the pressures of daily life. It is difficult to determine a hierarchy of the above-described functions. The case of the women *bishi* suggests that the socio-cultural and psychological functions are more important than the financial ones. When the socio-cultural and/or psychological function in a lottery ROSCA dominate, the obligation of paying financial contributions keeps the whole group together. Non-cooperation in this matter can be punished by exclusion from the next cycle of the financial mutual. Such an incentive is of crucial importance when the husbands of the participants object to social gatherings of their wives, but allow them when gatherings are connected to saving in a financial mutual.

There were no signs of a taboo of speaking about money or an attempt to hide the significance of the economic value of a ROSCA as Ardener (1995:9) suggests for Almedon's description of an Ethiopian ROSCA. This finding supports Almedon's idea that the socio-cultural and psychological functions of ROSCA gatherings may be as important as the financial ones.

To sum up, ROSCAs are multi-functional organizations. If the ultimate goal is finance, social control mechanisms have to be developed and/or maintained as instruments to reach that goal. Then the socio-cultural and psychological aspects act as glue to keep people together. However, if socio-cultural and psychological functions are stressed as the ultimate goal, the regularity of contributions of saving provides the platform on which these activities take place. Furthermore, in cultures where social gatherings of women are not appreciated by their spouses, a financial function can help to ensure the acceptance of such gatherings, which provide pleasure particularly for women, by allowing them to get relieved from daily stresses.

Trust in community-based and business-like organizations

A financial mutual requires mutual trust among the participants. When default occurs, they are all, possibly one more than another, likely to be harmed. In order to reduce risks, newcomers are only allowed to withdraw their fund at the end of the cycle, which enforces them to pay all their contributions before they receive the fund. Such participants appear to have what Granovetter (1973) calls weak ties and a *Gesellschaft*-like way of living, where people's behavior is determined by rational judgement and processes of individualization (Tönnies 2001). Here, trust generally has to be earned, i.e. that it is obtained by showing positively valued behavior and transactions, which is then expected to be continued in the future (Knorringa 1999:70).

When a newcomer in a financial mutual is from the same (religious, caste, ethnic or political) community as the other participants, such measures are often not required, because they know this person's behavior from other occasions. This brings us to the question what defines a community. This is rather difficult, because the concept is multifaceted and multi-interpretable. For the purposes of this paper, a community should be seen as a *Gemeinschaft*-like way of living, which is often associated with 'traditional' homogeneous societies, where people are seen as affective social beings, motivated by feelings of togetherness and mutual solidarity. Here, people know each other from face-to-face and employ multiple activities together (Tönnies 2001). In terms of Granovetter (1973), people have strong ties, leading to a powerful 'us' feeling. Moreover, trust relations are ascribed, because the trust is associated with the status one has, which may be derived from the family background or ethnicity (Knorringa 1999:70). If in such a community, ROSCA participants are harmed by others' default, such incidents may involve personal affairs and can lead to big quarrels (Van der Harst 1974:69; Bouman 1978:37-38). Non-cooperative behavior within a ROSCA may lead to exclusion of the financial mutual in the next cycle or even from the community.

The Mandula can be seen as a *Gemeinschaft*-like community, where norms and values prescribe how to behave. After having been settled in Hyderabad, their community structure is still omnipresent. A traditional male elite, who employs its own legal system with rules and regulations, including punishment and fines, rules the Mandula community. The traditional income-earning activities, such as trading and moneylending, have diversified. While women have mainly developed their own trade, men have also become employed as businessmen, laborers and government employees. The traditional elite developed an 'informal' financial center, through which they could generate additional income. In comparison with the Mandula's own financial mutuals, the financial mutuals which are part of the financial center, are commercial and profit–oriented.

Although the Urban Community Development Department of the Municipal Corporation of Hyderabad introduced a neighborhood community structure with committees, the traditional power structure was maintained. It was the traditional male elite, which dominated the new structure. Moreover, non-Mandula were excluded.

Gemeinschaft-like communities also existed among other classes and religious groups such as Hindus, Muslims and Christians. For example for Muslims, it could be religious values, as illustrated below.

> In Sangli, a group of Muslims started an ASCRA in 1984. The initiators discussed how to cope with the Islamic interest principles in relation with their *bishi.* Although there are different interpretations about the Islamic interest principles (see e.g. Shagil 1989; Qureshi 1983), the bishi was organized around interest free transactions. The Muslims starting the ASCRA managed it successfully. After one year, they had second thoughts about this lack of interest with a view to enlarging the loan fund of their ASCRAs so that more members could be attracted. In order to

> increase the supply of loans, it was decided to introduce interest on credit and the payment of dividend to the participants in their *bishi*. More people, Muslims as well as Hindus, joined the ASCRA and the loan fund increased. (Smets 1992:50-54).

This example shows that it was difficult for the Muslims to stick to their specific financial values in a mixed neighborhood with Hindus, Muslims and Christians. Here, it is shown that a community does not always equal the neighborhood, but only a specific group within the neighborhood. It appears that urban neighborhoods where only one ethnic, caste or religious community lives are scarce. Nowadays, one will find more groups with their own binding social capital in a neighborhood. Even within the settlement of the Mandula, others are settled. They were seen and treated as outsiders. They were considered as not belonging to the community. When there is a strong community feeling, including mutual trust and confidence, community members appear to be more motivated to participate in a financial mutual. However, financial mutuals in their turn probably have the potential of enhancing the solidarity in a neighborhood. This may look like a tautology, but in reality both processes do take place.

To understand the influence of the neighborhood on decisions to partake in a financial mutual, it is important to distinguish the neighborhood as the place of work and of living. In the neighborhood as a place of work, fellows can meet on an almost daily basis and get to know more and more about their peers' character and behavior. Co-workers can join hands at their place of work for many reasons such as overcoming periods of a decline, as shown by Weitering (2003) in his study on railway coolies in Mumbai and Smets (1992:73) in his study on Sangli:

> In 1966, Market Yard was quite a new area in Sangli with shops and storehouses. Coolies were working for wholesalers, who had their storehouses there. There were no proper roads. In the rainy period trucks could not reach the storehouses. During this period, coolies did not obtain work and income. The wholesalers were asked to provide them with money. The wholesalers got fed up with this situation and some of them combined to start a *bishi* for the coolies. In this way, the coolies could save for the slack season and the wholesalers also had a source of working capital. In the 1990s, roads were constructed and the work went on for 12 months a year. In the meantime, more *bishis* appeared in the Market Yard area. In 1988, a group of coolies started the first cycle of their own *bishi*, because these coolies could not easily get loans from the *bishis* in Market Yard. The big shopkeepers were dominating other *bishis*. They took big loans and the coolies were often told that they could not get any credit. The wholesalers took most of the loans. In the new *bishi* of the coolies there is no problem of loan disbursement.

Here, employers and employees initially joined hands, while the employed were not so pleased when it appeared that most of the loans went to the better off. As a reaction they started their own financial mutual. The composition of the last group was more homogeneous and proved to serve more participants better. When one looks at the neighborhood as place of residence, the composition of the neighborhood population influences the existence of and participation in local financial mutuals. When people strongly maintain the links with their place of birth or the neighborhood they grew up in, it becomes more difficult to establish new trustworthy bonds in a new area of settlement.

To trace influences of the place of residence on participation in financial mutuals in Sangli, Smets (1992:43-49) has surveyed two neighborhoods; Ramanata Nagar and Indira Nagar. Ramanata Nagar was originally given to the untouchables or outcastes by the former king of Sangli. In the 1980s, people plotted this agricultural land and sold it. The new owners have constructed their shelter illegally on these plots. In pockets of the area settlers have created their own infrastructure and basic facilities; such as roads, water and electricity connections. These self-help practices appear to have spread towards the organization of and participation in local-based financial mutuals. A *bishi* organizer even set up an ASCRA with the motivation of creating a community feeling in his own neighborhood. Here, the existing co-operation of settlers offers a basis of trust and confidence within the community. *Bishis* therefore have the potential to enhance solidarity in a neighborhood, or part of it. Another neighborhood, called Indira Nagar, is a settlement created by the Municipality of Sangli. Here, squatters from roadside settlements were resettled. For their new place of settlement, each household had to pay a rent of a few Rupees per month. Most settlers have constructed their own shelter, while a small minority could profit from a governmental housing scheme. The population is very fragmented and 2/3 live below the poverty line. Here, self-help is quite individually based, and for basic facilities and infrastructure the settlers depend on the municipality. The weak community feeling among the settlers is also reflected in the organization and participation of local *bishis*. Most settlers have their networks outside the neighborhood and when they participate in a *bishi*, they tend to do it outside the settlement.

One could see that especially the more complex financial mutuals, the auction ROSCA, the ASCRAs with a high number of participants, and the SAVAs tend to be managed by one person or a board in a more business like way. Often profit had to be made. Here, the selection of participants would be done by the organizer(s). It was tempting to welcome only kin, but selection was also based on other criteria, such as: admit only those who are unlikely to leave the community, admit only those who have proven their creditworthiness, or take no chances at all with new members. In larger financial mutuals, face-to-face relations decline. Consequently, formal control mechanisms are increasingly needed for the survival of the larger group of participants. Here, my empirical findings support Hechter's (1987:105, 110-111) theoretical insights.

For example, ASCRAs have to attract participants to enlarge their loan fund. Money within an ASCRA is not lent during the whole cycle. In the beginning, the loan fund remains unused, while at the end of the cycle problems may arise in recollecting outstanding debts. If loans are not recovered in time, ASCRA organizers face problems with closing down their accounts at the end of the cycle. For filling up this gap they may cooperate with other ASCRAs. Money will be transferred temporarily from one ASCRA to another. For example, an ASCRA, which closes down in October, can use a part of the loan fund of an ASCRA, which has a cycle from August till August. The ASCRA first mentioned may close down the accounts and pay back the money lent by the time the outstanding loans are recovered from the defaulters. In this way, some flexibility for the repayment of loans is built in, without damaging other members of the ASCRA concerned. For these transfers *bishi* organizers create their own networks. These networks are maintained by personal contact. A *bishi* organizer may create or extend his own network by motivating friends to start an ASCRA. If necessary s/he may guide and advise them and provide her/himself the possibility of transfers. In Sangli such transfers took place. This could be seen as a first attempt to establish networking between financial mutuals.

To be independent of such an external network, an organizer can organize two ASCRAs with a different cycle to solve problems of loan recovery. In one ASCRA problems may arise potentially leading to the closure of that specific ASCRA, if loans are not repaid in time. The organizer can then transfer money temporarily from the fund of the second ASCRA to the first one. The money transferred will be paid back to the ASCRA when loans are recovered. A popular combination for this purpose is one ASCRA which has a cycle from August to August (Independence Day till Independence Day) and another *bishi* with a cycle from January to January (Republic Day till Republic Day).

If due to good management an increasing amount of money circulates in a financial mutual from cycle to cycle, it could be difficult for organizer(s) to refrain from using the mutual's finance for own purposes. This can have repercussions for the trust in the organizer(s), the financial mutual in general, and among settlers in the neighborhood as shown below.

> In the 1970s, social workers were running ASCRAs in a neighborhood in Sangli, called Sangli Wadi. In one ASCRA the organizers decided to provide the participants with a bigger share in the profits, compared with other financial mutuals in the same area. This *bishi* was well managed and people had confidence in this financial mutual. Every cycle more people became members. Even the total amount of contributions increased every year. Members of the board and their family put big claims on the mutual fund. Problems arose when the third cycle was coming to its end. The money had not been recovered in time. Just before the money had to be paid back to all members, the person responsible committed suicide. Some people even told me that the account books were burned, because the total collection of Rs. 500,000 was gone. After this incident, eight other *bishis* were closed down. The organizers of these *bishis* were afraid that the same thing might occur in their *bishi*. On the other hand, people became hesitant to participate in *bishis*, because they were afraid of losing their money. In Sangli Wadi, only three *bishis* continued. One of these *bishis* stopped in 1976. The president concerned had been running the *bishis* already for seven years. During the last year he faced problems with the secretary. The secretary made false accounts. He disbursed loans on paper,

> but not in practice. The missing money was channeled to his relatives for solving some domestic problems. At the end of the cycle, Rs. 9,000 were lacking. To close down the *bishi* and to pay every member his share, the president took credit from friends and a bank loan. Since 1978, new *bishis* have spread in Sangli Wadi. In the beginning of the 1990s, the members of the board of the *bishi* discussed first are political leaders. They have large sugar cane fields and are related to the sugar factory. Many people are dependent on them for their jobs. Most of the people do not want to speak about the suicide incident. They seem to be afraid of saying negative things about these leaders. Most of the people merely say that it is their own fault that something like this could have happened (Smets 1992:72).

This case shows that default can have repercussions on neighborhood relations. Distrust among the settlers grows very quickly and no one dares to partake in a financial mutual in the neighborhood for many years.

Up till now, the focus of this paper has been on informal financial mutuals. Now the attention will shift to auction ROSCAs that are under control of the Central Bank of India, of which an example will be provided.

> The Chit Fund Corporation Magadarsi in Hyderabad, registered since 1982, organizes three types of auction ROSCAs with twenty participants each. The individual monthly contribution in these *chit funds* is Rs. 500, 1000 or 2500, resulting in a total fund of Rs. 10,000, 20,000 and 50,000 respectively. In total, 25 *chit funds* are operational. The financial turnover is Rs. 27,500 per month.
>
> The minimum auction amount is 5%, which is in fact the commission taken by the organizers. The maximum auction amount is 30%. During the first 7-8 months the maximum amount was always reached and a lottery had to take place to allocate the fund. The auction takes place from 10.30 a.m. onwards. For the different groups there are different timings. A maximum of about hundred people is present at the small office/shop. For the auction itself only 5 minutes are available.
>
> At the 5th of each month, the participants are expected to pay their contributions and at the second Sunday of each month the bidding activities will take place. The time gap offers an opportunity to collect the remaining contributions. Even when people do not pay their contribution until right before the start of the auction, they are still allowed to partake. When a participant is well known by the organizer, the organizer may advance his payments. In this instance, however, a customer should not have delayed payments before. In case of late payments, a penalty of 3% per month will be charged. All financial transactions are noted down in the passbook of each participant.
>
> The organizer employs three staff members and three agents, who motivate people to participate. For each participant brought in, they obtain a commission. Only people with government jobs or well running businesses and those who can bring forward a government employee as guarantor are accepted as participants in a scheme. When a participant wants to have the fund in one of the first months, such a person will be refused. New members are asked to take part in the auction in the 5th-6th month when they have paid regularly his contributions.

The Chit Fund Corporation Magadarsi is registered as a non-banking financial institutions, which are placed under the control of the Central Bank of India. The *chit fund* organizers have to obey the governmental rules and regulations. For example, the organizer has to go to the registration office where he has to submit the number of operational *chit funds*, including registration bylaws and the application forms. Moreover, 50% of the chit value has to be deposited with the register of chits to ensure that all participants will obtain their auctioned amount. Moreover, they want to know how many people are participating in the auction and see the receipt of the amount given to the highest bidder. Besides this, people from the registration office come to inspect the office. This is done to circumvent default.

The manager of the Chit Fund Corporation Magadarsi said that the registration offers a reduction of the risks that a person can run away after receiving the fund. In case of default of participants, the organizer can file a court case. In a period of 10 years, he filed 5-6 court cases, which were solved within 6-7 months. The result was that the defaulter had to pay the outstanding debt, costs of the lawyer and a penalty fixed by the court. Although court cases were pending from 2-3 up to 6-7 years, another *chit fund* organizer stressed that the register should not intervene in case of defaults of one of the participants, but is more focused on preventing default behavior of the organizers.

Participants in a registered *chit fund* need to have a regular and large enough income (often twice the size of the fund of the *chit fund*) and are often required to be backed up by a guarantor. Participants can also pledge goods or papers, or provide a bank guarantee. Once participation is accepted, the contributions have to be paid personally at the office, but some companies employ a *pygmee agent*, who collects the contributions. Such a *pygmee agent* (recovery boy) has a fixed monthly salary, but he is responsible for losses of the collections made.

Longer ROSCA cycles can be found with registered *chit funds*, but are not preferred due to their high default rates. Interviewed organizers of registered *chit funds* report that the length of a cycle should not exceed a maximum of 20 months in order to maintain the social control mechanism. In reality, one can even trace cycles of 50 months.

Recapitulating development trajectories

SAVAs, ROSCAs and ASCRAs can be found simultaneously in the same region or city. Each financial mutual may serve its own clientele that has different needs. The emergence of the different types of associations may suggest that there is a parallel development and that there is no fixed development path from one specific financial mutual into another type. However, when one looks over a relatively long period of time, one can detect ontogenetic development patterns. During cycles, the best solutions for coping with specific circumstances survive and a kaleidoscope of variations on the different types of financial mutuals (SAVA, ROSCA and ASCRA) develops. It is hard to follow the same financial mutual from one cycle to another, but this is tried as far as it was possible As a consequence, an enormous number of financial mutuals had to be interpreted. The development trajectories, which I could trace, can be distinguished in an institutional and functional path.

Institutional development can be observed at two levels; the organizational set-up and the kind of management practiced. At the organizational level, the case study of the Mandula shows a development from the SAVA towards the ASCRA. In the established financial center, apart from the ASCRAs, auction ROSCAs were also introduced. It appeared that there was a shift from community-based to more business-like organizations. Such development could be expected when more money circulates due to a boosting economic development. In Sangli, this was accompanied with a simultaneous shortage of banks. If banks are available at all, they tend to be difficult to access by low-income groups. This development applies only when participants share in the economic growth and do not remain in an economically marginal position.

Finding 1: If the local economy boosts and *access to banks is restricted, if available at all, financial mutuals develop from community-based to more business-like forms.*

In the financial mutuals studied, it appears that participants and organizers develop all kind of incentives, based on especially social control mechanisms to diminish cheating and defaulting behavior. Mutual trust has mostly to be earned and ascribed trust to be proven over time. The peer pressure or pressure from the organizer to pay the contributions in time is strong and default rarely occurs. Sometimes the participants even have to sell or pawn goods or take out a loan in order to meet the obligations towards the financial mutual in which they participate. To ensure an increase in the welfare of all participants in a financial mutual, selective incentives of an informal or more formalized nature are used.

Nowadays, the question is whether financial mutuals should be brought under control of the Central Bank. De Soto (2001) expects a lot from the legalization of property owned partly or entirely outside the judicial system. Once legalized, property can help people to obtain credit, insurances and utility services.

The registration of chit funds as financial non-banking institutions shows that the rules and regulations accompanying such registration circumvent default behavior to a certain extent. However these chit funds lose their flexibility of adjusting to the needs of clients. In fact, they have already specialized by focussing on auction as a suitable method for allocating the fund. The chit fund corporations are commercial and ask their clientele for sureties and large contributions, only the better off can cope with. This way, poorer sections of the population are excluded.

Finding 2: If financial mutuals are legalized, they only serve the better off and tend to keep the poorest sections of society out of the system.

Among the Mandula, the management of the financial mutual was and stays authoritarian according to the norms and value pattern in their own community.

In other examples of financial mutuals, it appears that when the participants organize and manage the financial mutual as a group, a democratic way of management is practiced. In a more complex ROSCA, such as the auction ROSCA, and the ASCRA the organization and management is the responsibility of one person or a small number of people. Moreover, SAVAs are generally organized and managed by a few persons, while more people participate.

Finding 3: If the size (participants and/or money) of financial mutuals with a savings and credit component increases and the organizational set-up becomes more complex, the management style tends to shift from a democratic to an authoritarian form in the hands of a few.

The second development trajectory deals with the function the financial mutual has for its participants. A financial and insurance function is often combined with a social function, but in Hyderabad to a lesser extent. In Hyderabad as well as Sangli, the social function dominates the ROSCA for middle and high-income women and finance plays here a minor role. However, for low-income women the finance is of importance; they do need the finance from the financial mutual for coping with expenditures for the household.

Finding 4: If elite women participate in a ROSCA together, the main function of the mutual can shift for them from finance to social issues.

Apart from development trajectories, it may also happen that there is a drawback in development. In such circumstances, devolution takes place. This happens in Sangli Wadi where well-organized and well-managed ASCRAs attracted an increasing number of participants when a new cycle started. However, the organizer(s) faced problems in dealing with this growing amount of finance. Default behavior has led to a collapse of the financial mutual. Consequently mutual trust between the organizer(s) and the participants collapsed leading to mistrust among the inhabitants of Sangli Wadi.

Finding 5: If the collapse of a successful financial mutual was caused by default of the organizer(s), mutual trust among neighborhood settlers and the operation of other financial mutuals will be severely affected for many years.

The ontogenetic development patterns as shown above provide insight in the development of specific financial mutuals and cover only a period of a few decades. To trace phylogenetic development trajectories, the findings may be used as hypotheses, which will have to be tested for other localities and periods.

Notes

1 This article draws heavily on my research in the Indian cities of Hyderabad and Sangli in the 1990s. I want to express my gratitude to Christine Delhaye, Hotze Lont, Ton Salman and Heike Schröder for commenting earlier versions of this paper.

2 The informal financial sector encompasses savings, borrowing and lending activities, which are beyond the reaches of the official regulation and control of the Central Bank (Bouman 1989:5-6).

3 During the time of research, the Mandula were classified as a backward community and not any more as a scheduled tribe, because they were not living in isolation.

4 One Indian rupee (Rs.) equals 0.033 US $ (1993-1994).

5 In general, the poorer sections of society face serious problems in obtaining access to 'formal' banks, if they obtain it at all (see for housing finance Smets 2004:173-176).

6 *Makar Sankranti* is a Hindu festival, which is held on the occasion that the sun enters the sign of *Makar*, corresponding to Capricorn. It occurs on the first day of the solar month *Magh*. On this day the sun reaches its most southern point and will start moving to its most northern point of the Zodiac. This period is called *Uttarayana*, whose days are reckoned as lucky ones (Balfour 1967:799-800).

7 *Narali Purnima*, or coconut full moon day, is a Hindu festival, which corresponds with the full moon of the month *Shravan* (July-August). On this day sisters tie an amulet, called *rakhi*, around the wrist of their brothers. *Narali Purnima* is considered auspicious to break a coconut at a shrine on starting any enterprise (Sharma 1975:438).

References

Adams, D.W.
1992 'Taking a Fresh Look at Informal Finance.' In: D.W. Adams & D.A. Fitchett (eds), *Informal Finance in Low-income Countries*. Boulder: Westview.

Adams, D.W. & M.L. Canavesi
1989 'Rotating Savings and Credit Associations in Bolivia.' *Savings and Development*, XVIII(3):219-235.

Almedon, A.M.
1995 'A Note on ROSCAs among Ethiopian Women in Addis Abada and Eritrean Women in Oxford.' In: S. Ardener & S. Burman (eds), *Money-Go-Rounds: The Importance of Rotating Savings and Credit Associations for Women*. Oxford/Washington: Berg.

Anderson, R.T.
1966 'Rotating Credit Associations in India.' *Economic Development and Cultural Change*, xiv, 334-339.

Ardener, S.
1995 'Women Making Money Go Round: ROSCAs Revisited.' In: S. Ardener & S. Burman (eds), *Money-Go-Rounds: The Importance of Rotating Savings and Credit Associations for Women*, 1-19. Oxford/Washington: Berg.

Ardener, S.
1964 'The Comparative Study of Rotating Credit Associations.' *The Journal of the Royal Anthropological Institute of Great Britain and Ireland*, 94, 201-229.

Bähre, E.
1996 'We Organize Each Other.' Financial Self-help Groups and Civics in the Townships of Cape Town, South Africa. MA thesis, University of Utrecht.

Balfour, E.
1967 *The Cyclopeadia of India and of Eastern and Southern Asia*, II. Graz: Akademische Druck u. Verlagsanstalt.
Bouman, F.J.A.
1978 'Indigenous Savings and Credit Societies in the Third World.' *Development Digest*, XVI, 336-47.
1989 *Small, Short and Unsecured: Informal Rural Finance in India.* Delhi: Oxford University Press.
1995 'ROSCA: On the Origin of the Species.' *Savings and Development,* XIX(2):117-145.
Bouman, F.J.A. & O. Hospes
1994 *Financial Landscapes Reconstructed: The Fine Art of Mapping Development.* Boulder, etc.: Westview Press.
De Soto, H.
2001 *The Mystery of Capital: Why Capitalism Triumphs in the West and Fails Everywhere Else.* London: Black Swan.
Economic Research Group
1993 'How to Build your own Dream House.' *Deccan Chronicle*, Business Finance section, 13-14, Monday September 20.
GAP (Government of Andhra Pradesh)
1977 *Report of the Andhra Pradesh Tribes Enquiry Committee*, 1, 1961-1962. Hyderabad: Education Department.
Geertz, C.
1962 'The Rotating Credit Association: a "Middle Rung" in Development.' *Economic Development and Cultural Change*,(10)3:241-263.
Granovetter, M.S.
1973 'The Strength of Weak Ties.' *American Journal of Sociology,* 78(6):1360-1380
Hechter, M.
1987 *Principles of Group Solidarity.* Berkeley,[etc.]: University of California Press.
Hospes, O.
1995 'Women's Differential Use of ROSCAs in Indonesia.' In: S. Ardener & S. Burman (eds), *Money-Go-Rounds: The Importance of Rotating Savings and Credit Associations for Women*, 127-148. Oxford/Washington D.C.: Berg.
Knorringa, P.
1999 'Trust and Distrust in Artisan-Trader Relations in the Agra-footwear Industry, India.' In: P. Smets, H. Wels & J. van Loon (eds), *Trust & Co-operation: Symbolic Exchange and Moral Economies in an Age of Cultural Differentiation.* Amsterdam: Het Spinhuis.
Lont, H.
2002 *Juggling Money in Yogyakarta. Financial Self-help Organizations and the Quest for Security.* PhD thesis, University of Amsterdam.
Nayar, C.P.S.
1986 'Can a Traditional Financial Technology Co-exist with Modern Financial Technologies? The Indian Experience.' *Savings and Development*, 1:31-56.
Qureshi, A.I.
1983 *Islam and the Theory of Interest.* Delhi: Idarah-I Adabiyat-I Delli.
Radhakrishna, R. & S. Galab
1994 *Informal Mutual Credit Associations in India: a Case of Slums in Hyderabad.* Hyderabad: Center for Economic and Social Studies.

Radhakrishnan, S. et al.
1975 'Chit Funds.' In: S.L.N. Simha (ed.), *Chit Funds and Finance Corporations.* Madras: Institute for Financial Management and Research.
Raghaviah, V.
1968 *Nomads.* Hyderabad: Bharateeya Adimajata Sevak Sangh.
Ranga Raju, K.P.
1969 'Mandulavaru Vari Jeevitha Vidhanamu (Mandulas and their way of living).' *Tribal,* VII(1&2):75-82. (Translated by G. Ramalakshmi).
Schrader, H.
1991 *Rotating Saving and Credit Associations – Institutions in the 'Middle Rung' of Development.* Southeast Asia Programme Working Paper 148, Bielefeld: University of Bielefeld, Faculty of Sociology.
Schrieder, G.R. & C.E. Cuevas
1992 'Informal Financial Groups in Cameroon.' In: D.W. Adams & D.A. Fitchett (eds), *Informal Finance in Low-income Countries.* Boulder/San Francisco/Oxford: Westview.
Scott, J.C.
1985 *Weapons of the Weak. Everyday Forms of Peasant Resistance.* New Haven, London: Yale.
Seibel, H.D. & H. Schrader
1999 'Dhikuti Revisited: From ROSCA to Finance Company.' *Savings and Development,* XXIII(1):47-55.
Seibel H.D. & B.P. Shrestha
1988 'Dhikuti: The Small Businessman's Informal Self-help Bank in Nepal.' *Savings and Development,* XII(2):183-198.
Shaghil, M.
1989 *Islamic Economics: A Global Perspective.* New Delhi: Ashish Publishing House.
Shanmugam, B.
1991 'Socio-economic Development through the Informal Credit Market.' *Modern Asian Studies,* 25(2):209-225.
Sharma, J.S.
1975 *Encyclopaedia Indica.* New Delhi: Chand & Co.
Smets, P.
1992 *My Stomach is my Bishi: Savings and Credit Associations in Sangli, India.* Urban Research Working Papers, 30. Amsterdam: Vrije Universiteit.
1996 'Community-based Finance Systems and their Potential for Urban Self-help in a New South Africa.' *Development Southern Africa,* 13(2):173-187.
1998 'Money-Go-Rounds for women: Finance as Instrument or as Ultimate Goal in Lottery ROSCAs.' *Anthropos,* 93:209-215.
2000 'ROSCAs as a Source of Housing Finance for the Urban Poor: An Analysis of Self-help Practices from Hyderabad, India.' *Community Development Journal,* 35(1):16-30
2004 *Housing Finance and the Urban Poor.* Jaipur, New Delhi: Rawat.
Smets, P. & A. Broekman
1996 Turkse vrouwen en hun *güns* in Amsterdam. In: M.Van der Linden & J. Sluijs (eds) *Onderlinge hulpfondsen. Historische en etnografische essays.* Amsterdam: Stichting beheer IISG.

Srinivasan, S.
1995 'ROSCAs among South Asians in Oxford.' In: S. Ardener & S. Burman (eds) *Money-go-rounds. The Importance of Rotating Savings and Credit Associations for Women.* Oxford, Washington: Berg.
Summerfield, H.
1995 'A Note on ROSCAs among Northern Somali Women in the United Kingdom.' In: S. Ardener & S. Burman (eds) *Money-go-rounds. The Importance of Rotating Savings and Credit Associations for Women,* 209-215. Oxford, Washington: Berg.
Thurston, E. & K. Rangachari
1975 *Castes and Tribes of Southern India,* IV. Hyderabad: Cosmos Publications.
Tönnies, F.
2001 [1957] 'Gemeinschaft and Gesellschaft.' In: J.J. Macionis & N.V. Benokraitis (eds) *Seeing Ourselves: Classic, Contemporary, and Cross-cultural Readings in Sociology.* New Jersey: Prentice Hall.
Van der Harst, J.
1974 *Financing of Housing by Low-income Groups.* Joint Research Project IV for Urban Development and Slum Improvement. Karachi: University of Karachi.
Weitering, D.
2003 'Carrying the Load Together. Mumbai Railway Coolies and their Quest for Labor, Income and Social Security.' Master Thesis Cultural Anthropology, University of Nijmegen, The Netherlands.

CHAPTER 7

Varieties of mutualism

Marcel van der Linden

Introduction

Many thousands of voluntary, independent financial self-help societies and organizations existed in Europe and North America in the nineteenth and early twentieth centuries. In England, for instance, many working class neighborhoods had 'draw clubs,' usually made up of twenty women who deposited a specific sum every week in a kitty, and could then spend the entire week's kitty on purchases from a local shop. There were also 'mutuality clubs' offering a type of regular loan, and many 'friendly societies' that organized mutual insurance to cover the cost of illness or funerals (Roberts 1973:33; Carr-Saunders et al. 1940:120-123; Gosden 1961). Organizations in other countries had different emphases: in France, for example, small producer cooperatives were relatively more common.

Most forms of collective self-help disappeared in Europe or became part of the state bureaucracy with the advent of welfare states following the Second World War, or when the bank and credit system became more accessible to an increasing number of people. Large-scale anonymous structures replaced the old arrangements, which had been much smaller and more vulnerable. For a long time neither historians nor social scientists have shown much interest in these voluntary associations of the past. This has begun to change since the late 1980s (see e.g. Yeo 1988). There are several reasons for this shift: not only has a more flexible, informal economy fostered the revaluation of small-scale structures, it has also affected historical research.[1] Moreover, the crisis in the traditional labor movement stimulated exploration of less heroic and more defensive aspects of labor history. The growing interest in the development of mutual insurance is one sign of this (Van der Linden 1996).

The social sciences have experienced parallel developments. Anthropologists and ethnographers have become interested in micro-financial institutions in the Third World. Although cooperative loan societies were mentioned in the late nineteenth century, such information was hardly used for analytic purposes (e.g. Smith 1899:141-145, 152-160, 179-195). It was only in the 1960s, when Clifford

Geertz developed a comparative perspective in an influential article that explored the similarities and differences between rotating credit associations in different areas of the world (Geertz 1962), that this began to change. Soon after, a second groundbreaking essay appeared by the British anthropologist Shirley Ardener, who critically amended Geertz's analysis (Ardener 1964). From the 1980s onwards, research in this field gained momentum. This surge of interest is probably directly related to the international debt crisis, which reached a first climax in August 1982 when Mexico declared itself insolvent. The enormous financial problems in parts of the Third World have led to a revaluation of previously neglected financial sources (Essombé Edimo 1998:861). There is clearly excitement and hope that 'much poverty can be alleviated' by providing financial services to low-income households through micro-financial institutions (Murdoch 1999:1569).

Never before have so many different disciplines shown so much interest in the present and past of autonomous micro-financial institutions. The essays in this book reflect this new interest and provide important contributions to the growing literature. Their value is to be found not only in the description of hitherto unknown examples, but also, and especially, in their attempts to interpret these examples from a comparative historical perspective. This concluding chapter will attempt to integrate two elements: to place the results presented in this collection of essays in the wider context of the literature on this subject, and to connect many of the existing individual historical and social-scientific studies. Of course, what follows is only tentative and provisional.

This collection of essays focuses on the different varieties of 'mutualism.' Mutualism is a concept that goes back to the nineteenth century,[2] and includes *all voluntary arrangements in which people make contributions to a fund, which is given, in whole or in part, to one or more of the contributors according to specific rules of allocation.* What is the basis for mutualism? This can most easily be answered by borrowing from rational choice theory, without necessarily accepting the theory in its entirety (van der Linden 1997). There are goods in everyday life that people 'desire but cannot provide at all, or as efficiently, for themselves as individuals.' (Hechter 1987:33) Such goods can consist of labor, commodities, or money. There are two possible reasons for the existence of such goods. On the one hand, there are many things in any society that individuals cannot possibly create on their own within a reasonable period of time. To do this they need other people to help them. The concept is also referred to as intrinsic jointness. Second, there are tasks that an individual could well perform, but which would have significant negative effects on the person involved: for example, because working to obtain something on one's own may be frightening or stultifying. In both instances, individuals benefit by asking others for help (Figure 1). In return for this help they can perform a similar (reciprocal) task or pay for it.[3]

FIGURE 1 **Decision-making tree diagram of a rational individual who pursues an object**

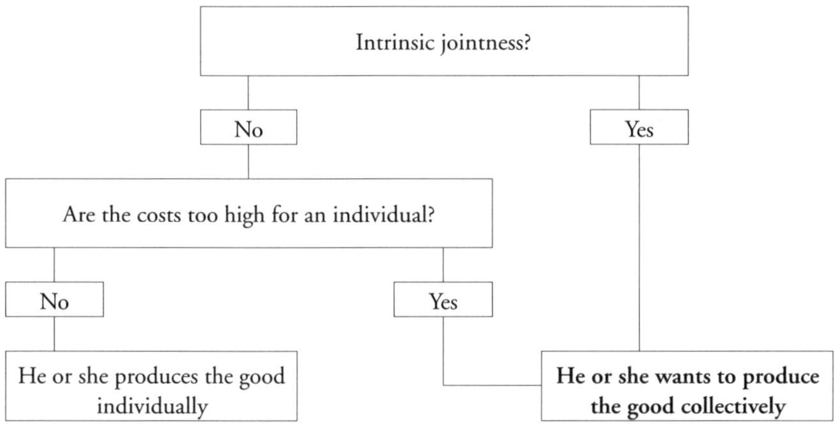

Typology

Labor Mutuals

In such mutual arrangements different people contribute labor, commodities, or money to a shared project. I will first examine mutual institutions in which the fund consists of labor. Such institutions can either rotate labor or use labor for the production of one object from which all can benefit. In the first example (rotation), the labor of the others in the group is first 'consumed' by one person, then another has his turn, and so on. Such forms of labor rotation are known around the world (see e.g., Epstein 1962:73; Dawley 1976:57; Wong 1987:120). Nicolaas van Meeteren, for example, described such widespread arrangements in Curaçao, which were common there up to the first decades of the twentieth century:

> Whenever one needed to weed, plant or harvest, the custom was implemented that was known as 'saam.' All neighbors then agreed to work for each other once or twice in the week in the evening by moonlight. The person for whom the work was done provided rum and refreshments. As the workers encouraged each other by singing in turns in 'guenee' or 'Macamba,' the work went smoothly and everyone benefited by it. (Van Meeteren 1947:35)

Van Meeteren thinks that a *saam* had an advantage because 'the work was done much faster, as each worker encouraged another,' which is very important, especially for labor in the fields (Van Meeteren 1947:35). Other writers confirm this. David Ames offers two explanations: working in a group stimulates competition among workers and is more agreeable: 'Working with one's companions, joking and singing, is obviously less tedious than solitary labor.' (Ames 1959:231)

Work in the fields is of course not the only form of labor that can be rotated. The barn raisings that were very common in the United States in the nineteenth century are another example: every first Sunday of the month a group of farmers built a new barn for one of their members, until every member of the group had had his turn (Besley, Coate & Loury 1993: 793note). In yet another type of arrangement women take care of each other's children in turns, or help each other with other tasks.

In the second form of labor mutualism, the joint effort results in a *shared* product. The members of the collective come together once or several times to work for the production of the product from which they all hope to benefit when it is finished.[4] The collective building of a community center or church are good examples.

Labor mutualism is often less important when money becomes more central to the local economy, or when social inequality increases. The tendency to purchase labor tasks with money usually increases when this happens. Returning to the example of Curaçao, we find that van Meeteren observes that the *saam* largely disappeared after the 1920s or 1930s. While similar trends occurred in many places (Erasmus 1956; Karunanayake 1979; Brown 1987), there are also exceptions to this rule. For the Maka in Southeastern Cameroon, the rise of cash crop cultivation has actually stimulated labor rotation because the Maka refuse to perform wage labor for the other villagers (Geschiere 1995).

Rotating savings and credit funds (ROSCAs)

It is a small step from labor mutuals to mutual institutions in which the fund consists wholly or partly of goods or money. Labor rotation exactly corresponds to the simplest kind of rotating and credit savings mutual, the ROSCA, in which labor input is replaced by a contribution in kind or in money. The cycle in the simplest ROSCA can be represented as in Table 1 (compare Ardener 1964:214).

TABLE 1 **A simple ROSCA**

	Contribution|Sum received			
Member	*1st meeting*	*2nd meeting*	*3rd meeting*	*Total*
A	10|0	10|30	10|0	30|30
B	10|30	10|0	10|0	30|30
C	10|0	10|0	10|30	30|30

For example, an anthropological study in the early 1960s recorded that Indian migrants on the island of Mauritius had a ROSCA that was called *cycle* or *cheet*: 'A man or a woman calls together a group of friends and neighbors. Suppose there are ten of them, and each puts in Rs. 10. They then draw lots and the winner takes the Rs. 100. (Sometimes the organizer automatically takes the first 'pool'.) The following month each again puts in Rs. 10, and another member takes the resulting Rs. 100; and so it continues for ten months until each member has had his Rs. 100'

(Benedict 1964:341). In other words, sums of money were deposited in the *cheet*, but for the rest the logic was the same as in labor rotation. It is therefore not surprising that some researchers believe ROSCAs originated in rotating labor pools.[5] Whether this hypothesis is true can only be determined by further empirical research.

But ROSCAs can also be much more complex than the simple case outlined above. The allocation of the order of rotation is central to ROSCAs. This can be determined by (i) a common arrangement between the participants, (ii) an allocation by the organizer, (iii) by auction, or (iv) by drawing lots. In an auction participants can of course exert a strong influence on the order of allocation, and this method can therefore lead to complex relations of debt and credit within the arrangement (Calomiris & Rajaraman 1998:211-215). To return to the Mauritius example, we find that, like the Indian immigrants on the island, the Chinese also had ROSCAs, but these functioned in a different way:

> The Chinese on the island as elsewhere operate a variant of the cycle in which the 'lenders' (late drawers) in effect receive interest payments from the 'borrowers' (early drawers). The participants bid for turns; a man in need of quick cash may bid to take Rs. 90 instead of Rs. 100, if permitted to draw first, or he may agree to put in a total of Rs. 110 over the cycle if he can have Rs. 100 immediately. Thus the other members of the cycle receive in due course more than their contributions; the difference is a form of interest paid to them by those in more urgent need of money. If the second and third drawings are bid for as well, the total interest payments to the more patient members increases. (Benedict 1964:341; Freedman 1979)

The number of varieties of allocation by ROSCAs is staggering, and the complexity of the arrangement could become significant.[6] Why some ROSCAs are more complex than others is still largely unknown.[7] But it is perhaps no coincidence that the most complex varieties occur in village communities with a long history. Perhaps newcomers, such as migrants who have only recently become acquainted where they are newly settled, prefer less complex arrangements, whereas groups that have a very tight, stable, and relatively old community culture are more likely to experiment with the rules and sometimes develop complex varieties along those lines.

Savings and loan associations (SLAs)

The sum that has to be deposited at every meeting of a ROSCA can vary considerably. Erik Bähre observed in Cape Town: 'On average, the participants contributed R200 to a monthly ROSCA and R60 to a weekly ROSCA. There were also ROSCAs with much higher contributions, like a 'BMW 518 Stokvel' where 50 members each contributed R1,000 per fortnight. The members each received R50,000 in turn and purchased a BMW 518. This ROSCA was an exception that indicates that ROSCAs were not only for the poorest. Most Africans, however, could hardly afford to dream of a car' (Bähre 2002:26).

There are goods that are too expensive to pay for with ordinary ROSCAs. Houses are a clear example of this. In general, they are so expensive that households have to save many years for them (if they can save that amount of money at all). In such cases a ROSCA can be set up so that the members do not receive a payment in every round, but only after several rounds. If, for instance, ten families each want a house worth 10,000, and if these families deposit 1,000 every year in a shared fund, then one family can buy a house after one year, and after ten years all families have a house. Such extended ROSCAs were established in the United States in the first half of the nineteenth century, and afterwards they were introduced in many other countries. In Germany they were known as *Bausparkassen* (Block 1931; Scholten 2000). ROSCAs of this type were also referred to as 'terminating societies,' because they were discontinued when all the founders had had their turn.[8]

Simultaneous allocation

As the ROSCAs are in a sense similar to forms of rotating labor, the second form of labor allocation has a counterpart in the domain of goods and money. In this type a group saves a certain amount of money by means of periodic contributions. The group can subsequently do one of three things with this sum. It can buy a common object that remains a collective possession (a joint object), it can redistribute the sum saved among the participants (individual allocation of money), or it can buy goods that will subsequently be distributed among the participants (individual allocation of goods).

Joint goods can be anything. In the 1950s Harry Hoetink gave a very common example of 'the system that occurred in the Netherlands in which several housewives buy a washing machine together, and use it in turn' (Hoetink 1956:43). An important form of joint goods allocation is represented by the production cooperatives of small commodity producers (craftsmen, farmers), such as the cooperative dairies, which in their original form 'consisted merely of a group of dairymen banded together on the basis of turning the milk into cheese, each man being left with his cheese to dispose of as best as he could' (Hibbard 1930:522). Similar arrangements occur around the world. The *mahaber* is an Ethiopian example: 'It usually has the purpose of providing assistance to those who are still in the countryside, not having migrated to an urban area. Thus, the residents of a principal city will meet periodically, and provide funds to support some project back in the home village or in the countryside, such as building a school, hospital, road, community hall, or furnishing one of these facilities, or some other needy purpose.' (Gerdes 1975:219) Bouman and Harteveld provide an example from Western Cameroon around 1970: 'Sometimes all money is pooled for a specific purpose as with the Cornmill Societies, to enable women to buy a corn mill to relieve them of the tedious maize-grinding by hand' (Bouman & Harteveld 1976:107).[9] Such a savings association would have a structure of the type indicated in Table 2. This type of a savings association can be effective even if there is only one meeting, providing that single round is sufficient to purchase the joint good.

TABLE 2 **A simple savings association for joint goods**

	Contribution/Sum received			
Member	*1st meeting*	*2nd meeting*	*3rd meeting*	*Total*
A	10/0	10/0	10/0	30/0
B	10/0	10/0	10/0	30/0
C	10/0	10/0	10/0	30/0

The situation is different in the case of *individual allocation of money*, an arrangement that is also known as a savings association (SAVA) in the literature (Smets 1996:178). Erik Bähre gives an example of an unofficial settlement near Cape Town: 'Each month the members met at a member's house and deposited R150. One of the members, Nofurniture, saved R300 per month; R150 for her and R150 on the name of a fictive person. The money was deposited in a group account at NedBank. Ten months later she received about R3,000, which she used to rebuild her house in Transkei.' (Bähre 2002:215 note) Migrant workers in Cameroon have an institution which they call a *family meeting* or *country meeting*. These are associations of people from the same region or from an area where the same language is spoken. 'They help members to find jobs and to adjust to the new conditions of life, and give aid in times of trouble. The meetings are mainly social occasions, but they also have some important economic functions.' (Delancey 1977:319) Delancey (1977:320) wrote the following about this:

> The ethnic associations in anglophone Cameroon are a regular feature of the lives of a large proportion of those who live in a migration 'location': 80 per cent of those who come from 'outside' are members, as well as 40 per cent of those whose origin is in the neighborhood. The meetings range in size from 10-12 to about 100, and are usually held soon after pay day in a plantation camp or a centrally-located town.... The get-together frequently opens with some business transactions. Members contribute money to be held as savings by the associations until the end of the year, and the treasurer deposits these funds in a bank and/or may make interest-payable loans to members and, occasionally, to non-members. All savings and accumulated interest are returned to the members in November or December, and this enables them to pay their heavy Christmas expenses. But many immediately return a large proportion of the accrued funds to the savings program for the next year, which opens at the same meeting.... During the year as many as 30-60 per cent of the members may take such loans, and although in most meetings these cannot exceed what the borrowers have saved in the society, the amount may sometimes be raised to the extent that other members are willing to pledge their savings as a guarantee of loan repayment. In case of default, the sureties lose their savings.

In SAVAs one round is of course never sufficient. The individual contribution would then be equal to the individual payment, and consequently the arrangement would lose its raison d'être.

The last variety is the *individual allocation of goods*. This includes, for example, the simplest consumer cooperatives, which are also known as 'dividing stores.' The following example illustrates this. Arthur von Studnitz, a German social reformer who traveled across the United States in 1876 to do research, reported a conversation with a mule spinner from Fall River. The spinner's story was as follows:

> The seven of us were working in a factory when prices rose so much that we could hardly afford to buy food anymore. So we decided to pool our dollars and cents to buy what we needed more cheaply. Each of us calculated his family's needs for the next month. We drew up a budget of ninety-eight dollars and appointed a secretary, who footed up everything we needed. Next, we sent someone to purchase the goods. We rented an area, brought the items there, and distributed them. When everything cost less than expected, we would refund the balance. When it cost more, we paid what was due. We called our area the Mule Spinners Cooperative Store. We purchased our clothes the same way, except that we agreed to buy from the dealer that offered us the biggest discount. The dealer gave us stamps entitling us to a discount, thus saving us ten percent on clothes and twelve percent on sewing supplies. (Von Studnitz 1879:206-207)[10]

Simultaneous allocation with credit facilities

A fund created for simultaneous allocation can also be used as a credit facility. In that case all the members of the group regularly deposit money in the fund, but they can also temporarily take money from it, promising to pay it back later. Usually a member who takes out a loan will have to pay interest on it. Such an arrangement is also referred to as an accumulating savings and credit association (ASCRA) (Bouman 1994:376-377). Smith describes nineteenth-century Chinese religious societies whose purpose it was to enable members to go on pilgrimages to five sacred mountains. To cover the cost of such a journey, 'traveling mountain societies' (*hsing-shan hui*) were established to which members contributed a specified sum of money every month. The societies were usually set up so that a pilgrimage could be undertaken after three years. In the meanwhile short-term loans could be drawn from the fund at a high interest rate (Smith 1899:141-143). Marjorie Topley described the so-called *pork societies* in Hong Kong's New Territories in the late 1950s:

> Each member contributes $2-$3 a month and the money is used to buy pigs for slaughter at the Chinese New Year. (Pigs are cheaper when bought in bulk.) The meat is usually distributed in equal weight among members, the best cuts apparently going to those reckoned to have the highest social standing in the group. In lineage-based associations the allocation of the various cuts may be according to kinship status. Loans from funds of pork societies may be available to members for from two to ten months. Amounts lent are said to vary from about $50-$200 per member, with interest working out at about 5 per cent a month. (Topley 1964:178)

Producer cooperation

When a group of people sets up a fund to buy some means of production (instruments, etc.) to start a business on their own, this is actually a combined purchasing, production, and selling cooperative that employs the members. Such arrangements have a long history. One example of this is the association set up by fourteen unemployed piano makers in Paris one and a half centuries ago.

> They began ... by collecting contributions of a few pennies from each member. Since they worked from home, most owned some of the necessary material for their trade: they contributed to the society in kind. On 10 March 1849 they established the society with 2,000 francs worth of inventory and 229.50 francs in cash. Following this major accomplishment, the society was ready for clients. None came for two months. Of course, the members obtained neither profit nor salary; they survived by pawning their personal belongings. The fourth month they found a bit of repair work and earned some money. Dividing it amongst themselves, they obtained 6.60 francs apiece. Each member kept 5 francs from this modest dividend. The surplus (i.e., 1.60 francs per person) was used for a fraternal banquet with their wives and children to celebrate the association's auspicious beginning.... In June, a few weeks later, they had a windfall, an order for an entire piano costing 480 francs! (Gide 1923:19-20)[11]

Mutual insurance

It is also possible that a fund can be set up on the basis of periodic contributions, which is paid out, partly or entirely, only when a calamity occurs. The savings fund is then used as insurance. Again there are two varieties: the money is used to cover individual or collective risks.

There is *collective coverage of risks* when the group is threatened by a common danger, a danger that can only be averted by spending on joint goods. Daniel Defoe (1697: section 'Of Friendly Societies') gave an example when he wrote about

> our marshes and fens in Essex, Kent, and the Isle of Ely, where great quantities of land being with much pains and a vast charge recovered out of the seas and rivers, and maintained with banks (which they call walls), the owners of those lands agree to contribute to the keeping up of those walls; and if I have a piece of land in any level or marsh, though it bonds nowhere on the sea or river, yet I pay my proportion to the maintenance of the said wall or bank; and if at any time the sea breaks in, the damage is not laid upon the man in whose land the breach happened, unless it was by his neglect, but it lies on the whole land, and is called a level lot.

There is *individual coverage of risks* when the members of the association are individually threatened by a danger, such as illness, death, or disabilities caused by labor. In those cases all members contribute to the fund periodically, but only those members requiring a payment for a specific reason receive a benefit from the fund. Such an arrangement is represented in Table 3.

TABLE 3 **Simple mutual insurance association**

	Contribution|Sum received			
Member	*1st meeting*	*2nd meeting*	*3rd meeting*	*Total*
A	10|0	10|0	10|0	30|0
B	10|0	10|0	10|90	30|90
C	10|0	10|0	10|0	30|0

Interactions and transformations

It is not uncommon for mutual associations to be linked with one another, directly or indirectly. People are sometimes members of several associations of the same type at the same time. Often members 'repay debts with debts.' (Lont 2002:233)[12] Bouman and Harteveld (1976:111) observed how such multiple memberships cause ROSCAs and ASCRAs to become no longer 'small, separated societies,' but 'a system of linked credit rings' in which money continually flows from one association to another. Associations of different types can also be connected. In the west of Cameroon, in addition to ROSCAs (*djanggi*), there are also 'special fund societies,' a type of ASCRA. These special funds 'sometimes take the form of a trouble fund and are combined with djanggis, making the latter all the more flexible and better adapted to the needs of its members. A member, unable to honor his djanggi-subscription at a particular meeting, can take a loan from the trouble fund against 5 % interest monthly.' (Bouman & Harteveld 1976:107) Moreover, an association can change from one type to another (a SAVA can, for example, become an ASCRA). A mutual arrangement can also be transformed into a commercial enterprise or a game of chance.[13] Other forms of organization can also be transformed into mutual associations. In Piedmont mutual insurance associations were formed to replace the guilds that had existed earlier but were prohibited in 1844 (Allio 1998:441).[14]

A special kind of transformation occurs when mutual associations become permanent or are institutionalized. We have seen that the life span of rotating societies, which is limited in principle, can be extended by starting again after each cycle. But the rotating principle can also be removed from rotating associations, becoming institutionalized in this way. In the past, this happened fairly often with savings and loan associations, for instance, by allowing people to become members who did not want to buy a house for themselves but regarded the association as a good investment (Block 1931:170f.). Institutionalized forms of non-rotating arrangements, such as ASCRAs, are well-known, for example, credit unions. As is the case with many ASCRAs, members of such associations have some common bond, such as religion or profession. They have a corporate structure, and their function is mainly to provide short-term cash credit to members at nominal rates of interest. In the course of the twentieth century, credit unions have spread from North America to many other areas of the world (e.g. Shapiro 1968; Runcie 1969).

Interconnections

The typology shows that in the past mutualism came in many forms, and still does. Yet there are patterns and relationships. Two criteria seem especially important: rotation versus non-rotation and scheduled versus contingent allocation.[15]

Rotating versus non-rotating allocation

In the case of rotating allocation, there is always a maximum number of participants because everyone wants to have his or her turn within a reasonable period of time. With rotating labor, 'the number of households comprising the group is relatively small, not usually reaching double figures.' (Moore 1975:272)[16] The membership of a ROSCA varies from two[17] to several hundred people, but the average is probably somewhere between ten and twenty people (Besley, Coate & Loury 1993:796 note). The larger the membership the more unstable the organization becomes. Erik Bähre (2002:155-156) made the following observation in his South African case study:

> Whenever ROSCAs became large, they tended to fail.... For example, a ROSCA in the 1970s in the township Langa had, at that time, up to more than 300 participants. Everybody had to wait their turn and the kitty became very large, up to R53,000. The cycle became very long and some worried that the ROSCA would collapse before they had had their turn, and there were some members who bribed the organizers in order to jump the queue. Corruption led to the expulsion of some members in 1978 and a split in the organization. In 1995, the ROSCA still existed but had sixty-five members and new members were not allowed. Although sixty-five members was still a lot, it offered a denser network with more possibilities for social control and the participants were content with the financial mutual.

The problem of limited membership can be solved partly by dividing ROSCAs into sub-ROSCAs. In the 1950s Bascom described the Yoruba-*Esusu*, large ROSCAs with up to 200 members, who were split up in four or more subgroups with different coordinators. The payment was made according to a system of *double rotation*: there was rotation of subgroups as well as within the subgroups (Bascom 1952:64). Table 4 shows (in a somewhat simplified manner) how this system functioned.

TABLE 4 **Double rotation in a ROSCA with twenty members and four subgroups**

First subgroup	*Second subgroup*	*Third subgroup*	*Fourth subgroup*
1st turn to receive the kitty	2nd turn	3rd turn	4th turn
5th turn	6th turn	7th turn	8th turn
9th turn	10th turn	11th turn	12th turn
13th turn	14th turn	15th turn	16th turn
17th turn	18th turn	19th turn	20th turn

This arrangement does not really solve the problem, however. The situation is fundamentally different in all non-rotating mutual arrangements (SAVAs, ASCRAs, producer cooperatives, and mutual insurance associations). There is no technical limit to the membership, and therefore these associations can contain large groups of people. There are instances of mutual insurance associations having many thousands or even hundreds of thousands of members. Of course, a growing membership can lead to problems in coordination and management, which usually result in a more formal, more professional, and more bureaucratic organization.

A second important difference between rotating and non-rotating arrangements is that rotating arrangements are always limited in time, while non-rotating arrangements are not. Indeed, rotating arrangements come to an end when the cycle is completed. Most ROSCAs continue for up to one or two years, although arrangements are known that have existed for five or ten years.[18] In contrast, non-rotating arrangements can continue indefinitely. Some savings arrangements and mutual insurance associations have continued for decades. As a matter of fact, this difference between rotating and non-rotating associations is only relative. Rotating arrangements can also be made permanent by linking several cycles that may include the same or different participants. These finite arrangements can thus be combined indefinitely. We read, for example, of an Ethiopian ROSCA, the *ekub*,

> The *ekub* continues until each member has been a winner, and then a fresh start is often made. However, an *ekub* may last indefinitely, with no person being able to win a second time until each one has done so once. Membership will remain the same throughout the *ekub*, unless a participant is unable to pay the full agreed contribution each period, in which case additional or replacement member(s) may be admitted. In case of death, the deceased heirs, usually his wife or children, may continue in the *ekub*. (Gerdes 1975:214)

On the other hand, non-rotating arrangements often have a fairly short life span at first. Savings funds were often distributed among the participants at the end of the calendar year or on the occasion of a holiday. Sometimes the money was squandered collectively. The limited life span of the arrangement in such cases was not so much a necessary consequence of the technique used as of the unwillingness of the participants to save money for a longer period of time.

Scheduled versus contingent allocation

The need for mutual arrangements can be contingent or scheduled. The contingent demand occurs when a need for money, goods, or labor arises that is not planned and mostly undesirable: death, unemployment, illness, natural disaster, etc. The mutual arrangements that can be useful in this context are accumulating funds (SAVAs, ASCRAs), and especially mutual insurance. There are two kinds of scheduled demand: one-time and recurring. *Single expenses* may be incurred for ceremonies or parties on the occasion of rites of passage, such as weddings or funerals. On such occasions, the individuals or households involved are in acute need of a large amount of goods or money that they cannot supply in a short period of time by themselves. Included among these single expenses are purchases of large commodities or investments in capital goods.[19] In his description of the Nigerian Ngwa, Nwabughuogu (1984:47) gave an example of a mutual association that responded to a single scheduled demand:

> [*Isusu*] existed to provide young men with the cash they needed to get married. In pre-colonial Ngwa society adultery was punishable either by death or by the sale into slavery of the offending man. Young men tried, therefore, to get their own wives early in life; but they had the problem of raising the money to pay the bridewealth (or 'dowry' as it is conventionally called in English throughout southern Nigeria). Those sufficiently astute began to make regular savings from their earnings, keeping them in the custody of reliable elders.... From this small beginning the *isusu* expanded to become a club embracing the whole village.

The second variety of scheduled demands are the *regularly recurring expenses*, such as the periodic strain on household resources at the end of the month. In these cases, mutual associations can also provide a solution. In the west of Cameroon, for example, people set up SAVAs to pay the annual poll tax (Bouman & Harteveld 1976:114).[20]

In combination these two main distinctions generate three families of mutual practices (Figure 2).

FIGURE 2 **Three mutualist families**

<table>
<tr><td rowspan="2">Scheduled</td><td>* Rotating labor
* ROSCA
* Savings and Loan Association</td><td>Rotating</td></tr>
<tr><td>* Simultaneous allocation
* ASCRA
* Producer Cooperative</td><td rowspan="2">Non-rotating</td></tr>
<tr><td>Contingent</td><td>* Mutual Insurance</td></tr>
</table>

Men and women take part in all forms, but rotating associations are often made up mainly of women, whereas men comprise a relatively large part of contingent associations. A satisfactory explanation of this difference in gender composition has not yet been given (see also Ardener & Burman 1995).

Threats and securities

As in any other collective activity, mutual associations can also fail in many ways. To be able to assess the specific nature of these threats, it is useful to return to the essence of mutual funds. In all cases, members contribute money, goods, or labor to a shared fund, from which subsequently payments are made to some or all members. In some cases, especially in scheduled non-rotating associations, members can also borrow money or goods from this fund for a certain period of time.

FIGURE 3 **The basic mutualist structure**

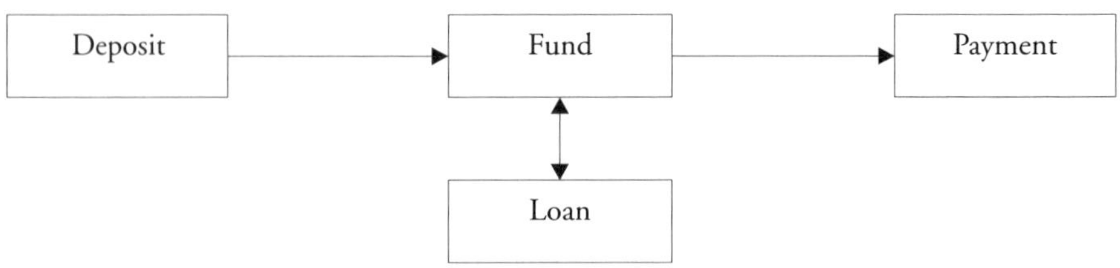

We can now distinguish between two fundamentally different kinds of threat. There are external threats, i.e., threats against which participants in an arrangement can do very little on their own. These threats can take the following forms (compare Ardener 1995:5-7).

1) Circumstances make it impossible for members to deposit money or goods or pay off a loan. This may be true for mutuals in a working-class area where families are almost completely dependent on one employer for their income. In that case the bankruptcy of the employer will also endanger the mutual arrangements in that working-class neighborhood.

2) The funds of mutuals are threatened by violence, inflation, or some other dire event. For example, in China at the end of the nineteenth century, 'the T'ai-píng rebellion, with its long train of sorrows, and the continual famines and floods of later years in Northern China, tended to bring loan societies into discredit, because experience has shown that thousands of persons have put into them what could never be recovered' (Smith 1899:157).

3) Especially in contingent associations there is a danger that an ecological disaster or an economic conjuncture can affect an entire population so that many or all members of a mutual ask for a payment at the same time and the fund is overcharged. A friendly society, for instance, whose members work in the building trade, will get into great difficulty when there is a recession in the building indus-

try that causes widespread unemployment among many members of the association at the same time and causes them to apply for a benefit.

Apart from these external threats, there are also internal threats caused by individual imperfections.

4) Individual members do not pay the deposit agreed upon. The severity of such default varies considerably. In rotating societies there is a big difference whether a participant failed to pay his contribution before he received his payment or afterwards. In the first instance the damage is limited; in the second one the other participants suffer a significant loss.

5) The administrator takes money from the fund or manages it badly. The person who has the kitty in his home is continually tempted to borrow money from it 'just for a short while.' Lont remarked that this is not uncommon in Java. He wrote that administrators 'usually try to repay the loan before the association needs the money.' In this way their actions remain hidden and they continue to have access to this convenient source for financial emergencies. Sometimes, however, they lose control and the fund suffers from that (Lont 2002:188).[21]

6) Especially in contingent organizations, members may claim a payment on false grounds by simulating illness, unemployment, etc.

7) Members may claim and receive a loan on false grounds, or not repay a loan in time, or only partly, or not at all.

Mutuals cannot do much against *external* threats, like wars or crises. At best in some cases they can try to be less vulnerable by spreading the risk. Friendly societies, for example, reduced the likelihood that all members would suffer the same adversity at the same time through supra-regional amalgamation, which ensured that members came from different regions and trades. And some ROSCAs deliberately tried to recruit members of different economic backgrounds (Anonymous 1959:437). Mutuals have many more ways of combating *internal* threats. Mutuals that are part of a very tightly knit community will suffer relatively little fraud and default. Shirley Ardener (1954) pointed out how much people in such circumstances were prepared to do to save face. Cases are known of fathers who would prefer that their daughters become prostitutes rather than fail in their obligations to the local mutuals. Sometimes 'technical' factors make it more difficult to commit fraud. It is, for instance, no coincidence that many mutual insurance associations focused on funerals in the beginning, because it is very difficult to simulate death (Van der Linden 1996). Verification becomes more difficult if the social bonds between the members of a mutual are not so strong or, in an even more extreme case, if members of a group do not even know each other personally. The latter is relatively unusual, although there are several examples of this (Kane 2000: 23f.; Bijnaar 2002). When there is asymmetrical information (the founder of a mutual has insufficient information about the reliability of a candidate member), precautions become crucial.

In principle there are three kinds of precautions. First, there are *rules for selection*: the threat to the arrangement can be reduced by only allowing members who are likely to meet their obligations. Here are some examples (see also Hechter 1987:110-111).

- Only admit persons with whom you have not just a financial relationship, for instance, relatives, or people with the same ethnic background, or people who went to the same school (compare Gerdes 1975:215).
- Only admit persons who are not likely to 'disappear' suddenly without leaving a trace. If the mutual has a kitty that is more or less permanent, it is especially important to find an administrator who is firmly tied to a place in one way or another. In ROSCAs in Jamaica, for instance, it was a rule that the administrator should be a person 'with real property, such as a home' and 'with a permanent address where he can always be found.' (Anonymous 1959:436) Similarly, mutual benefit societies often entrusted their kitty to publicans or clergy who would be at great risk if they committed fraud.
- Have new, unknown members pass through a trial period or (in the case of rotating arrangements) put them at the end of a cycle so that potential deceit does little harm.
- Select other members on the basis of their reputation, their name, i.e., the beliefs the others hold about the potential member's preferences or feasible actions (Ellis 1992:331-332).
- Have others stand surety for dubious members. In the Ethiopian *ekub* (a ROSCA), every member was obliged to supply one or more guarantors who would pay in case of default, regardless of the reason why the member concerned had failed to meet his obligations (Gerdes 1975:214).
- Have new members pay an entrance fee to encourage their loyalty and/or ask for a security on the loan.

Monitoring provides a second means of security.[22] This is especially important for mutual insurance. In his study of mutual aid societies in Paris in the early nineteenth century, Michael Sibalis showed how closely members kept an eye on each other. On the one hand, *visiteurs* were appointed who were supposed to visit those who received sick benefits both to check them out and as an act of charity. In this context the articles of association state that 'The obligations of the visitors consist of surveillance, benevolence, and humanity. The interests of the Society are entrusted to them; they should not make an exception for anyone.' It was also pointed out that sometimes the member of the board who was responsible for the selection of *visiteurs*, 'is not allowed to select them either from among his friends, or from among the neighbors who are too close to the sick person.' (Sibalis 1989:17) The ordinary members often spontaneously kept watch on each other as well, as was shown in 1823, when 'a society of engravers cancelled the sick benefits of a member named Vialard when someone spotted him drunk in a wine shop' (Sibalis 1989:16-17).

Sanctions are a third precaution. We can distinguish between external and internal sanctions. For internal sanctions, members of a mutual mete out the punishments themselves. It is important to know in such a case who the interested parties are in seeing that the rules of the mutual are not transgressed. If all the members have to pay for a loss together, they all benefit by punishing the offender. But if it was agreed that the coordinator of a ROSCA should personally act as guarantor for default or fraud (as in the *cundina*, see Kurtz 1973), only that person has an immediate interest in the punishment. For external sanctions, either official bodies (the authorities) can mete out punishment, or the larger community (such as the entire village) can do so. Such sanctions sometimes have a formal character, but they can be more informal as well: the defaulter loses his reputation. In the case of the Ethiopian mutual insurance *idir*, 'any members in arrears for two or more consecutive periods may be expelled.' This news quickly spreads, and an ex-member may be barred from joining another *idir* (Gerdes 1975:215-216).

Why mutualism?

As Abram de Swaan pointed out in the introduction, mutual arrangements were and are practiced all around the world. But the frequency of their occurrence varies considerably depending on the social context. Associations with scheduled allocations seem to be especially common in poor countries and among migrants in poor *and* rich countries. Associations with contingent allocations seem to be universal, but in advanced capitalist countries they no longer consist of small groups that do not operate bureaucratically; that is, wherever such associations have not been replaced by governmental arrangements. What makes mutuals so popular in certain social and historical circumstances and not in others?

There have always been alternatives to mutuals (see e.g. Smets 2002: Ch. 4). Indeed, anyone who has needed money, goods, or labor regularly is usually able to borrow on an individual, private basis from people in his or her direct social environment. For fairly small sums of money, it is usually possible to call on relatives or acquaintances. For larger amounts, however, it is more customary to approach a superior to ask for credit. In all these arrangements, a relationship of dependence is formed, which may have an impact on personal freedom; where it is a matter of patronage by a superior, it can even result in debt bondage. It is therefore likely that an individual would only resort to this kind of solution if, for some reason, other solutions were not possible.[23]

These other solutions fall, broadly speaking, in two categories: mutuals and formal institutions such as banks and insurance companies. What factors play a part in the choice between these alternatives? No doubt it is an important aspect of this choice that mutuals are usually more than just a form of microfinance. Apart from their function in redistribution, mutual associations usually have a latent function as well: they satisfy a need for company and a sense of community. Especially among new immigrants there is a great need for clubs and similar organizations because they help newcomers adjust.[24] Gorsky (1998:308-309) argues that in nineteenth-century Britain 'the geographic distribution of early friendly societies in areas of in-migration and industrialization suggests a primary appeal to young newcomers who had relinquished rural support structures for the higher wages of the town, but lacked a Poor Law settlement or entitlement to charity.' Most ROSCAs are also embedded in a broader context of sociability (see also Weisser 1985). Oscar Lewis' remarks about the Mexican working-class family Gomez in the 1950s in his famous study *Five Families*, for instance, are revealing:

> The sense of community is strong, particularly among the young people who belong to the same gangs, form lifelong friendships, attend the same schools, meet at the same dances held in the patios and frequently marry within the same *vecindad*. Adults also have friends whom they visit, go out with, and borrow from. Groups of neighbors organize raffles and *tandas* (informal mutual savings and credit plans), participate in religious pilgrimages together, and together celebrate the festivals of the *vecindad* patron saints, the Christmas *Posadas*, and other holidays. (Lewis 1975:63)

The sociable character of mutual arrangements and their roots in communities make for several important differences from banks and insurance companies. In the first place, mutuals offer a solution to people who lack the will to save a certain amount of money or goods on their own. It is through mutual associations that an individual may reach what the Norwegian philosopher Elster (1979: Ch. 2) called 'imperfect rationality': an individual recognizes his or her own weakness and voluntarily appeals to external compulsion to realize what he or she would not achieve by him or herself (De Swaan 1988:144-145). Aspha Bijnaar (2002: Chap. 4) reveals how this 'social constraint' functions in ROSCAs. In banks and similar institutions, such pressure is often absent. An account of Jamaican ROSCAs (referred to as *partners*) once explained the difference:

> every thrower [participant] feels it to be his most important obligation to obtain the money for his throw. He foregoes all other purchases to make that payment and exerts strenuous efforts to find ways of earning money. When a member has accumulated the money for his throw, he takes it immediately to the banker [administrator], so that he will not be tempted to spend it in any other way. On the other hand, the government savings bank engenders no such pressure. Throwers report that, even if they plan to deposit a certain amount in the bank each week, it is almost impossible to do so. Their resources are so small in comparison with their needs that they always see something that they need desperately on their way to the bank with the money and, more often than not, spend it and never get to the bank. (Anonymous 1959:439)[25]

A second difference is that mutual associations are often psychologically and/or practically more accessible than banks: (i) official institutions are sometimes located at a great distance, and it may be necessary to travel a long way to get to them; (ii) banks require surety or guarantors for a loan, while mutual arrangements need not do that because the participants know each other personally. It is not just the practical difficulties that prevent them from 'disappearing' when they owe a debt, because doing so would result in serious loss of face within the community (Adebayo 1994:396); (iii) official institutions are impersonal and formal, whereas mutual associations are personal and informal (Bouman & Harteveld 1976:115-116); (iv) official institutions sometimes have considerable financial or legal barriers.[26]

As banks and insurance companies became more interested in smaller customers, they began to lower the barriers and compete with the mutual arrangements. In some cases banks set up their own savings associations. Christmas Clubs that spread over the entire United States from 1909 onwards are an example of this. These clubs were administered by banks, and the members were supposed to contribute a small sum of money for fifty consecutive weeks, receiving a small stipulated amount of interest. On 10 December, the final sum was paid. The banks regarded the Christmas Club as 'an advertising undertaking' familiarizing wage earners who had 'almost no knowledge of banking activities' with large savings and credit institutions (Crosgrave 1927).

In spite of such attempts, commercial banks and insurance companies have certainly not yet replaced mutuals everywhere. Even if formal institutions succeed in lowering the psychological and practical barriers to entry, and even if they provide a substitute for 'the social constraint,' mutual arrangements are often less expensive than their commercial counterparts for the simple reason that the personal and sociable character of mutuals are associated with lower transaction costs (Vollmer 2000).

All in all, mutualism is not a relic from the past or an ill-advised form of traditionalism; it is a rational form of self-help for millions of people in all parts of the world.

Notes

1 In a groundbreaking essay, Sabel and Zeitlin (1984), for example, argued that the rise of modern mass production was not an inevitable effect of economic forces, but the contingent result of a historically 'open' process in the nineteenth century. They argue plausibly that originally there had been an efficient alternative to large centralized factories, namely, networks of decentralized small companies.

2 The term was probably coined by the French social anarchist Pierre-Joseph Proudhon (1865). Also compare Kropotkin, 1902.

3 Mutuals need not always be centered around money. They can also involve goods or services. Bähre mentions 'a brandy *umgalelo* that consisted of seven members who met each month. They gave two bottles each to the member whose turn it was. The twelve bottles (six times two) were used for special occasions, such as the initiation of girls and boys.' (Bähre 2002:26).

4 Apart from rotating labor (which in the literature is also called cooperative or exchange labor), there is also festive labor, i.e., labor that is organized *ad hoc* at the request of one villager, who rewards the workers for their efforts with food and drink (Erasmus 1956; Moore 1975). Swindell (1985:133) suspects that in tropical Africa festive workgroups 'may well form the basis of contemporary hired gang labor, inasmuch as their lack of reciproc-

ity is a means of transferring labor from poorer farmers to 'big-men' and emergent capitalist farmers.'

5 Reading about Ngwaland in the Imo State of Nigeria, we see: 'The Ngwa have a tradition of pooling labor to break farm bottlenecks. Transition from labor pools to pooling money resources was easy enough.' (Nwabughuogu 1984:47). And we also find the following comment about the *Njangi* (ROSCA) in Cameroon: 'The *njangi* is really the monetized form of a traditional method of organizing co-operative labor, namely what might be called a 'rotating land-clearing association.' Several men agree to work as a group, first on the fields of one member, and then in succession on those of everyone else in the group. Indeed, some *njangi* members report that the money they save is used to hire labor to clear their farm land.' (Delancey 1977:319)

6 Here is an example from China in the 1930s, the so-called *yao hui* (Fei 1980:270-273).

– An organizer who was in immediate need of money was the starting point. He brought together fourteen other people. Everyone contributed $10. The organizer paid $10 on every meeting (that is 14 times in total) plus an interest of $3 each time. The organizer paid 14 x $10 + 14 x $3 = $182 in total, whereas he received 14 x $10 = $140 on the first meeting. In other words, he paid an interest of $42.

– Every time, all participants received half the contribution of the organizer divided by the number of participants ([$13/2]/14 = 0.464). This was called the 'organizer's surplus.' The order of the players was decided by lot.

– Every session, the fourteen participants received in turn a fixed sum of $70 ($140/2). Thus, the person who received $70, actually received $70 + $0.464 = $70.464.

– If a member had received $70, he would pay $70/14 = $5, plus an interest of ($1.5) (that is $6.5 in total) at every subsequent meeting. A person who had received $70 was called a *debtor*; a person who still had to receive his share was called a *depositor*. As the rotating cycle proceeded, the number of debtors increased and the number of depositors diminished.

– The first session began when the organizer had received his $140. During this session, the first debtor appeared. $70.464 was paid and $13 was received (from the organizer). A grand total of $57.464 was spent. There were thirteen depositors and their 'subscription' was therefore $57.464/13 = $4.420.

– In the second session, it was the second debtor's turn to receive $70.464, while the organizer again paid $13. In addition, the first debtor paid $6.5 - $0.464 = $6.036. The society paid a grand total of $70.464 - $19.036 = $51.428. This amounted to $4.286 for each of the twelve depositors.

– In the third session, the third debtor received $70.464, the two debtors paid 2 x $6.036 = $12.072, and the group as a whole consequently $70.464 - 25.072 = $45.492. This amounted to $4.126 (or actually 4.127) for each of the eleven depositors. And so on.

– In the tenth session, the tenth debtor received $70.464, the nine debtors of the preceding sessions paid 9 x $6.036 = $54.324, and the organizer paid $13. Consequently, the association as a whole paid $70.464 or $67.324 = $3.14. That amounted to $0.785 for each of the four depositors.

– In the eleventh session, the group realized a positive balance. $70.464 was paid and $13 + (10 x $6.036 = $60.360) = $73.360 was received. The remainder was consequently $2.896. Thus, the three remaining depositors then received a sum of money, namely $0.965.

– In the fourteenth and last session $70.464 was paid and $13 + (13 x $6.036 = $78.468) = $91.468 was received. There was a positive balance of $8.004 and no depositor.

7 In their Mexican case study, Kurtz and Showman (1978:70) make a suggestion that could be taken further: 'The fact that participants in the *tanda* do not acquire their position in the rotation order either by bidding or gambling, as is common in some Asian associa-

tions, points to the consumer-oriented function of the *tanda*.' Not every member need have exactly one share. Bascom (1952:64) writes on the Esusu: 'A single individual may hold more than one 'membership' in a given *esusu* group by regularly making more than one contribution and receiving the fund more than once during a single cycle. Conversely, a single 'membership' may be shared by two or more individuals who are not able to afford the entire contribution separately.'

8 The serial society was a variety of this. In this kind of organization, new groups of members (new 'series') could join the society (every year or month) and start their own cycle.

9 Similar arrangements can be found in European history. See Tann 1980; Banfield 1998.

10 Apart from that, a transition from the ROSCA is possible in this case. This is an example from Western Cameroon: 'Other djanggi have taken on a supply function. People preferring zinc roofs to thatched houses for the sake of convenience and status have started djanggi where all funds are kept by the president who then buys zinc sheets to distribute over the members instead of money. Buying in large quantities he is likely to claim a discount. The same procedure might suit agricultural purposes.' (Bouman & Harteveld 1976:114)

11 An account of an eyewitness can be found in Huber 1895:923-933. There is little agreement on the exact definition of producer cooperatives. Most experts would probably agree with Doucouliagos (1990:46), however: 'Worker *ownership* is not sufficient. There must be worker *control*. A firm owned by workers is not labor-managed if its operations are controlled by management or external financiers.' See also Bonin, Jones & Putterman 1993:1291-1292.

12 See also Bascom (1952:64): 'It is also common for a single individual to belong at the same time to several different *esusu* groups, which may have different contributions and varying intervals of payment.'

13 Little attention has been paid to this kind of lottery in the standard literature. See for instance Clapson 1992; Munting 1996.

14 The direct transition from guild to mutual insurance association was certainly not unusual in European history. Gorsky (1998:306) reports that 'The rulebooks of the earliest Bristol benefit clubs suggest the direct influence of the declining craft guilds on the rules of order that governed their business and social arrangements. There was home-visiting, to ensure observation of guild ordinances, just as friendly society stewards visited members' homes. Fines, to enforce decorum, the duties of office and attendance at meetings and funerals, were common to both types of association, as was participation in the election of officials, with guilds voting at an annual meeting, and the societies selecting members as stewards and balloting for president from nominees. In both cases democracy was tempered with respect for hierarchy. Other similarities were the use of a box with multiple locks and keys held by separate officials, and the central importance of members receiving a decent funeral. Both set great store on conviviality, with guilds celebrating patron saints' days and civic ceremonies, and benefit clubs diverting monthly sums for beer on club night and enjoying an annual feast, often around Whitsun.'

15 There are, of course, other possible criteria for classification of the arrangements. We could, for example, further specify the payments. Are they made to individuals or groups? Is the payment made in money, kind, or labor? Is it possible to borrow from the fund?

16 Swindell (1985:130) says that in Africa it is 'rarely above ten [households],' and Epstein (1962:73) describes it as 'about six men' for South India.

17 'A very simple institution known as *chilemba* ... appears in Northern Rhodesia. In its most common form, two wage-earners agree to give part of their monthly wages to each other in turn, and a man may make several such bilateral agreements. Occasionally three men join together in such an arrangement.... It may be argued that where, as is usual

here, only two participants are involved, the term 'association' is inappropriate. However the elements of rotation and regularity appear, and the existence of groups of three participants shows that *chilemba* may be regarded as an embryonic form of the institution.' (Ardener 1964:207)

18 Of course, the duration of a ROSCA depends on the number of payments (the number of meetings) and the period of time between the meetings. A ROSCA that comes together every week and has thirteen members thus has a term of three months.

19 The distinction between ceremonial expenses and consumer expenses recurs throughout the literature. Kurtz and Showman (1978:72), for example, wrote that 'Blue-collar workers and their wives use the *tanda* primarily in two ways: to purchase consumer items that would otherwise be unobtainable, such as clothing, electric food blenders, radios, phonographs, and the like, and to finance ceremonial expenses such as celebrations for a saint's day, or their children's birthdays, graduations, or weddings, which are as lavish as possible.'

20 '[R]otating credit associations are used to save money in order to meet expected and unexpected needs.' (Kurtz & Showman 1978:64).

21 This risk is absent from ROSCAs in which members periodically come together in person. As the kitty is (re)distributed at each meeting in the presence of all the participants, the problem cannot, in fact, occur. 'The fact that each fund, instead of being kept by a treasurer, is immediately handed over to one of the members, excludes the possibility of embezzlement.' (Bouman & Harteveld 1976:112)

22 See also the theoretical considerations in: Banerjee, Besley & Guinnane 1994:492-501.

23 Perhaps this also explains why the importance of patronage in advanced societies has diminished. See also the discussion on the subject between Theobald and Korovkin (Theobald 1983 and 1992; Korovkin 1988). The Jewish soft loan societies in the early twentieth century that provided money to poor newcomers, without any surety, from people who were well off were a kind of transitional phenomenon between paternalism and self-reliance (Godley 1996; Tenenbaum 1993).

24 ROSCAs are very common among migrants. We can read, for example, about Papua New Guinea in the 1970s that ROSCAs are known among migrants in the towns as 'sundaying' or 'fortnighting.' And the author adds: 'it is a characteristic of the laboring and lower income groups from all parts of Papua New Guinea; it is not typical of public servants or other white collar workers. In a sample of 28 working families in Lae, 22 heads of family engaged in 'sundaying' and in a sample of 89 migrant workers around Goroka, 59 'sundayed,' percentages 66 and 79 respectively.' Skeldon regards this as a process of adaptation: 'The system appears to recreate in a modified form the cycles of debt and credit, of exchange and reciprocity in the traditional society. It helps to integrate the migrant into a network of social responsibility in the urban environment.' (Skeldon 1979-80:252-253)

25 Another advantage of ROSCAs is that after the money has been contributed, 'one could not withdraw money on impulse, as could be done from a bank or building society account.' (Burman & Lembete 1995:41).

26 In Papua New Guinea, for instance, for a long time the colonial authorities had established restrictions to access by Chinese migrants to banks. 'According to Chinese informants, the first bank loan was not granted to a Chinese until the 1950s.' (Wu 1974:570-571).

References

Adams, D.W.
1992 'Taking a Fresh Look at Informal Finance in Low-Income Countries.' In: D.W. Adams & D.A. Fitchett (eds), *Informal Finance in Low-Income Countries*, 5-23. Boulder, CO: Westview Press.

Adebayo, A.G.
1994 'Money, Credit, and Banking in Precolonial Africa: The Yoruba Experience.' *Anthropos*, 89: 379-400.

Allio, R.
1998 'Welfare and Social Security in Piedmont: Trade Guilds compared with Mutual Aid Societies.' In: A. Guenzi, P. Massa & F. Piola Caselli (eds), *Guilds, Markets and Work Regulations in Italy, 16th-19th Centuries*, 436-446. Aldershot [etc.]: Ashgate.

Ames, D.W.
1959 'Wolof Co-operative Work Groups.' In: W.R. Bascom & M.J. Herskovits (eds), *Continuity and Change in African Cultures*, 224-237. Chicago [etc.]: Chicago University Press.

Anonymous
1959 'Partners: An Informal Savings Institution in Jamaica.' *Social and Economic Studies*, 8:436-440.

Ardener, S.
1964 'The Comparative Study of Rotating Credit Associations.' *The Journal of the Royal Anthropological Institute*, 94:201-229.
1995 'Women Making Money Go Round: ROSCAs Revisited.' In: S. Ardener & S. Burman (eds), *Money-Go-Rounds. The Importance of Rotating Savings and Credit Associations for Women*, 1-19. Oxford and Washington: DC: Berg.

Ardener, S. & S. Burman (eds)
1995 *Money-Go-Rounds. The Importance of Rotating Savings and Credit Associations for Women* Oxford and Washington: DC: Berg.

Bähre, E.
2002 *Money and Violence. Financial Mutuals among the Xhosa in Cape Town, South Africa.* PhD thesis, University of Amsterdam.

Banerjee, A.V. et al.
1994 'Thy Neighbor's Keeper: The Design of a Credit Cooperative with Theory and a Test.' *Quarterly Journal of Economics*, 109:491-515.

Banfield, J.
1988 'Consumer-Owned Community Flour and Bread Societies in the Eighteenth and Early Nineteenth Centuries.' *Business History*, 40(4):16-36.

Bascom, W.R.
1952 'The *Esusu*: A Credit Institution of the Yoruba.' *The Journal of the Royal Anthropological Institute*, 82, 63-69.

Benedict, B.
1964 'Capital, Saving and Credit among Mauritian Indians.' In: R. Firth & B.S. Yamey (eds), *Capital, Saving and Credit in Peasant Societies*, 330-346. London: George Allen and Unwin.

Besley, T. et al.
1993 'The Economics of Rotating Savings and Credit Associations.' *American Economic Review*, 83:792-810.

Bijnaar, A.
2002 *Kasmoni. Spaarzame levensgenieters in Suriname en Nederland.* PhD, Universiteit van Amsterdam.

Block, A.
1931 *Bausparen in England, Amerika und Deutschland.* Berlin: Bauwelt-Verlag.

Bonin, J.P. et al.
1993 'Theoretical and Empirical Studies of Producer Cooperatives: Will Ever the Twain Meet?' *Journal of Economic Literature*, 31:1290-1320.

Bouman, F.J.A.
1994 'ROSCA and ASCRA: Beyond the Financial Landscape.' In: F.J.A. Bouman & O. Hospes (eds), *Financial Landscapes Reconstructed: The Fine Art of Mapping Development*, 375-394. Boulder, CO: Westview Press.

Bouman, F.J.A. & K. Harteveld
1976 'The Djanggi, A Traditional Form of Saving and Credit in West Cameroon.' *Sociologia Ruralis*, 16:103-118.

Brown, P.F.
1987 'Population Growth and the Disappearance of Reciprocal Labor in a Highland Peruvian Community.' *Research in Economic Anthropology*, 8:225-245.

Burman, S. & N. Lembete
1995 'Building New Realities: African Women and ROSCAs in Urban South Africa.' In: S. Ardener & S. Burman (eds), *Money-Go-Rounds. The Importance of Rotating Savings and Credit Associations for Women* 23-47. Oxford and Washington: DC: Berg.

Callier, P.
1990 'Informal Finance: The Rotating Savings and Credit Association: An Interpretation.' *Kyklos*, 43:273-276.

Calomiris, C.W. & I. Rajaraman
1998 'The Role of ROSCAs: Lumpy Durables or Event Insurance?' *Journal of Development Economics*, 56:207-216.

Carr-Saunders, A.M. et al.
1940 *Consumers' Co-operation in Great Britain. An Examination of the British Co-operative Movement.* Revised edition. London: George Allen & Unwin.

Clapson, M.
1992 *A Bit of a Flutter. Popular Gambling and English Society, c. 1823-1961.* Manchester and New York: Manchester University Press.

Crosgrave, L.M.
1927 'Christmas Clubs.' *Quarterly Journal of Economics*, 41:732-739.

Dawley, A.
1976 *Class and Community. The Industrial Revolution in Lynn.* Cambridge, MA, and London: Harvard University Press.

Defoe, D.
1697 *An Essay Upon Projects.* London: Tho. Cockerill.

Delancey, M.W.
1977 'Credit for the Common Man in Cameroon.' *Journal of Modern African Studies*, 15(3):316-322.

De Swaan, A.
1988 *In Care of the State. Health Care, Education, and Welfare in Europe and the USA in the Modern Era.* Cambridge: Polity Press / New York: Oxford University Press.

Doucouliagos, C.
1990 'Why Capitalist Firms Outnumber Labor-Managed Firms.' *Review of Radical Political Economics*, 22:41-66.
Ellis, C.J.
1992 'Reputation.' *The New Palgrave Dictionary of Money & Finance*, 331-332. London: Macmillan.
Elster, J.
1979 *Ulysses and the Sirens. Studies in Rationality and Irrationality.* Cambridge [etc.]: Cambridge University Press, and Paris: Editions de la Maison des Sciences de l'Homme.
Epstein, T.S.
1962 *Economic Development and Social Change in South India.* Manchester: Manchester University Press.
Erasmus, Ch.J.
1956 'Culture, Structure and Process: The Occurrence and Disappearance of Reciprocal Farm Labor.' *Southwestern Journal of Anthropology*, 12:444-469.
Essombé Edimo, J.R.
1998 'Dynamique financière des tontines: quels enseignements pour le financement des petites entreprises en Afrique?' *Revue Tiers Monde*, 39:861-883.
Fei, Hsiao-Tung
1980 *Peasant Life in China.* Preface Bronislaw Malinowski. London: Routledge & Kegan Paul / first edition 1939.
Ferber, R.
1964 'Saving.' In: J. Gould & W. Kolb (eds), *A Dictionary of the Social Sciences*, 616-617. New York: Free Press.
Freedman, M.
1979 'The Handling of Money: A Note on the Background to the Economic Sophistication of Overseas Chinese.' In: M. Freedman, *The Study of Chinese Society: Essays.* Selected and Introduced by G. William Skinner, 22-26. Stanford, CA: Stanford University Press.
Geertz, C.
1962 'The Rotating Credit Association: A "Middle Rung" in Development.' *Economic Development and Cultural Change*, 10:241-263.
Gerdes, V.
1975 'Precursors of Modern Social Security in Indigenous African Institutions.' *Journal of Modern African Studies*, 13:209-228.
Geschiere, P.
1995 'Working Groups or Wage Labor? Cash-crops, Reciprocity and Money among the Maka of Southeastern Cameroon.' *Development and Change*, 26:503-523.
Gide, C.
1899-1900 'Productive Co-operation in France.' *Quarterly Journal of Economics*, 14:30-66.
1923 *Les obstacles au développement des Coopératives de production.* Paris: Association pour l'enseignement de la Coopération.
Godley, A.
1996 'Jewish Soft Loan Societies in New York and London and Immigrant Entrepreneurship, 1880-1914.' *Business History*, 38(3):101-116.
Gorsky, M.
1998 'Mutual Aid and Civil Society: Friendly Societies in Nineteenth-Century Bristol.' *Urban History*, 25:302-322.

Gosden, P.H.J.H.
1961 *The Friendly Societies in England 1815-1875*. Manchester: Manchester University Press.
Hechter, M.
1987 *Principles of Group Solidarity* Berkeley [etc.]: University of California Press.
Hibbard, B.H.
1930 'Agricultural Cooperation.' In: *Encyclopedaedia of the Social Sciences*, vol. I, 521-529. New York: Macmillan.
Hoetink, H.
1956 'Curaçao en Thorstein Veblen.' *Mens en Maatschappij*, 31:40-46.
Huber, V.A.
1895 'Skizzen aus dem französischen Genossenschaftsleben.' In: K. Munding (ed.) *V.A. Hubers Ausgewählte Schriften über Socialreform und Genossenschaftswesen*, 923-933. Berlin.
Kane, A.
2001 *Les caméléons de la finance populaire au Sénégal et dans la diaspora*. PhD Thesis, University of Amsterdam.
Korovkin, M.
1988 'Exploitation, Cooperation, Collusion: An Enquiry into Patronage.' *Archives Européennes de Sociologie*, 29, 105-126.
Kropotkin, P.
1902 *Mutual Aid: A Factor of Evolution*. London: William Heinemann.
Kuper, H. & S. Kaplan
1944 'Voluntary Associations in an Urban Township.' *African Studies*, 3, December:178-186.
Kurtz, D.V.
1973 'The Rotating Credit Association: An Adaptation to Poverty.' *Human Organization*, 32:49-58.
Kurtz, D.V. & M. Showman
1978 'The Tanda: A Rotating Credit Association of Mexico.' *Ethnology*, 17:65-74.
Lewis, O.
1975 *Five families. Mexican case studies in the culture of poverty.* Introduction by Margaret Mead New York: Basic Books. [Originally 1959].
Lont, H.
2002 *Juggling Money in Yogyakarta. Financial Self-Help Organizations and the Quest for Security.* PhD Thesis, University of Amsterdam.
Moore, M.P.
1975 'Cooperative Labor in Peasant Agriculture.' *Journal of Peasant Studies*, 2:270-291.
Moss, B.H.
1975 'Parisian Producers' Associations (1830-51): The socialism of skilled workers.' In: R. Price (ed.) *Revolution and Reaction. 1848 and the Second French Republic*, 73-96. London & New York: Croom Helm.
Munting, R.
1996 *An Economic and Social History of Gambling in Britain and the USA*. Manchester/New York: Manchester University Press.
Murdoch, J.
1999 'The Microfinance Promise.' *Journal of Economic Literature*, 37:1569-1614.
Norvell, D.G. & J.S. Wehrly
1969 'A Rotating Credit Association in the Dominican Republic.' *Caribbean Studies*, 9 (1969-70)1:45-52.

Nwabughuogu, A.I.

1984 'The *Isusu*: An Instititution for Capital Formation among the Ngwa Igbo; its Origin and Development to 1951.' *Africa*, 54(4)46-58.

Proudhon, P.-J.

1865 *De la capacité politique des classes ouvrières*. Paris: no publisher.

Regnault, F. & M.Waton

1893 'Les nouvelles compagnies ouvrières.' *Revue d'économie politique*, 7:625-653, 796-814.

Roberts, R.

1973 *The Classic Slum. Salford Life in the First Quarter of the Century*. Harmondsworth: Penguin.

Runcie, N. (ed.)

1969 *Credit Unions in the South Pacific: Australia, Fiji, New Zealand, Papua and New Guinea* London: University of London Press.

Sabel, C. & J. Zeitlin

1984 'Historical Alternatives to Mass Production'. *Past and Present*, 108:133-176.

Schnapper, B.

1965 'Les sociétés ouvrières de production pendant la Seconde République: l'exemple Girondin.' *Revue d'histoire économique et sociale*, 43:162-191.

Scholten, U.

2000 'Rotating Savings and Credit Associations in Developed Countries: The German-Austrian Bausparkassen.' *Journal of Comparative Economics*, 28:340-363.

Shapiro, E.

1968 *Credit Union Development in Wisconsin*. New York: Columbia University Press, 1947; reprint New York: AMS Press, 1968.

Sibalis, M.D.

1989 'The Mutual Aid Societies of Paris, 1789-1848.' *French History*, 3(1) March:1-30.

Skeldon, R.

1979 'Regional Associations among Urban Migrants in Papua New Guinea.' *Oceania*, 50:248-272.

Smets, P.

1996 'Community-Based Finance Systems and Their Potential for Urban Self-Help in a New South Africa.' *Development Southern Africa*, 13(2):173-187.

2002 *Housing Finance and the Urban Poor: Building and Financing Low-Income Housing in Hyderabad, India*. PhD thesis, Vrije Universiteit Amsterdam.

Smith, A.H.

1899 *Village Life in China. A Study in Sociology*. New York [etc.]: Fleming H. Revell Company.

Swindell, K.

1985 *Farm Labor*. Cambridge [etc.]: Cambridge University Press.

Tann, J.

1980 'Co-operative Corn Milling: Self-help During the Grain Crises of the Napoleonic Wars.' *Agricultural History Review*, 28:45-57.

Tenenbaum, S.

1993 *A Credit to Their Community: Jewish Loan Societies in the United States, 1880-1945*. Detroit: Wayne State University Press.

Theobald, R.

1983 'The Decline of Patron-Client Relations in Developed Societies.' *Archives Européennes de Sociologie*, 24:136-147.

1992 'On the Survival of Patronage in Developed Societies.' *Archives Européennes de Sociologie*, 33:183-191.

Topley, M.
1964 'Capital, Saving and Credit among Indigenous Rice Farmers and Immigrant Vegetable Farmers in Hong Kong's New Territories.' In: R. Firth & B.S. Yamey (eds) *Capital, Saving and Credit in Peasant Societies*, 157-186. London: George Allen and Unwin.

Van der Linden, M. (ed.)
1996 *Social Security Mutualism. A Comparative History of Mutual Benefit Societies.* Bern: Peter Lang.

Van der Linden, M.
1997 'Old Workers' Movements and "New Political Economy": The Uses and Drawbacks of Rational Choice Theory.' *Traverse: Revue d'histoire/Zeitschrift für Geschichte* [Zurich]: 128-143.

Van Meeteren, N.
1947 *Volkskunde van Curaçao.* Willemstad: no publisher.

Von Studnitz, A.
1879 *Nordamerikanische Arbeiterverhältnisse.* Leipzig: Duncker & Humbolt.

Vollmer, U.
2000 'Warum gibt es (immer noch) Kreditgenossenschaften? Eine institutionenökonomische Analyse.' *Jahrbuch für Wirtschaftswissenschaften*, 51:53-74.

Weisser, M.R.
1985 *A Brotherhood of Memory: Jewish Landmanshaftn in the New World.* Ithaca: Cornell University Press.

Wong, D.
1987 *Peasants in the Making. Malaysia's Green Revolution.* Singapore: Institute of Southeast Asian Studies.

Wu, D.Y.H.
1974 'Kill Three Birds with One Stone: the Rotating Credit Associations of the Papua New Guinea Chinese.' *American Ethnologist*, 1:565-583.

Yeo, S. (ed.)
1988 *New Views of Cooperation.* London/New York: Routledge.

Contributors

Erik Bähre (1969) studied cultural anthropology and wrote a doctoral thesis on *Money and Violence. Financial Mutuals among the Xhosa in Cape Town, South Africa* (University of Amsterdam, 2002). He works at the University College Utrecht, Utrecht University, and at the Amsterdam Institute for Metropolitan and International Development Studies (AMIDSt), University of Amsterdam. His research at AMIDSt is on emerging insurance arrangements in urban South Africa (NWO-WOTRO research grant).

Aspha Bijnaar (1966) is a sociologist and researcher at the National Institute for the Dutch History of Slavery and its Heritage (NiNSee). Her doctoral thesis on Surinamese rotating credit and saving arrangements in Paramaribo and Amsterdam was published as *Kasmoni. Een spaartraditie in Suriname en Nederland* (Amsterdam: Bert Bakker, 2002).

Abram de Swaan (1942) is Distinguished University Professor of Social Science at the University of Amsterdam and held the chair of sociology from 1973 until 2001. He was co-founder and dean of the Amsterdam School for Social Research (1987-1997) and is presently its chairperson. His publications include *In Care of the State. Health Care, Education and Welfare in Europe and the USA in the Modern Era* (Cambridge/ New York, 1988); *The Management of Normality. Critical Essays in Health and Welfare* (London and New York, 1990), and *Words of the World. The Global Language System* (Cambridge, 2001).

Hotze Lont (1971) is an anthropologist working at the Institute for Social Studies, The Hague. His doctoral thesis was *Juggling Money in Yogyakarta. Financial Self-Help Organizations and the Quest for Security* (University of Amsterdam, 2002). He published, with Otto Hospes, *Livelihood and Microfinance. Anthropological and Sociological Perspectives on Savings and Debt* (Delft, 2004).

Peer Smets (1958) teaches at the Faculty of Social Sciences, Free University Amsterdam. He wrote a doctoral thesis on *Housing Finance and the Urban Poor: Building and Financing Low-Income Housing in Hyderabad, India* (Free University Amsterdam, 2002). He published apart from chapters in books, also articles on microfinance in *Development Southern Africa, Anthropos, Community Development Journal, Housing Studies* and other academic journals.

Abdoulaye Kane (1970) teaches at the Department of Anthropology, University of Florida at Gainesville. He wrote a doctoral thesis on *Les caméléons de la finance populaire au Sénégal et dans la diaspora* (University of Amsterdam, 2001).

Marcel van der Linden (1952) is Research Director of the International Institute of Social History, Professor of Social Movement History at the University of Amsterdam, and the editor of the *International Review of Social History* (Cambridge, UK). His publications include *Social Security Mutualism. The Comparative History of Mutual Benefit Societies* (Bern, 1996), *New Methods for Social History*, with Larry J. Griffin (Cambridge, 1999), and *Transnational Labour History: Explorations* (Aldershot, 2003).

Index